THE MORMON
TABERNACLE
CHOIR

MUSIC IN AMERICAN LIFE

A list of books in the series
appears at the end of this book.

THE MORMON TABERNACLE CHOIR

A BIOGRAPHY

MICHAEL HICKS

UNIVERSITY OF ILLINOIS PRESS

URBANA, CHICAGO, AND SPRINGFIELD

Library of Congress Cataloging-in-Publication Data
Hicks, Michael, 1956–
The Mormon Tabernacle Choir:
a biography / Michael Hicks.
pages cm. — (Music in American life)
Includes bibliographical references and index.
ISBN 978-0-252-03908-9 (cloth: alk. paper)
ISBN 978-0-252-09706-5 (ebook)
1. Mormon Tabernacle Choir—History.
I. Title.
ML28.S27M674   2015
782.506'0792258--dc23   2014033692

"MUSIC IS DIVINE BECAUSE IN ITS ESSENCE IT IS SO HUMAN."
—ADOLF WEISSMANN

CONTENTS

Illustrations follow page 84

INTRODUCTION

AT BARACK OBAMA'S SECOND inauguration on 21 January 2013, Senator Charles Schumer announced that "The Battle Hymn of the Republic" was about to be sung by the "award-winning Tabernacle Choir." Then, with a playful smile, he added, "the *Brooklyn* Tabernacle Choir." The audience laughed, because who could not be in on the joke? The *Mormon* Tabernacle Choir had been the only "tabernacle choir" to sing at a presidential inauguration before—six times, to be exact. Since Ronald Reagan dubbed them America's Choir at his first inauguration, they had been known by that nickname. They had become the state choir of the republic to which the battle hymn was devoted—and the group that won a Grammy for its version of the "Battle Hymn" in 1959. As one writer put it, the Mormon Tabernacle Choir was "the anointed voice of America's civil religion."[1] But the pivot toward a new tabernacle choir seemed fitting, not only for a new era, but for the specific circumstance: Obama had beaten Mitt Romney, a Mormon, in the election.

The moniker America's Choir seems both ironic and inevitable for the Mormon Tabernacle Choir. In the mid-1840s, Mormons fled the boundaries of the United States to set up their own kingdom, ostensibly the Kingdom of God, which all generations of U.S. Protestants, at least, had themselves preached and pursued. Mormons thought it not only unlikely but impossible that they could build it within "America." But within fifty years, their territory of Utah, the theocracy on which it was founded now having been threshed out of it, became the forty-fifth state. From then on, its Tabernacle Choir has hunted down national respectability like a marksman. No other choir in the democratic world has done that, and if "official" national status were its only achievement it would be an incomparable one.

But the phrase America's Choir also suggests a "people's choir." And in that, too, they can boast. The social (though not racial) diversity of the Choir has always been apparent. As Heber Wolsey deftly, if over-cleverly, wrote in 1967:

> Architects, attorneys, and an agricultural statistician sing in the choir. There are bankers, beauticians, and business men. College professors, carpenters, chemists, contractors, and chiropractors make the twice-weekly rehearsals. Doctors, a dentist, and a dairyman add their special talents. Two electrical linemen participate in the singing. Nearly thirty per cent of the choir members are homemakers. Another thirteen per cent are school teachers. A lady realtor sings soprano. A missile engineer is part of the tenor section. A baritone sells autos six days a week. And his friend who sings bass is an experienced welder. One family boasts a tenor-alto-soprano trio. A carload of choir members travels over 10,000 miles a year just to attend the rehearsals.[2]

This is not a professional choir, despite tremendous quasi-professional success in broadcasting and recording. And its repertoire is hardly stuffy—although that repertoire has been a century-long tug of war.

The Tabernacle Choir is also a close-knit family. And close-knit families often stiffen their ranks against outsiders. The current handbook of the Choir may not be shown to anyone who is not a member of the Choir. Choir members are not to write about the Choir in blogs. And they are pledged to secure permission from the Choir President before speaking to "the media." Even then, the Choir member is urged to "avoid commenting on any projections or assumptions."[3] I plead innocent to representing "the media," but I still met current Choir members who felt it a violation of the terms of their membership to tell me of their experiences. That's a pity, but not a blow to this book. Because not only does silence give me a sort of implicit consent, but it may speak more than it withholds.

Vivian Gornick wrote of a great nonfiction narrator that he or she is always "possessed of a sense of history, proportion, and paradox."[4] If not possessed of them, I do aspire to inhabit those same three traits in this book.

My pursuit of Tabernacle Choir history has its own history. I have been an observer of the Choir for decades, a friend and even music teacher of many Choir members, and an avid Choir researcher and note taker since the mid-1980s, when I began writing my related book for the University of Illinois Press, *Mormonism and Music: A History*. After writing that and three other historical books, I've developed my own ways of working, quirky habits of organizing, even filing, laying pages around the floor, and so on. As for my sources, though, I try to work from the "inside," seizing and milking as many journal entries, letters, and other old documents as I can find—or, in cases like this one, as I am allowed to see. Mormon historians know that Church archives have opened and shut like poppies for years. Overall, more materials have opened to historians than have closed in the past two decades. But much remains concealed, according to the so-called SPC constraints of official Church archivists: journalists or academics, they tell me, may not see "sacred," "private," or "confidential" documents.

While I keep myself open to what any document can teach me, like anyone else, I have my predilections. I like to find the story or stories that seem most true to human nature, as I understand it, viewing it from atop a perch of nearly six decades on earth and the occasional reading of Jeremiah. So, as I roam through the tens of thousands of pages that circumnavigate the life of the Tabernacle Choir, I look for those that most illuminate the humanity etched into the music. Although a skeptic, I'm also a sentimentalist. I deeply believe in the epigraph printed at the front of this book: what makes music divine is the humanity from which it springs.[5] The history of any success, unless utterly serendipitous, is a history of manipulating failures into their opposites, walking one way only to walk back, but wiser. And that's the history of this Choir.

Predilections, of course, shape proportion. Mine inevitably shape this book's. Not everyone—maybe no one—will agree with the amount of space I give to or withhold from any given moment in the life of this Choir. I sometimes dwell on an obscure detail (say, a paragraph from a Mormon Apostle's talk), yet barely mention some massive undertakings (say, any number of elaborate but routine concert tours). That's because, for me, some things more than others illuminate the strivings of character that determine institutional progress or detour.

Also, I think of this book as cinematic in its construction. Here you have a huge musical group that records, broadcasts, concertizes, and evangelizes, a group whose sounds and exploits are assembled by Apostles, Choir Presidents, conductors, singers, engineers, and, of course, huge cultural trends and markets. I have to keep shifting the angle of my lens to try to take it all in—which, of course, one can never do. But I try to stay conscious of all the simultaneities, not to mention the needs and personalities that sometimes gallop in different directions at the same time. So one will see lots of crosscutting in this narrative.

Access to sources also affects proportion. A large cache of firsthand documents proffered me allows me to saturate myself with the language and vision of their times. At the same time, a trove of documents withheld (or never produced) pushes me to other sources—reminiscences, newspaper accounts, and even my own speculation, those "educated guesses" whose diplomas I always try to have on the wall. So the character of this narrative—the lighting and set decoration, to extend the film metaphor—might shift now and then. Knowing that, I try to keep the story brisk and inviting enough to draw the reader into each new lighting scheme and layout of furniture.

Paradox (the third of Gornick's ideal traits) actually seems the least of my worries—at least if one lets ironies speak for themselves. But rather than telegraph the paradoxical themes here, I'll leave them to emerge from the tales themselves.

So much of the insight and vision of this book—however perfunctory it seems in the shadow of its looming subject—I owe to far more people than I can remember to name. Still, many names from the past year of earnest authorship come readily to mind.

Friends and faculty colleagues who've had everything from infatuation to skirmishes with the Choir have volunteered their recollections on this or that point (or trend), including Mark Ammons, Kurt Bestor, Carol Cornwall Madsen, Daren Bradford, Thomas Durham, Rosalind Hall, and Brett Stewart. Durham was among those who sat down for longer interviews; others include Jon Holloman, Luke Howard, Ron Staheli, and Shane Warby. More distant friends, many of them my onetime students and now accomplished professionals, offered anecdotes: Alisha Ard, Justin Findlay, Marie MacArthur, and especially Mark Porcaro, who probably knows more about the Choir's recorded repertoire than anyone. Ruth Eldredge led me to useful sources, while Jared Oaks shared many interesting documents from his personal archive. Heidi Reed expertly proofread a full draft fresh from my printer. Jeremy Grimshaw read and discussed various large and small clumps of pages along the way.

So many people gave simple but strong encouragement, many of them the Facebook friends who "Liked" my intermittent reports on the book's progress from November 2012 through October 2013. I also was spurred, happily, by the exhortation of noted editors Lavina Fielding Anderson, Kristine Haglund, and two others to whom I have longer and stronger ties: University of Illinois Press's Laurie Matheson and, of course, her predecessor Judith McCulloh, who first invited me to pursue a book about Mormon music almost thirty years ago.

A few archivists should get a royalty from this book (but won't), most notably Bill Slaughter at the LDS Church History Library, Liz Rogers at Marriott Special Collections at the University of Utah, and John Murphy at the L. Tom Perry Special Collections of the Harold B. Lee Library at Brigham Young University. One also serendipitously gets those offhand but incredibly generous ad hoc patrons like Ron Fox, who shared with me many fascinating photographs.

My wife, Pamela, however, will get half of the royalties, or thereabouts, and deserves more than that for all the craven obsession I lavish on projects like this. I'm off the hook for thanking my kids, though: they're mostly off having kids of their own.

THE MORMON
TABERNACLE
CHOIR

CHAPTER 1

BOOKS AND ANGELS

"HE THAT IS FOUND GUILTLESS . . . HATH
IT GIVEN UNTO, HIM, TO DWELL, IN THE
PRESENCE OF GOD IN HIS KINGDOM,
TO SING CEASELESS PRAISES WITH THE
CHOIRS ABOVE."

WHEN JOSEPH SMITH dictated those words into what became the Book of Mormon, he knew a bit about angels. For almost a decade this twentysomething upstate New Yorker had visits from spirits awash in heavenly light. One of those spirits, an angel named Moroni, had led him repeatedly to a local hillside where a stone box of gold plates lay buried. After Moroni finally let Joseph hoist the plates from their hole, the young prophet spent months "translating" them through visionary means, dictating the text in a broken King James English transcribed by friends—including his wife—who were convinced of his divine prowess. The result was the thick, ungainly, but spiritually potent Book of Mormon, which collated the sermons, battle histories, and sacred anecdotes of ancient Hebrew tribes in the Western Hemisphere.

Buried in its jangling prose were four passages that mentioned heavenly "choirs." One is the promise that the prophet Mormon makes above—heavenly choir membership as a reward to the faithful. Another is when the pious monarch King Mosiah predicts that his death will soon arrive and his "immortal spirit may join the choirs above in singing the praises of a just God." The most interesting statement, though, uttered twice in the book, comes from the visionary patriarch Lehi, who "saw God sitting upon his throne, surrounded with numberless concourses of angels in the attitude of singing and praising their God." Note the language: he doesn't hear them, but *sees* them in "the attitude of singing"—head erect, mouth open, eyes ablaze, perhaps. Sadly, no sound is described. And they apparently had passed their auditions not by musical skill but by righteousness.[1]

All these passages would have made sense to a young religious American in the 1820s. Smith had grown up with Christmas carols that spoke of angels singing to announce the birth of the Son of God. Smith had read the Book of Revelation, in which the masses of redeemed souls in heaven jointly sing "a new song." He had probably seen pictures in books depicting heavenly beings with mouths agape, harps and trumpets beside them. And he had certainly heard tales of celestial voices singing in the dreams and visions of charismatic preachers in the revivalist meetings of his youth.[2]

He even knew about Emanuel Swedenborg, that great visionary of the eighteenth century. In his visions, Swedenborg sometimes "heard" (i.e., perceived) angelic choirs for hours at a time and even devised a taxonomy for different types of angelic choirs, their tone colors and timetables. Even the "pillar of cloud" described in the book of Exodus, he wrote, was actually an angelic choir.[3] Swedenborg, Smith allegedly said, "had a view of the world to come."[4] And indeed, some of Smith's visions resembled Swedenborg's, illuminating the degrees of heavenly glory, for example, or even celestial marriage. But Joseph Smith never mentioned hearing angel choirs in his visions.

That might have surprised his followers, who in the early 1830s had begun to flock around him because of the Book of Mormon and other revelations he declared. Many Christians of Smith's era believed that angel choirs could and even should be heard on earth in the right circumstances. Those circumstances often included how close the hearer was to death. By 1600 the idea was so ingrained in the Christian psyche that in *Hamlet* (act 5, scene 2) Shakespeare has Horatio utter his classic line, "Good-night, sweet prince; / And flights of angels sing thee to thy rest." In 1842, the Irish author Aubrey de Vere fleshed out the idea:

> When a Christian lies expiring
> Angel choirs with plumes outspread,
> Bend above his death-bed singing,
> That when death's mild sleep is fled,
> There may be no harsh transition,
> When he greets the heavenly vision.[5]

With angelic choirs as part of the heavenly template, one would expect churches to mimic them, filling earthly chapels with the praises of disciplined, well-regulated, harmonious troupes of singers. That was true of some churches, including the Presbyterian church that most of the Smith family attended in the 1820s. At the February 1824 installation of a new pastor there, the *Wayne Sentinel* praised the effort and effect of the choir, noting that "the pieces were selected with judgment and performed in a manner which we presume has never been equaled in this place. It is indeed a subject of felicitation that our singers, although their number be limited, are manifesting a laudable ambition to excel in this sublime and delightful part of public worship." The Methodist church in town—to which young Joseph was partial—also had a choir, "led by a man with a very large head of hair" who fascinated the children by clinking a tuning fork against his teeth, then holding it to his ear for the pitch.[6]

But for most churches in Smith's environs, earthly choirs were a transgression. One needs to recall that, as choir historian Arthur Mees pungently puts it: "When, in 1620, the Pilgrim Fathers landed at Plymouth Rock, they brought with them a hatred of musical culture which has no parallel in history."[7] Christianity, from its beginnings, had had its full measure of anti-music in the rhetoric of patrists, scholars, and even popes, who argued that its pleasures held secret dangers, the seductions of pleasure and flesh-gratification.[8] Gradually, music charmed even its enemies, who over time became the sponsors of some of the greatest musical art in the Western world. Still, reformers often tried to reverse or at least buck the trend of musical acceptance. The fiercest of those reformers, in the English-speaking world, at least, headed for America.

Some of these reformers—especially among Quakers and Baptists—questioned singing at all by Christians well into the nineteenth century. The Quaker point of view at the time was the most extreme: sacred music deludes the mind by "producing an excitement mistaken for devotion."[9] But even among Christians for whom singing in church was the norm, choirs or singing by note should not upstage free-form congregational singing. Peter Cartwright, the so-called Backwoods Preacher, had a prayer that typified the sentiments of Protestant purists: "Lord, save the Church from desiring to have pews, choirs, organs, or instrumental music . . . like other heathen Churches around them."[10] Such formality mimicked the debased "popery" of Catholicism and those Protestant movements—including Anglicanism, Episcopalianism, and Presbyterianism—that seemed to echo the formalities of Rome. Many nonmetropolitan U.S. congregations opposed any "singing by note" (i.e., musical literacy), choirs, and musical instruments in church. Those were all *state-church* practices, many felt, that the New World should exclude.

As it turned out, musical literacy triumphed in New England. "That music in New England should have not only recovered from the blows dealt by Puritan intolerance but in its reproductive branches, and particularly that of chorus singing, should have risen to a certain degree of artistic independence as quickly as it did, is little short of marvelous."[11] This miracle had begun to reshape the expectations of even circuit-riding evangelists. Consider the remarks of famed evangelist Charles Finney. Trained in the choral traditions of the East Coast, he described his reaction to some congregational singing in the upstate New York village of Antwerp in 1824. "I cannot call it singing," he said, "for they seemed never to have any church music in that place. However, the people pretended to sing. But it amounted to this: each one bawled in his own way." After recalling his own musical training, he noted that he was tempted to flee the scene of such caterwauling. Then, "I finally put both hands over my ears, and held them with my full strength. But this did not shut out the discords. I stood it, however, until they were through; and then I cast myself down on my knees, almost in a state of desperation, and began to pray."[12]

Still, the anti-choir, anti-music-literacy strand of American Protestantism kept up throughout the nineteenth century. In 1840, a large group of Ohio Presbyterians publicly objected to musical literacy, arguing, "Is the chief end now to *worship the music*? This is idolatry, however refined it is" (original emphasis). To sing from written musical notation was "an outrage upon Divine institution, a violation of solemn vows, and a manifest insult to common sense."[13] In 1854, the anti-choir members of an Ohio Methodist congregation heckled the choir whenever it tried to sing, hoping to "bring discredit on the singers by creating discord." The chief heckler defended his tactics by arguing "there could not be a revival of religion with a choir tolerated in the Church" because "choir singing originated with the devil."[14] In another Midwestern Methodist church in about the same year, members of the choir, weary of being condemned by some of their hearers, quit coming to meetings and let the multitude musically fend for itself. Of these schismatic meetings one writer recalled that "sometimes one [choir member] was present, and sometimes all; and sometimes the choir would sing, and sometimes there was no singing by any body in the church."[15] As late as 1862, the *Associate Presbyterian* called singing by the musically trained a "stupendous Babel" by which "people may become infatuated by music" until "artistic display takes the place of decent and unified praise to God."[16]

These conflicting visions of musical literacy lived on in the church Joseph Smith founded in 1830 as the Church of Christ and twice rechristened until it became the Church of Jesus Christ of Latter-day Saints ("saints" being the catch-all term for his new disciples). The ideal of literacy undergirded that Church: the angel Moroni had delivered a *book* to Smith. And in honor of that book, the Church's members became known as Mormons. Smith was also biased toward *musical* literacy. He had been born in Vermont, where New England religion had favored singing by note. His angelic visits were in and around Palmyra, New York, whose bookstores carried Little and Smith's *Easy Instructor* and *Sacred Harmony*, Hastings and Warriner's *Musica Sacra*, and other books of musically notated multi-part sacred songs and hymns. Most importantly, according to Smith's brother William, their father (Joseph Sr.) "was a teacher of music by note to a conciderable extent."[17]

Smith also balanced his quest for visions with a thirst for conventional education. He organized a School of the Prophets (i.e., of the elders of his Church) that taught, among other things, Hebrew and Greek. In 1833, he delivered a revelation that Latter-day Saints should "seek ye out of the best books words of wisdom, seek learning, even by study and also by faith." That revelation does not mention songbooks, of course. But it does privilege written, printed sources of knowledge and at the same time relegates the Book of Mormon to a larger pantheon of contenders for readers' attention. Worship and sanctification did not depend only on looking inward. It meant looking outward, even if that meant into the pages of a book.

Nevertheless, many converts to the Church were primitivists or "seekers," on the hunt for primitive Christianity. For them the old way of worship suggested that one could only sing in the "old way," which they believed went back (via the synagogues) to the original Christian church: the preacher would chant a line of text and the congregation would sing it back, slowly, individualistically, in a whining or moaning—though pious—single line. Those who argued for this practice traced it to Jesus' own time. Many early Mormons in Kirtland, Ohio—the Church's largest central gathering place for most of the 1830s, its first decade—converted from churches founded by Alexander Campbell, who had taught against the singing school movement. "Psalm and hymn singing," he wrote in 1827, "like every other part of Christian worship, has been corrupted by sectarianism." To learn hymns by note, he wrote, was a "desecration" of the hymns.[18]

Smith had to reconcile these competing views of musical worship. He did so in an extravagant and doubtless unforeseen way: by reviving the temple tradition of the Old Testament and linking it to a singing school.

In the 1830s, Mormon missionaries were new circuit riders in the soul game that became known as the Second Great Awakening. Itinerants who—per Jesus' dictum—went "without purse or scrip" from town to town and home to home, in effect begging for food, drink, and lodging, this new wave of Mormon preachers still carried at least some books with them, because their message was about a new book and, of course, one needed samples for would-be readers. At the same time, one would encounter not just preachers from other sects carrying Bibles, but singing masters who rode the same circuits carrying song books. Each singing master would enter a town seeking room, board, and a small fee for setting up a class that taught proper vocal production, how to read notes, and even a little theory, "the knowledge of which," says Mees, "he was, as a rule, entirely innocent."[19] He would have picked (or even written and published) a book to serve as a text for the class, usually an oblong four-part book with four-shaped noteheads (square, oval, triangle, diamond) to convey the solfège (fa-so-la-si) syllables that matched the placements of the notes on the musical staves. With a sack of these books at hand for sale to his students, he would find a rehearsal space—usually a schoolhouse—and recruit for his course, a several weeks–long affair in which the patrons, young and old, would have the good, clean fun of harmonizing. The usual result: the graduates would end up sitting together at church, sing in harmony, and become, de facto, a choir.

Joseph Smith's decision to erect an extravagant temple in Ohio spawned the first Mormon singing school. A costly building for worship—the kind primitivists such as Alexander Campbell had vigorously opposed—seemed to require high-church traditions of formality, dignity, and aestheticism. Since such a temple needed a choir, Smith recruited a newly baptized singing teacher to organize one. One feels the tension that must have surrounded this new venture in Smith's journal account of it. He writes on 4 January 1836 that he met at the local chapel "to make arrangements for a Singing School." There, "after some altercation," he writes, "a judicious arangement was made, a committee of 6 was chosen, to take charge of the singing department." Years later, when Mormons could not imagine any objection to choirs, Smith's phrase "after some altercation" was changed to "after some discussion."[20]

But "altercation" makes sense. A Mormon singing school laid bare a basic rift in the early church. The Church newspaper *Millennial Star* put it succinctly: "In this last dispensation God will send forth, by his servants, things new as well as old, until man is perfected in the truth."[21] Those who had converted to Mormonism because of its "restoration" of ancient Christianity were, in principle, pursuing the old. Those same converts then had to accept, often suddenly, the very new that flowed from Smith's inspiration—new doctrine, new church organization, new ordinances, and new social habits. The dilemma became: what of the old ways should one preserve and cherish as authentic (and not merely habitual) versus what of the new ways should one embrace as progress (and not just erosion)? For many who had converted from reformist churches such as Campbell's, or from Methodism, or from any of the "seeker" traditions, the genuine church could not have a choir. But to others, choirs and singing schools might signify prophetic advancement, a step in building a more orderly and beautiful Kingdom of God on otherwise American soil. In singing as in doctrine, old ways suggested security, new ways growth.

The Kirtland singing school begged a basic question: how many voices does one need to make a bona fide "choir"? History gave few clues. Just as when the *Wayne Sentinel* wrote the Palmyra Presbyterian choir's numbers were "limited," one has no idea how large the singing school—also referred to as the Temple Choir—was. If they filled all the four choir lofts built into the temple, they would have numbered perhaps two hundred members or more. But since only 250 families lived in Kirtland at that time, that number seems implausible. Whatever its size, the Temple Choir steered clear of high ambition. The scribe at the dedication, held on 27 March 1836, dutifully preserved the titles of the two hymns the choir sang, both with newly written texts and one set to a well-known tune known as "Sterling." That tune essentially provided chanting chords for whatever text one assigned to it. Although four-part harmonizations of "Sterling" appear in various tunebooks of the time, we can only guess what the choir made of the hymn in phrasing, dynamics, and general expression. But it was probably as simple a setting as one could have found.

It turns out that at least some people, unaccustomed to hearing trained choirs in this new church, assumed that the songs were sung spontaneously, without rehearsal but propelled by the Spirit.[22] Others claimed they heard angel choirs singing with the Temple Choir—thus answering Smith's dedicatory prayer that his saints' voices would "mingle" with heavenly seraphs in "singing Hosanna to God and the Lamb!"—which were the final words of the choir's closing song. If the choir was split into four locations around the room, one would arguably have a hard time discerning the source of voices one heard.

Whether the Temple Choir sounded impromptu or angelic, Smith assessed it in nondescript but positive terms: they sang "admirably," he said after one rehearsal, then called them "excellent" at the dedication. These assessments, though, may have been less an aesthetic judgment than more manifestations of what he called "my native cheery temperament."[23]

As far as we can tell, this choir sang without accompaniment. And indeed, amid many, perhaps most, U.S. Protestants of the time, instruments were even more taboo than choirs. So, at this inaugural temple festival, which itself had trappings of high-church religiosity, why risk more offense? In the new Mormon canon, God had only revealed his pleasure in the singing voice—"the song of the righteous is a prayer unto me," a July 1830 revelation had said—not instrumental sound.

In 1839, after often vicious clashes with neighbors in Missouri and a series of financial collapses in Ohio, the majority of Church members moved en masse to the town of Commerce, along the banks of the Mississippi River in west-central Illinois. Digging trenches to drain the mosquito-breeding swampland on which they were settling, the Saints changed the name of their new home to the more optimistic—and fundamentally aesthetic—name of Nauvoo, Smith's transliteration of the Hebrew word meaning "beautiful place." Beyond repurposing the land and building homes, one of their early acts of civilization was to organize the University of Nauvoo. "University," of course, was a hopeful affectation: the range of schooling among the Saints no doubt varied according to their upbringing. But the university regents determined, according to Smith's bookishness, that they would promote literacy of all kinds.

After the Temple dedication, the Kirtland singing school had kept meeting every Sunday night, doubtless with as much social as aesthetic purpose. Early accounts of Nauvoo also say that "singing meetings," or choir rehearsals, continued.[24] What brought the university and the singing school together was a late-1841 petition the choir brought to the "University Regents" requesting a Department of Music in the university with a "Professor" heading it and a board of four wardens who would "regulate" music in the four wards of the city. The chancellor of the university, Mayor John Bennett, accepted the proposal with a proviso, vaguely recommending that the regents "instruct the board . . . to prohibit the flat sound of the notes, and adopt the broad." Smith, who was at the meeting, quipped, "I move the instruction, for I was always opposed to any thing flat."[25]

As the Mormon populace grew in Nauvoo, the validation of angelic descants no longer sufficed. The city of the Saints needed to show both its self-sufficiency and its equivalence to rival municipalities. Nauvoo could boast of a large populace—although like most cities, certainly on the U.S. frontier, it probably inflated its statistics for the sake of bragging rights. But Nauvoo also needed to stake its claim on cultural legitimacy. Mormons could arm themselves against the physical persecution rooted in mob mentalities. But the best antidote to the mocking of newspapermen and journalists was culture. Mormondom welcomed, even pursued, settlers from the East Coast and Europe. Each new immigrant to Nauvoo—most came from Great Britain—brought a set of expectations and, if the city was lucky, skills to contribute. That happened as much in choral music as in any other trade.

When the new university department met, Gustavus Hills presided. The "Professor" had come from New England and now, in Nauvoo, promoted Lowell Mason's Boston Academy version of singing schools, with more rigorous, European-style training and better harmonizations in their tunebooks. Two of the four university music wardens (Benjamin Wilber and Stephen Goddard) would eventually take turns directing the Church choir, while the other two (Titus Billings and John Pack) would focus more on instrumental music. Hills and the rest in attendance voted to call their department "The Teacher's Lyceum of Music in the University of the City of Nauvoo," with Hills as its ex-officio president and the wardens its ex-officio directors. They divided up other duties (secretary, treasurer, etc.), formulated rules for matriculation and class absences, agreed to meet in class once a week, and adopted two textbooks. First was Lowell Mason's *Manual of Instruction* as a textbook "for the examination of teachers in the elements of the science of Music, and as a guide for instruction in the art of sacred singing in the schools of this city." The second was Porter's *Cyclopedia of Music* "for those who wish to pursue the science beyond the elementary principles." These two books suggest how the Church wanted to move from mere "singing by note" to a whole philosophy and dogma of choral practice.[26]

While most of the *Manual of Instruction*'s 252 pages deal with vocal technique and fundamentals of notation, it begins with four chapters of introduction to the ideals behind the practice. The first chapter primarily surveys the uses and benefits of learning to sing, to wit: Singing can be learned; God gave almost everyone the ability to learn to sing. And it ought to be learned; God wants everyone to learn beautiful things. From a pragmatic, almost humanistic, viewpoint, singing improves one's vocal apparatus, general health, intelligence, and emotions. Finally, the manual makes the argument that musical training creates discipline and improves the social order, from the family outward into the community. The second chapter deals with instructional methods; the third treats the materials of teaching (room, blackboards, blank music books, etc.). Finally, the fourth chapter details the qualifications of a proper teacher. These should include piety, an ability to compose, and a knowledge that this is a divine art, one which has the traits enumerated in the first chapter.

Porter's *Cyclopedia* is not a manual but a reference book, with hundreds of cursory or detailed entries on musical topics, from timings to modulations to tunings to orchestration. The entry under "choir" trenchantly surveys and critiques such institutions. It first defines the nature of a choir, without reference to size, quality, or criteria for membership: it is simply "the company of singers associated together for the performance of sacred music in a church." Its duties are to "excite, in the bosoms of the congregation, those emotions which are indicated by the sentiment of the words sung." After these boilerplate observations, it then takes up at great length "the failings of the vocal performers," of which "it is equally painful to speak. Were a spectator, from the celestial world, to come into most of our congregations, he would regard the singing as any thing else than a devotional exercise." If heavenly beings did "mingle their voices" with human choirs, that is, it would soil their own music. "The causes of the desecration of this sacred service are various," Porter then says.

In the eight "causes" he then lists, one sees many of the issues that would both energize and daunt Mormon choirs for generations.

1. Irreverence, indifference, and distraction among the singers. If they are flipping through pages or chatting, instead of focusing on the task at hand, they can't properly lift their hearers.

2. "Too great fondness for display." If the singers can't move their hearers, they will try to dazzle them with virtuosity.

3. Hiring non-church singers to sing in church. The problem here is twofold: hiring people to sing in church at all (church service should be volunteer), and having unworthy singers (this is divine, not secular service).

4. "Extreme jealousy of interference." The choir serves the church but often refuses to listen to the clergy that governs it. "Singers frequently persuade themselves, that the psalmody is entirely their province." When their church leaders try to control their repertoire, sound, or methods, the choir members push back.

5. "The character and pretentions of the chorister. The same remarks apply to him as above to the choir, only with more force."

6. "Bad taste in the choice of tunes and style of performance. In almost every department of art and science, simplicity is the soul of excellence." Often choirs pursue ear-pleasing display or overwrought arrangements.

7. "The inattention of the congregation, who, by their listlessness, appear to regard the time of singing as a season for relaxation; or an intermission, to give them an opportunity of attending to their little private concerns."

8. "The disregard and employment of the clergyman, who is often turning over the leaves of his sermon, or looking out the next hymn, which ought to be done at home, or looking for a chapter in the bible, or in adjusting the bible &c. about the pulpit. Can he blame the choir, for handling their books and instruments during prayers, while he sets such an example?"

Summing up, Porter says that "we need a general reformation in the moral character of our choristers and choirs, and in our singing schools; and also in the conduct of ministers and congregations, before sacred music can become truly the handmaid of religion."[27]

Reflecting on the new Lyceum, in 1842 the Church newspaper *Times and Seasons* praised "the laudable zeal manifested by some of our *musical* friends, to bring about a uniform and tasteful style of sacred singing." Noting the "different prejudices and habits" of the Saints, the editorial celebrated "the improvements made, and the judicious order established within a few months past." It went on: "By the by, we peeped in the other evening, during the performance of the Musical Lyceum, and heard what will make us try to peep in again." Then it gave a purple-prosed reflection on the aims of singing, along with a spiritual anecdote:

A proper and expressive articulation of the words constitute the life and soul of music; intelligence thus clothed with the robes of melody, and harmonic numbers, moves gently over the spirit, imprints her heavenly footsteps, and awakens all its energies. We should not be so sure that the performances before hinted at were good, were it not that we are sure we have a tolerable good ear for music, or an ear for good music and we were delighted, where as our devil, who is known to have a bad ear for good music, and a good ear for bad music, was quite differently affected; he crowded in edgewise, but soon deserted,—said he could not stand the racket.[28]

Unfortunately, the account and mini-manifesto had a biased provenance: that very issue of the newspaper introduced its new assistant editor as one Gustavus Hills.

Despite his auspicious beginnings in Nauvoo, Hills's reputation crashed when it came out, within days after the Lyceum began, that Professor Hills had impregnated a choir member out of wedlock.[29] He had breached the moral rigor that a true choirmaster needed, especially one who presided over the sacred music of God's newly restored Church. But the choir carried on. While there may have been small "choirs" here and there—possibly within single families—the records of the Church at that time normally refer just to "the choir." For general Church meetings or other large events, there was one main, general choir, whose unauditioned membership would doubtless vary in size and tone quality. We do know a few things about it, though.

One is that the choir got bigger and better, mostly through the immigration of new members from Great Britain. In the fall of 1840, after proselyting in England for a few months, Apostle Brigham Young wrote to his wife that the missionaries had converted "a grate meny musisions." Meanwhile, Apostle Wilford Woodruff wrote that at Herefordshire "church ministers are alarmed" in part at the "numbers . . . of musicians [being] baptized."[30] Many of these converted musicians sailed to the New World to join with the main body of the Saints. As they did so, the Mormon Church in the United States began to be both enlarged and constrained by this new swelling of the ranks. Church rolls lengthened, of course, but the education, biases, and cultural habits of the Church veered more and more toward the Old World that was now expanding its U.S. membership.

We know little about the sound of the Nauvoo choir. But we do know that they lacked the advantage of good acoustics. They almost always sang outdoors. The main events for which the choir would sing—funerals and large Church meetings—occurred in the Grove, the huge natural amphitheater that sloped down to the Mississippi from the city plat (a map of which was ably drawn up and published, in fact, by Gustavus Hills). One 1842 account from an outsider describes the choir singing to the assembling congregation before a grove service started. The choir was "directed by one who appeared to be a professional singing-master," probably Hills.[31] A longer and more florid account of the choir from that year comes from a Mormon who gleefully praised the choir's rendition. At the funeral of Ephraim Marks, Lyman Littlefield writes that the choir sang three numbers. After the procession to the grove where Smith would preach the funeral sermon, "the choir broke the solitude of the noiseless scene; and with the artful modulation of harmonious voices, 'chanted forth a hymn to the living God.' . . . Again the choir swelled their heavenly music on the busy air. . . . [right before the close, before the procession to the graveside] solemn music of the choir re-echoed through the grove."[32]

We also don't know if performances by the choir were used as a source of income for the Church, as sometimes happened in other churches in urban centers such as Chicago (probably the only Illinois city larger than Nauvoo at the time).[33] Given the Church's and city's socialistic aims—outlined in Smith's revelations—the choir probably sang in church and funerals and provided entertainment without pay. If so, that was a generosity the Mormon church choir would overcome in future incarnations.

Helen Mar Whitney's reminiscences of the Nauvoo choir give the best set of facts about how it operated, both generally and on one specific occasion:

- One of the city's musical wardens, Stephen Goddard, conducted
- The group usually practiced outdoors on the hill next to the temple site
- Most of the men were also militia band members who might play their instruments in addition to (or instead of) singing
- When singing a New Year's Eve (1843–44) serenade to Joseph Smith and his family, they sang one or two "anthems"
- On that occasion she recalls ten singers by name and says there were "many more, too numerous to mention"[34]

That would be Smith's last New Year's Eve. On June 27, 1844, a mob cornered him and his brother Hyrum in a ragtag "jail" a few miles outside Nauvoo, gunned them down, and ran off. After being wagoned back into Nauvoo, the Smith brothers' oozing, bloated corpses lay in state at the Mansion House, the hotel where Joseph and his wife had been raising their family. Then, at the Smith family graveyard, Goddard's choir sang before the bodies were lowered into the ground.

Earlier that year, workers had finished constructing the first large indoor space in Nauvoo, the Masonic Hall. It came at the front end of a number of public construction projects that included not only a temple but a concert hall for the choir and other musicians to use. Shilling for people to buy shares to build the hall, Lyman Littlefield used the choir as his bait: their "zeal can only be made manifest by the difficult circumstances under which they are laboring, by singing in the open air and that too frequently in windy weather." The choir's constant outdoor singing meant that "we have an imperfect idea of the thrilling delight such a body of music placed under different circumstances would produce." Waxing hyperbolic in typical Victorian fashion, Littlefield extolled "the leader of the choir"—Goddard—at length, ending with a forced but reverential wordplay. Littlefield mused on being in "the great congregation of an assembled multitude" of five to ten to even twenty thousand (presumably in the grove), hearing the choir sing "the high praises of Jehovah." On that occasion, "every heart beat high in unison to the joyful lay as it echoes from the general throng [with] the loftiness, theme, and the grandeur, and harmony with which such scenes are associated." This spiritual grandeur leads us to "enquire who is the mover of this mighty mass. Notice being given for music, all eyes are eagerly placed upon one individual," who leads the choir to inspire "the enwrapt feelings of thousands." When that happens, it "forces the conviction on the mind that *God*(dard) was there."[35]

Singing outdoors, the choir had welcomed the accompaniment of the Nauvoo Legion military band to project their music to the crowd, even if the instruments overbalanced the singers. Now, at the dedication of the Nauvoo Concert Hall, both the Nauvoo Band and Choir held forth, sometimes together, other times independently, with a few speeches and solo performances sprinkled throughout the program. The choir performed two numbers generically listed as "Chorus," two more as "Song," and one as "Chorus, Duet and Chorus." Another was simply listed as "Dedicatory Hymn." But the four pieces listed by name reveal how far the choir had come: "Strike the Cymbal," "Heavenly Vision," "Jerusalem," and "Denmark." All were anthems, choral works slightly more elaborate than hymns. The first, a popular festival and dedicatory piece of the day, was Pucitta's bombastic poetic setting about David slaying Goliath. "Heavenly Vision" was William Billings's dramatic, episodic anthem based on texts from the Book of Revelation. "Jerusalem," and "Denmark" were slightly less complicated anthems common in tunebooks of the time. These performances showed three things. First, the choir had branched out from mere hymns. Second, it had not limited itself to the Lowell and Timothy Mason *Sacred Harp*, now being offered for sale in the *Times and Seasons* bookshop (adjacent to the newspaper printing shop). Third, it was ready to do full programs of choral music.

The Nauvoo Concert Hall was hardly a showplace, though. First, its acoustics were dubious. The building was thirty by fifty by eleven feet wide, but nowhere near high enough for good choral resonance. To offset that, the builders installed "sounding jars," resonating clay vases used to artificially enhance the sound properties of an otherwise-dead space. (How well they worked, if at all, we will never know—the building was demolished before the decade ended.) Second, the room had terrible ventilation. Goddard realized this two nights into the three-night dedication services, when he had the windows removed before the next concert. A reader of the *Nauvoo Neighbor* wrote to the newspaper to explain that this is why the music improved on the third night. He warned not only that "speakers [who] do not wish to injure their lungs . . . should be cautious about speaking in unventilated rooms or halls," but that the other two halls in town, the Masonic Hall and the new Seventies Hall, should have their windows fixed or replaced.[36]

Concerts continued in the hall, though without the choir. Six weeks after the hall's dedication, Goddard had fallen headfirst from the under-construction Nauvoo Temple walls as he was helping to remove the scaffolding. The floor joists broke his fall before he hit the stone floor of the basement, which would certainly have killed him. Still, his head wound bled heavily, it would be weeks before he could conduct the choir again, and no one seems to have taken his place during his recovery. In the meantime, soloists, both vocal and instrumental, joined the band in recitals. The rest of the time, the hall functioned mostly as an ad hoc meetinghouse.

At one of the Nauvoo Temple's several dedication services (6–8 October 1846), the choir sang seven times, with at least five of the numbers being hymns (among them "The Prodigal Son" and the temple dedicatory hymn introduced in Kirtland, "The Spirit of God").

But by then the populace was splitting into factions, of which the most stubborn—or stolid, depending on one's point of view—was Smith's own family, who bucked against Brigham Young and the Twelve Apostles he oversaw.

The Twelve formed part of the elaborate hierarchy—equal parts biblical, Roman Catholic, and federalist—that Smith had constructed before his death. The General Authorities who presided over the whole Church consisted of a three-man First Presidency (Smith and two counselors), the Twelve Apostles, Seventies (based on the seventy who Jesus called as missionaries in the book of Luke), and a three-man Presiding Bishopric. "Local authorities" headed up smaller units of the Church—"stakes" (from the notion of Zion as a tent with stakes to stabilize it) and smaller units that stakes comprised, called wards or branches. Stakes and branches had three-man presidencies, wards had three-man bishoprics; in each case, one man (the president or the bishop) had final authority, while his two counselors weighed in with advice or filled in when their leaders were away or incapacitated. Through the mechanisms of calling (summoning to church duty by the inspiration of higher leaders) and "sustaining" (pledging to uphold by congregational consent), this hierarchy took the

Church from the charisma of its founding Prophet into a long history of stable, even routinized formality.

While not everyone assented to the leadership of Young and the Apostles, most Mormons agreed to follow their counsel and flee Illinois. A few months before the temple's May 1846 completion in Nauvoo, thousands of Latter-day Saints had begun to migrate west, destination unknown. Young chose Stephen Goddard to be in the first company of wagons, apparently wanting a choir at the ready the moment they arrived at what a new trail song would vaguely call "the place which God for us prepared." The company temporarily settled in Iowa, calling the makeshift town simply Winter Quarters. In December 1846, Goddard set up a singing school there and revived the choir for its first performances since the dedication of the Nauvoo Temple in October. The following spring and summer, after months of wagoning and walking, hobbled by snow, malnutrition, and diseases, the company arrived in the Utah basin. Young told them to stop and settle. This was the right place to plant, survey, and start digging foundations. For public gatherings, they quickly pieced together a moderate-sized bowery where Goddard conducted a vestige of the Nauvoo-via-Winter Quarters Choir, still singing in "the difficult circumstances" of the unresonant out-of-doors.

While Smith is now best known for his trans-heavenly esotericism and visionary boldness, Young is known as a rough-hewn and somewhat brusque pragmatist. But not only were both men far more complex than their stereotypes, Young was, in fact, the musician of the two. For years he sang solos, duets, and trios at church meetings and parties, usually with his equally musical brothers. Smith's namesake nephew, Joseph F. Smith, wrote to Young's daughter Susa that "many times I have listened to duets by your Father and Uncle Joseph [Young], in which I thought it would be difficult, if not impossible for any two male voices to make better music or sweeter harmony than they did. A number of times I have heard three of the brothers, your Father, Joseph and either Phineas or Lorenzo . . . sing together as a trio as sweetly as any trio I ever heard." He added, "I am really conceited enough to believe I can distinguish good music from poor. Disharmony in duets, trios, quartettes, and concert and choir singing nearly shatters my nerves." In turn, Brigham, hearing Joseph F. sing a hymn in a Church meeting told him, "You have a good voice, and with training would make a good singer." However gifted he was as a singer, Young believed in vocal training and would promote the latest vocal methods in the Saints' new land.[37]

But Young also believed in providence. And that belief drew him to a large group of Welsh-convert singers who entered the Salt Lake Valley in 1849. Citizens of Wales typically grew up singing at almost every turn—at home, at school, at church, and at all sorts of public events, from politics to sports. So when Mormon priesthood leaders in Wales closed church meetings (or tried to start them), unquenchable singing often broke out, perhaps to bring some fervor and excitement to the otherwise potentially bland discourses that had preceded or might follow it. Thus, we find a local leader of the Church in Wales writing to the local Saints in 1851 the following:

> There is an excess of harmful singing. I visit many branches throughout the country, and the first thing that happens after a meeting is over, is singing. I am prevented from saying a word for an hour, when the true need is to give counsel to various persons. I have to listen to the singing, and by the time it is over it is time to go to bed. I enjoy hearing singing as much as anyone in the country; but there is a time for everything, and in the meetings there is a time to sing, or in singing practice, and on other occasions when circumstances allow. Instruct all to go to bed early, for their good health, and to receive wisdom, which is a commandment of the Lord to everyone. The priests and teachers are frequently prevented from officiating in their callings, because of singing when they visit the homes of the members, when everyone should be quiet at their entrance.[38]

As for their collective sonority, Welsh singing groups apparently tended to sound darker, chestier than typical U.S. church choirs, which had favored a younger, brassier tone well-suited to the outdoors. What Welsh singing may have suffered for in timbral sheen, it made up for in sheer volume. Welsh choirs sang lustily and flamboyantly, traits singers learned early on. And, perhaps more to the point, choral singing in Wales had become overtly competitive. Since about 1820, the centuries-old practice of *eistedfoddau*, public literary competitions, had begun to include choirs dueling in performance for social rank and position. So Welsh singing meant singing out, possibly less precisely than some might think proper, but always with more bravado.

As the first group of Welsh emigrants crossed the plains in 1849, one of them, William Morgan, wrote that when they first sang from their wagons, "we saw the English and the Norwegians and everyone, I would think, with their heads out of their wagons." Soon those wagons "were empty and their inhabitants running toward us as if they were charmed." People asked who the group's singing teacher was. "I said that the hills of Wales were the schoolhouse, and the Spirit of God was the teacher. Their response was, 'Well, indeed, it is wonderful; we never heard such good singing before.'"[39]

Once they arrived in Utah, these Welsh singers expanded the ranks of Goddard's choir, but only marginally, since many of them could not speak or read English. Nevertheless, they revamped the choral culture of the Church. J. W. Gunnison wrote in 1852 that typical Mormon worship in the Salt Lake Valley included "a large number of Welsh in the meetings," who, while they needed an interpreter to understand the sermons, formed choirs who would "exhilarate all present by singing one of their hymns, to one of their charming, wild romantic airs." One of these groups, or a combination of them, sang at events in the early 1850s as "The Welsh Choir."[40]

On 20 May 1849, as Welsh immigrants were still slogging across the plains, Young announced that the bowery would be dismantled and replaced. A new building would enclose the Saints in large meetings when the weather took a bad turn or the wind came up and speakers could hardly be heard even when shouting. It would be called a tabernacle.

BUILDINGS
AND PROFESSORS

A TRUE TABERNACLE, of course, in its original sense, was a large tent, the type of portable covering Moses had used in the wilderness. But for decades, Protestant churches in the United States had transposed the term to denote any decent church. The new Mormon version, their first tabernacle, would be a slightly oblong boxy structure—64 feet by 126 feet—not unlike some of the old Nauvoo halls. At the 6 April 1852 General Conference—a putative gathering of all Church members to vote for and hear talks by General Authorities—the Church dedicated this Salt Lake Tabernacle. The conference minutes name British emigrant James Smithies (about whose credentials we know virtually nothing) as the Choir director. What works the Choir performed during that first conference in the Tabernacle is hard to say—although the scribe of the conference wrote that they sounded "like a choir of heavenly angels."[1] While the minutes only mention "hymns," some by name and some with newly composed words for the occasion, scribes may have been loose in their terminology—would they know a simple hymn from a more elaborate and fulsome "anthem"? We do know that the main Church choir had sung multi-sectional, contrapuntal anthems such as William Billings's "Heavenly Vision" years earlier. And we know that the year after the Tabernacle's dedication the Choir sang the "Hallelujah Chorus" (from Handel's *Messiah*) in a General Conference in that building.

By 1855, two visitors from France could give this detailed description of the music at a Tabernacle service:

> The choristers and band belonging to the choir executed a piece of one of our greatest masters; and we feel bound to say that the Mormons have a feeling for sacred music, that their women sing with soul, and that the execution is in no notable degree surpassed by that which is heard either under the roof of Westminster, or the frescoes of the Sistine chapel. The music finished, the officiating priest extemporizes a prayer, often long enough, in which he returns thanks to God for his mercies, and makes known to him the wants of the people. At the end of the prayer all the faithful respond "Amen." Then the choir sing a hymn, after which one or more sermons follow. When the preachers have done, the choristers sing a Psalm, accompanied with music, at the close of which, the officiating priest pronounces a blessing on all present, and so the service ends.[2]

By that time, Brigham Young had led the quest for the advanced repertoire implied in that description. In February 1855, Young approved the formation of the Deseret Philharmonic Society, one of many organizations and businesses in these years that took up the name Deseret, the Book of Mormon word for "honeybee," for which the territory was now named. With Smithies appointed by Young as the Deseret Philharmonic Society's President and Conductor, the new group would coordinate and combine musical activities in the city and "promote the love and study of harmony throughout the territory." To wit, the secretary of the society, the well-known cultural and musical gadfly Jonathan Grimshaw, announced through the official Church newspaper in the United States, the *Deseret News*, that anyone on their way from Europe or the East Coast should bring scores with them. "We are much in want of the Oratorios of Handel, Haydn, Mendelssohn, &c and *new* works of merit; the whole *with full orchestral accompaniment* in separate parts, and as much as possible with *singing* copies in separate parts" (original emphasis). Orchestral and chamber scores were welcome too, as were any worthy members: "We shall also be glad if our musical brethren and sisters will report themselves to this society on their arrival here."[3]

This new enthusiasm may have dimmed somewhat during two sudden but brief phases in Utah.[4] One was the yearlong Mormon "reformation" that began in the fall of 1856. Thousands of Mormons not only had themselves rebaptized, but they committed to living what amounted to a more Puritanical life, one in which such potential vices as singing schools (and aestheticism of any sort) might harbor latent sinfulness. In 1857 this reformation overlapped with the brief Utah War, in which federal troops headed for Utah to put down what might be a budding theocracy in one of its territories. Young had people dig in, but also prepare to torch their cities and, once again, head west. Thankfully, these obsessions and threats tapered off. On one hand, the reformation relaxed; on the other, the troops backed off.

In August 1852, the Church had officially revealed its worst-kept secret: it encouraged the practice of Old Testament–style polygamy. Brigham Young was its most avid spokesman and practitioner, with his large multifamily estate laid out within a short walk of the Tabernacle. In the fall of 1860, Young added a large schoolhouse to his property, in which he could not only have his large polygamy-based brood properly taught, but begin vocal lessons for as many as two hundred children at a time under the direction of another British immigrant, David Calder, who championed a modified form of John Curwen's Tonic sol-fa method, which included hand signals to denote scale degrees and a notational system void of any notes or staves. This caught Young's fancy, since not only did he, like many Americans, still look to Europe as the gauge of cultural advancement, but he also craved novelty. Just as his own religion and marriage conventions transgressed U.S. conventions, any systems that did the same piqued his interest. Calder persuaded Young that Tonic sol-fa was the most efficient way to teach musical literacy. And it had the practical benefit of not requiring musical type. Any regular print shop could use the type at hand to print Tonic sol-fa song books with Mormon hymns. To add cachet to the new venture, the new singing school came up with a formal name: the Deseret Musical Association, with its honorary president none other than Brigham Young.[5]

The *Deseret News* promoted Calder's method in December 1860, and the 1861 and 1862 Tonic sol-fa classes at the Young schoolhouse became fashionable. Graduates of the classes sang in concerts beginning the following year in Young's latest big public construction project, the Salt Lake Theater. This building became the center point for all sorts of soirees, including plays with songs and underscoring, as well as concerts by soloists and groups of various kinds, especially touring professionals once the railroad was completed in 1865. The dedication of the theater in March 1862 featured a new anthem, "God Bless Brigham Young." Popularly known as "The Saints' National Anthem," it suggested that the Mormons now saw their society as self-contained, a new "nation" outside the nation they had left. The music to this new anthem was composed by the newly appointed director of the theater orchestra and, on Sundays, of the

Tabernacle Choir—Charles John Thomas. Young had known for months about this recent British convert—known professionally as C.J. and, to his friends, as Charley—and relished what he had heard of Thomas's exploits in the British musical scene as a theatrical conductor and composer.[6]

Historian (and son of the region's top music critic) Edward Tullidge saw Thomas's elevation to virtual overseer of music in Salt Lake City as a huge advance in the music of the Church's centerplace. And indeed, Thomas coordinated sacred and secular concerns adroitly, writing new music for both theater and Church, accompanying the Tabernacle Choir at public events with his theater orchestra, and using subsets of the Tabernacle Choir as the chorus in dramatic presentations. Tullidge remarked that before Thomas became the Tabernacle Choir conductor, the Choir "had never risen above the musical status of an ordinary choir of a country church."[7] Thomas expanded the Choir's repertoire not only in the classical realm, but also into the popular. He was certainly the first to have the Tabernacle Choir, under that name, sing a Stephen Foster song, "Hard Times Come Again No More" (in December 1862), which became a recurring number at General Conferences of the Church. Being a composer also meant that he wouldn't have to order music months ahead of scheduled performances to get the scores from back East. He could write serviceable new material at the drop of a hat—though was publicly excoriated by for sometimes writing "grammatically incorrect" music, that is, music with part-writing "errors" such as parallel fifths.[8]

Perhaps part of what elevated Thomas's stature in Utah musical history was his severity and self-regard. He bristled if someone did not use the title "Professor" before his name. One member of his theater orchestra thought Thomas "a very rigid disciplinarian." Those he conducted "knew it was their duty to [rehearse] to the best of their ability for the eagle eye of the conductor got on them constantly, and if any of them got a little careless or negligent, they were called to account immediately." Although he praised his musicians when praise was due, "he never allowed any one to slight his work. . . . The company learned to fear, respect and admire him."[9] Presumably, some of those traits bled into his choral conducting, though perhaps with a tinge of spiritual leaven. At the same time, Thomas looked after the vocal health of his singers, recommending as a cure for hoarseness the home remedy of "a few drops of nitric acid in a glass of sweetened water, twice a day."[10]

Yet despite Thomas's skill and aplomb, he received no pay for his conducting in either church or theater, only blessings from above, territorial bragging rights, and free advertising for the dozens of private and group music lessons he offered.

All musicians in Deseret, one player explained in 1864, "are expected always to be in tune, on all public occasions in the true Mormon style, without purse, or even city scrip" (alluding to Jesus' command to his apostles to travel and proselytize with no money or provisions).[11] Still, though Young did not believe in paying musicians (yet), he allowed Thomas to mount benefit concerts for himself in the theater rent free.[12]

Young touted Calder's vocal-notational system on visits he made to towns throughout the region. Its methods made some inroads in the settlements, egged on by well-publicized concerts at the theater featuring huge choirs of Tonic sol-fa trained children, during the evenings of the Church's semiannual General Conference. Of their December 1863 concert, one local critic said that the Deseret Musical Association showed "prophetic signs of the growth of a grand national institution for the 'lovers of harmony and sweet sounds.'"[13] The esteemed Mormon poetess Eliza Snow (one of Brigham Young's wives) even penned a poem about the event, simply titled "That Concert." In the children's massive choir, she saw "a type of the choirs above." She praised their diction, poise, and "pure strains." Someday, she hoped, they would "all join in the chorus with Gabriel's lyre, / At the crowning of Zion's great king."[14]

Around this time, adult choirs were forming in many smaller cities in Deseret, including Spanish Fork, Springville, Provo, and Ogden. New tabernacles began to be planned and erected in various townships, each with its choir loft, mostly for choirs of a few dozen singers. Meanwhile, on 6 April 1863, Young announced plans for a new Tabernacle on Temple Square. One of its architects, Truman Angell (brother of another of Young's wives), tinkered with plans for months. Along the way, he discussed with a Brother Sands, "leader of the singers," the choir seating in the building. Whether this "leader"—now understood to be Robert Sands, yet another British immigrant—was the same person as the "chorister" of the choir Angell later mentioned having met with is hard to say. In any case, Angell thought the latter "a very modest man."[15]

The centerpiece of the New Tabernacle's west end, planted like a massive tree trunk looming over the choir loft, would be a new organ specially built for the hall. Small instrumental bands had often accompanied the choir in the outdoors. In 1857, the immigrant Joseph Ridges had a decent organ imported from Australia and installed in the Old Tabernacle. But this huge king of instruments in the New Tabernacle would become a surrogate orchestra. It would also allow for bona fide instrumental recitals, which would be dominated in the early years by a precocious teenager named Joseph Daynes. The total cost of the new instrument was to be $40,000. That cost would keep growing, of course, as additions, upgrades, maintenance, and all sorts of tinkering would bless and dog the organ for the rest of its existence. But the cost paid off in the Tabernacle's esteem: Apostle George Smith later said that Mayor French of Boston declared the new organ "more handsome and sweeter-toned" than the renowned German organ in the Boston Music Hall.[16]

Just as the building construction was begun, Young abruptly sent Thomas to the southern tip of Utah, St. George, to teach music in the sweltering heat of Utah's rapidly growing Dixie (nickname for the territory's southlands). The move seemed calculated, in that Young had his eye on an even more accomplished British immigrant "professor," George Careless. According to Careless, Young asked him to oversee not only the Tabernacle Choir and Salt Lake Theater, but music in the Church generally. Careless said that Young told him he wanted Careless to "lay a good foundation" for music in Utah—an almost brazen statement, if true, considering what had already been accomplished. Young's call to Careless was to be "chief director of music throughout the church," which included, according to Careless, to "immediately [begin] development of the Tabernacle choir." Young said he wanted music that sounded like angels, although Careless insisted that worthy music not always sound "sweet." One added asset in this transaction was Careless's wife Lavinia: she sang like an angel, many said, and could possibly have a touring career outside of Utah. She was, Young's daughter later said, Brigham's favorite singer.[17]

In 1867, teams of workmen finished up the main part of the new Tabernacle, a building that looked, as one Apostle put it, like a giant tortoise shell or like "Noah's Ark turned bottom side up"—both apt metaphors for this refuge in the desert. Although engineers kept modifying the structure for decades, the dazzling and disheartening miracle of the new hall was its hypersensitive acoustics. The interior space was astonishingly "live," reverberating like an Old World cathedral. This was both a boon and a drawback for any choir who sang there, of course. The alluring acoustics would actually draw prospective audiences to the hall. Any choir would sound special in it. Yet one struggled to hear a speaker clearly, it turned out, and the room blurred every staccato passage the Choir sang. The Choir could easily get spoiled by this building. When they sang elsewhere, they would have to dramatically readjust their expectations of raw sonic warmth.

The minutes of the October 1867 dedication of the New Tabernacle record that the Salt Lake Choir of 150 voices was conducted by someone identified only as Elder Sands. While minutes from subsequent Conferences typically indicate that "the choir" sang, or even the "Tabernacle Choir" sang, the person who led that choir is only mentioned once—"Mr. Sands"—until in 1869 "Brother George C. Careless" finally is credited.[18] Whatever Robert Sands's abilities may have been, his name was usually omitted from lists of conductors of the Tabernacle Choir from the 1880s through the 1910s—that is, among lists made by the very people who witnessed firsthand who actually took charge. Sands may have been an acting director of the Tabernacle's Choir from time to time, or perhaps he was an understudy or apprentice to Careless. But Careless is clearly the direct successor of Thomas at the helm of the Tabernacle Choir, though he no doubt handed over some choral conducting duties when overwhelmed by his orchestral assignment at the Salt Lake Theater. The Tabernacle Choir could be a kind of spiritual moonlighting for "professors" busy with paying students and gigs.

Throughout the 1860s and 1870s, a variety of choirs sang in General Conference besides the Tabernacle Choir, the most popular being the Brigham City Ward Choir, usually referred to as Fishburn's Choir (after its conductor, John Fishburn). What did all these choirs sing? Mostly hymns, some anthems, and the occasional male glee, the latter being known for its upbeat, heraldic quality. As to how well they sang, one local paper said that, although Young had long preferred the Tabernacle Choir to any of its rivals, the Choir under Careless surpassed all previous incarnations of the group and any other choirs that sang in their company. For "beautiful music" and "genuine artistic efficiency," the Tabernacle Choir trumped the others.[19]

To get that "efficiency" the Choir needed disciplined rehearsal. That meant rehearsing not only right before performances, but also every Friday evening from 5:30 to 7:00.[20] In spring and summer, light would bleed into the Tabernacle enough to allow some visibility of the manuscript parts (bound or unbound) from which the singers generally read. Most of the time, though, a singer would have to hold a candle in one hand and the corner of the vocal part in the other. Each of these parts, hand copied by members of the Choir, had only the notes for their section and no text underlying them. The words would have to be memorized or read from the palm-size hymnbook of the Church, which a given singer would have to hold in a free hand, if, between candles and parts, one was available. This situation, of course, was intolerable. At his first rehearsal, right after Young called him in 1865, Careless demanded—and got—not only an oil-lit chandelier for the building, but also a stove for heating the cavernous space.[21]

In 1869–70, trying to correct the Tabernacle acoustics and accommodate almost four thousand more in the audience, Young had a thirty-foot-wide gallery built around 480 feet of the upper perimeter of the Tabernacle's interior walls. This addition proved a mixed blessing. More bodies surrounding the upper walls meant less reverberation and thus greater clarity for speakers at the pulpit. But more people, especially children, meant more ambient noise. After the gallery was installed, one Apostle remarked from the pulpit that, despite the improvement in acoustics, "if all who attend Conference will leave their coughing at home, sit still while here and omit shuffling their feet, they may have an opportunity of hearing pretty much everything that may be said." Even so, he said, a speaker would have to work hard to fill this space with one voice, "and that effort must be met by a corresponding effort on the part of the audience to preserve perfect stillness."[22] That, of course, would never happen. But a choir, especially one whose size kept growing, could indeed project its music through the hall admirably.

In reviewing the music of the April 1870 General Conference, the Church's *Millennial Star* newspaper said that "never before, we think, has the Tabernacle choir been in such a state of efficiency, and the highest credit is due to Professor Careless, the conductor, and to the brethren and sisters of the choir, for their excellent rendering of the various compositions sung." The review then asserted that "like most other professions here, [music] in days past has received but little attention, and has not been studied scientifically, hence its interpretations have been crude, and have lacked that finish and delicacy so necessary to the musical artist." But, "times are changing [and] the taste of the people, thanks to the exertions of Professors Calder, Thomas, John Tullidge, sen., Careless and others, is improving." The kingdom was now passing through a "transition state," which "promises before long to be followed by one as strongly characterized by taste, skill, and proficiency, as that of the past by a lack of these qualities."[23]

In 1872, Careless called together the conductors of choirs who had recently sung in the Tabernacle. After their discussion of the future of choral music in the Tabernacle, Careless wrote an open letter to "the choir masters and choristers of the territory."[24] He began by reaffirming his belief that his people's music should surpass that of others' and that "by study, perseverance and co-operation, in time they can do so." Toward that end, he and his colleagues had made two resolutions. First, all Mormon choirs should be singing from the same book. That would allow people to move from choir to choir or amalgamate into larger choirs without a complete disruption in repertoire. Second, all Mormon choral singers needed to become good sight readers, so they could advance to "a higher class of music" and thus perform it accurately and well. At the following General

Conference, April 1873, he proposed to have "an amalgamation of choirs on a larger scale" and wanted all choirs to begin rehearsing for that. He then invited any and all choir singers in the territory to join in this mega-choir, whose first non-Church concert appearance was slated for that November.[25]

The chief choral collection they used was *Thomas's Sacred Music*, one of the standard works in English-speaking countries at that time. It was filled with hymns (or "choruses") and anthems by the likes of Handel, Haydn, Mozart, and Mendelssohn, as well as lesser known composers, including its compiler, J. R. Thomas, who had the lion's share of new pieces in the book. The book used traditional—as opposed to Tonic sol-fa—notation, wrote the parts in four lines (SATB), and included an organ part, usually to double the vocal parts. It was a prime example of "modern" choirbooks rooted in European tradition, not the ragtag singing-school tradition of the U.S. South and Midwest, with their often dubious harmonies and voice leading. If Mormon choral music was now in the firm grasp of immigrant professors, this book embodied their doctrine.

Thomas's collection joined a torrent of newly published Mormon hymns, songs, and anthems, as well as publications of new music issued by the Church's Sunday School Union, which had now essentially institutionalized and brought under Church governance the vocal training of youth that Calder had begun. In the early 1870s, the combined Mormon Sunday schools of the region began to have annual concerts in the Tabernacle, pageants in which thousands of children sang, not only in thousand-voice choirs, but in trios, quartets, and even in the occasional solo rendition. In the summer of 1875, the Sunday School of the Church created a subsidiary: the Deseret Sunday School Musical Union. Its officers contained a who's who of Tabernacle professors: C. J. Thomas, now back in the city and directing a variety of local choirs, as president; as one of its vice presidents, Thomas Griggs, who would soon be voted in as the new Tabernacle Choir conductor; as chair of the Committee on Music, Ebenezer Beesley, who would become acting conductor of the Choir in Griggs's absence; and Joseph Daynes as organist. This meant that the children of Zion would all be trained by Tabernacle insiders, who would gain, in turn, long-term auditions for prospective recruits to the Tabernacle Choir. And for the composers of the hymns, it meant large choirs at the ready to run through the music.[26]

At the same time, Careless got Young to start paying musicians. That meant cutting the personnel of the theater orchestra; the seven who remained were paid fifteen dollars a week for their services. That lined their pockets and also set the scale for other gigs they might play—recitals, dances, weddings, and so forth—the usual fee for which was three to five dollars a night per player.[27] The Choir, however, was not as fortunate: Tabernacle Choir singers, unlike many members of church choirs, have always been unpaid volunteers. Careless himself, though, did receive what appears to have been the first salary paid to conduct the Tabernacle Choir, probably a thousand dollars a year.[28]

All of the professors in this widening network of British-led Mormon music making seem to have known that the next step for the city was to mount an oratorio—preferably the one oratorio that most choirs in the United States cut its teeth on: Handel's *Messiah*. The Moravians of Pennsylvania had sung it just a year after its premiere in 1741; and, beginning in 1818, Boston's Handel and Haydn Society choir sang *Messiah* almost yearly. But, although the Tabernacle Choir had been singing the "Hallelujah Chorus" since at least the early 1850s, it took until 1875 for Careless to bring together the theater orchestra and the Tabernacle Choir for a full performance of the work. The two groups had worked together before—in Thomas's 1866 Salt Lake Theater production of *Macbeth*, for example, a show that used both Thomas's original music and the Tabernacle Choir as advertising hooks to fill up the seats. But *Messiah* united these groups (and other musicians from the region) and allowed for Careless to conduct them across a new cultural threshold.

On 3 June 1875, a huge, fashionably dressed audience gathered in the Salt Lake Theater to hear the first oratorio performed in Utah, indeed, a work only one member of the entire combined forces had ever heard before. The newspapers, predictably, generally glowed about the performance, with occasional small jibes about this or that needing improvement. Criticism was leveled at the lack of punctuality, since the event was billed as beginning at 7:00 P.M. but didn't commence until 8:00. The undisputed hit of the night was Lavinia Careless's account of "I Know that My Redeemer Liveth," for which the audience demanded an encore.

Before the premiere, Young had listened to a rehearsal and quizzed Careless about the principles of the counterpoint he heard, then threw Careless the compliment that "the choir followed every motion of your stick."[29] The ability to lead a large group with the wave of a musical wand no doubt intrigued and inspired a religious despot like Young.

Whatever the highlights or flaws of the premiere performance, no event in Mormon musical history to this point vaulted into legend as this one did. In 1886, historian Edward Tullidge's assessment almost tumbled over itself. "Now the great and relative significance of the oratorio of the 'Messiah' in Salt Lake City is, that it marks the beginning of the musical culture in their supreme line of a people with the genius and subject of the 'Messiah' actually embodied in their whole history. . . . The very prophecies, in the history of the past of this peculiar community, proclaim with trumpet tongue that Salt Lake City in the coming time will be the city of America pre-eminent in the oratorio performances." This performance, possibly superior to any in London and definitely than any in Chicago, he wrote, compelled us "to affirm that Salt Lake City is one of the greatest musical cities in the world."[30]

Careless and Calder had by now merged their musical clout into a business alliance that ranged from vocal and instrumental lessons to sheet music to pianos to band instruments, all purveyed in a downtown Salt Lake storefront. The two professors also issued polemics, critiques, and even new music via a new magazine, the *Utah Musical Times*. The cast-metal musical fonts that Calder and Careless had imported into the territory via the new railroad allowed them to publish fresh scores in the magazine, from hymns to anthems to parlor songs to solo piano pieces. The journal ceased publication in 1878, though, not long after the August 1877 death of Brigham Young, whom the magazine called "the chief patron of the musical movements among the people over whom God made him a leader."[31]

For the leader's funeral, the Tabernacle Choir—now over two hundred voices strong—sang three laments, one newly composed by Careless. Tabernacle organist Joseph Daynes played two dirges by Mendelssohn and a third he had just written, a simple, minor-key trope on the pioneer song "Come, Come Ye Saints." Perhaps the underlying tribute was not the music itself but the confidence and self-containment the Tabernacle music crew displayed in the attempt.

Around the time of Young's death, a local musician's union formed, a labor cooperative that intended not only to correlate and govern large-scale musical projects in Salt Lake City, but also to oversee musicians' wages. Careless would have none of this sort of unionizing, feeling that no Mormon should take a part in such potentially coercive organizations. After four years of disagreements, the union threatened to strike the theater and, in the fall of 1880, Careless quit his position as the official conductor of both the theater orchestra and, as if to wash his hands of municipal conductorship altogether, the Salt Lake Tabernacle Choir.[32] He somewhat unconvincingly wrote to the *Salt Lake Herald* that John Taylor, Young's successor as President of the Church, had not forced him out of his leadership positions. Thereafter, Careless briefly continued conducting via his own eponymous ensemble, the Careless Orchestra, whose unnerving name perhaps forestalled its success.

On 19 August 1880, the Choir elected Thomas Griggs as the new conductor. At the time, Griggs was on a British mission, which he still had over a year left to serve.[33] In his absence, newly elected assistant conductor Ebenezer Beesley took charge. Fortunately for scholars, he also began taking minutes of the Choir's activities for the first time in its history.[34] Not only do those minutes suggest some of the rehearsal procedures that preceded and continued during Beesley's tenure, they also reveal how deftly Beesley led the Choir to monetize their Christian spirit and Mormon sense of self-reliance. They did so by pooling their means into two funds. One was the Careless Baton Fund, designed to raise $23.50 for a gold-and-silver-laced mahogany "heavily encased" baton for their former leader. The second was a Perpetual Benefit Fund, whose aim was "a higher standard of musical excellence" through financial independence. The Choir would take donations from its members (and generous outsiders), buy new music, mount concerts, add any profits to the fund, and reinvest in repertoire and new concerts as well as donate money to needy people or institutions in their orbit. An early ledger entry shows the fruits of this effort: the Choir grossed $597.50 for a concert at Brigham Young Academy, the new Church school in Provo, forty miles south of Salt Lake City. The Choir's expenses were $185. They donated $250 to the academy and put the remaining $162.50 in the Choir's bank account.

After the first rehearsal with Beesley at the podium, Thomas McIntyre wrote in his journal a terse assessment of the loss of Careless: "Beesley leads the choir. George is missed very much in the Anthem."[35] The roster of the Choir had now nearly halved, down to 111.

In November 1881, Griggs came home. Within a few weeks, he and Taylor decided to switch his calling with Beesley's: Griggs became assistant conductor, and Beesley remained in charge.[36] Immediately, Beesley wrote to Taylor, asking what he could expect his salary to be, given that as the Choir's director he would have to oversee the copying of parts into partbooks, keep the partbooks in good repair, write new music, rehearse, organize concerts, recruit new singers, and exert "general watchcare" over the spiritual health of the Choir. He pointed out that these duties would disallow other employment, so he would need to get paid at least what Careless had gotten.

Taylor replied with strong praise for Beesley's "promptness of action" with the Choir and placed a thousand dollars in an account for him, though with no firm commitment about future pay.[37] It was a down payment on growth. Expecting Beesley to build up the Choir's size, Taylor authorized a one-third increase in choir seats in the Tabernacle to two hundred, matching the number of singers

Careless had accumulated at the Choir's peak but would not have been able to squeeze into the existing loft. He also approved electric lighting in the building, to be turned on for the first time on 4 July 1882. The eight installed lights helped that concert dazzle the holiday crowd. When the increasingly forgetful Taylor saw the bill, he became angry until Sunday School President George Goddard reminded him he had approved the installation just weeks earlier.[38]

That March, U.S. President Chester Arthur had signed into law the Edmunds Anti-Polygamy Act, which targeted men who "cohabited" with more than one woman, revoking those men's right to vote, ability to serve on a jury, and ability to hold political office—all this in addition to the ongoing criminalization of cohabitation that President Lincoln had authorized two decades earlier. In the next six years, 1883–88, three Apostles and a multitude of midlevel Church leaders and lay members went to prison on the strength of this law. Even Taylor went into hiding for the final three years of his Presidency till his death in 1887.[39]

Mormon choral tradition, though, could not be suppressed, even behind bars. Not only did the Tabernacle Choir visit and sing to their brethren in prisons, but Mormon male prison choruses sprang up, appointing their own conductors, welcoming non-Mormons into their ranks, and even enticing at least one prison official to join. These groups favored songs about home on the one hand and, on the other, songs that mocked the legal system that had cut them off from their now criminally overpopulated families.[40] Back in Salt Lake City, though, male attendance at Tabernacle Choir rehearsals began to shrink. Some sopranos and altos, too, plural wives themselves, stayed home to shield their identities.

Still, the minutes of rehearsals and other meetings reveal how ambitious the Choir had become, even with falling attendance. In the October 1883 General Conference alone, for example, they sang twenty-four pieces, split about evenly between hymns and anthems. More astonishingly, for the first time ever in a General Conference, most of the words and all of the music were written by Mormon authors and composers. At the next General Conference, in April 1884, the Choir sounded so good that the *Utah Journal*, published in nearby Logan, published this backhanded compliment, reflective of the cattiness that went with choral rivalry among Utah's various tabernacle choirs: "The singing of the Salt Lake Tabernacle Choir is very fine and has improved of late. It promises to become as good as that of our Logan Choir. When it does[,] Utah will possess two splendid choral organizations." That fall, after more jibes had appeared in the *Journal*, the Logan Choir's conductor wrote a letter of apology for the affront to Beesley and his Choir, who, of course, accepted it.[41]

In the summer of 1884, a *Harper's Monthly* writer published his thoughts on the Tabernacle and its Choir. He described the building vividly, citing its dimensions and its relative invisibility amid the trees and wall that surrounded Temple Square, giving "the impression of an enormous building more than half buried." He admired the electric lighting, which, though it revealed "the chilling bareness of the huge whitewashed vault" was "relieved by hangings of evergreens and tissue-paper flowers." The sacrament area was "loaded with baskets of bread and tankards of water" to distribute to the thousands of people who met there on Sunday afternoons. The organ and organist rivaled those from New York. The Choir, though, did "not come up to a New York performance." Still, it was "conspicuously good for the material at hand and the locality." Backhanded praise indeed—but no doubt apt.[42]

Four months before the *Harper's* piece appeared, though, Beesley had already crafted new criticisms of the Choir, writing an open letter to the Choir, referring to the General Conference at which they had just sung.[43] First, he declared it an "ordeal" to have to prepare so much music for the event, given their limited rehearsal time. He had one positive thing to say about their execution: they stayed in tune. He offered reasons and remedies for his two negative comments. First, the Choir "lacked in execution in some pieces" because some members were not up to the task. Apparently, the Choir was unauditioned, because Beesley promised to begin "testing the voice and capability of each new applicant for membership" from then on. Second, some Choir members could not get a seat. Apparently, those who came early were letting family and friends sit with them in the choir loft. From then on, Beesley would issue tickets to Choir members to access the loft, appointing someone to check the tickets before a person could sit.

Beyond tickets, Beesley seems to have been the first conductor to formalize an attendance policy.[44] If a member didn't show up for four rehearsals in a row, he or she would be sent a form letter demanding that they attend the next rehearsal or they would be dropped from the Choir and have to reapply for admittance. Readmittance, of course, would require a solemn pledge of repentance and renewed zeal. The new policy showed that quality trumped quantity in Beesley's mind. Taylor had expanded the choir loft, but Beesley now insisted on deepening the Choir's prowess.

For the rest of the decade, the Choir proceeded with at least five apparent missions. One was its charitable communalism. Another was to staff conferences and services at the Tabernacle. A third was a series of "excursions"—one- or two-stop tours—to various places around the territory, including Provo, Nephi, and

Tooele to the south, and Ogden to the north. A fourth was to serenade Church dignitaries or other prominent people in need of cheer, the Choir singing outside their homes—something like caroling out of season. The fifth, and most lasting, was to be the sounding board for new four-part arrangements of every hymn in the Mormon hymnbook.

Since its founding in 1830, the Church had never officially published a hymnbook with printed music. Two ad hoc independent productions had appeared (in 1844 and 1857), while the Sunday School and Primary (children's) organizations had published tunebooks of their own. But the official canon of hymns had always existed in thick, pocketbook lyrics-only collections. In 1885, Beesley, Daynes, and Griggs sent a letter to Taylor, their president in exile, proposing that they compile and issue a choir book containing four-part settings of all the hymns in the lyrics-only hymnbook. Taylor turned them down, because "as there are many questions of importance connected therewith we would prefer not doing anything about this matter at present." Soon, with a five-man committee of professors—Careless and the young Welshman Evan Stephens added to the other three—Taylor relented.[45] The compilation flowed smoothly because many of the settings had already been published in other books and magazines and in many cases had been tested by the Tabernacle Choir, who rehearsed them and presented them in their Sunday meetings and General Conferences. In 1889, the committee issued the product, *The Latter-day Saints' Psalmody*, a hefty volume of hymns printed on heavy stock, typeset large enough so that a pair of singers could share the book easily. Each hymn was identified by its tune title only, although the texts were partially printed between the treble and bass parts. The musical style was almost entirely formal, staid, almost Anglican, at least in the newly composed settings, of which there were dozens. It was a choir book, miles in attitude and style from the congregational gospel hymnbooks that had become the rage in U.S. evangelical Protestantism.

Despite abundant incarcerations for polygamy, the Mormon populace remained belligerent toward the Edmunds Act. So in February 1887, Congress fought back by passing the Edmunds-Tucker Act, which disincorporated the Church and seized its assets. By that time, the Choir members and leaders had already complained bitterly about how it was being ravaged by federal officers. One 1885 entry in the minutes, for example, not only lamented the Choir's dwindling ranks under the older Edmunds Act, but took aim at prosecutors, who now tried "to harass and annoy honest and virtuous men who are members of the Church and have more wives than one."[46] While good men and women were being rounded up by men in badges, could it be that at the same time "prostitution houses of ill fame and associate crimes are smiled upon by the officials of the U.S. Government in Salt Lake City, and supported by those not of this Church, without fear of molestation from the 'law'?" The entry in the minutes ends with this threat: "A righteous God will ere long reckon with the wicked and adulterous." Within a year of that entry, despite continuous recruitment, the Choir rolls had shrunk back to only a hundred members, many of whom were absenting their way into being cut from the Choir. Now, with passage of this all-or-nothing act of Congress, the Tabernacle Choir threatened to become a mere vestige of a defunct U.S. sect. But what seemed the Choir's impending doom turned out to be yet another "transition state"—a kind of cocoon from which an enormous butterfly was about to burst.

CHAPTER 3

"MY TABERNACLE 'MORMON' CHOIR"

IN 1890 MORMONS OUTGREW two fads, one doctrinal, the other musical. First was the idea that the world would end between December 1890 and December 1891. This commonplace belief, which helped nurture Mormon ferocity in the face of anti-polygamy legislation, derived from a statement Joseph Smith had made in 1835: "I was once praying very earnestly to know the time of the coming of the Son of Man, when I heard a voice repeat the following: Joseph, my son, if thou livest until thou art eighty-five years old, thou shalt see the face of the Son of Man; therefore let this suffice, and trouble me no more on this matter."[1] He would turn eighty-five on December 5, 1890. We can never know how Smith might have tamped the idea down had he lived into middle age. But clearly the idea remained lively in the culture, as seen in statements opposing it. On 7 October 1889, for example, Apostle Francis Lyman spoke in General Conference against "the idea of the world coming to an end in 1891." A year later, George Q. Cannon—one of two counselors to Wilford Woodruff—Taylor's successor—said in General Conference, "Concerning 1891 I will say that the Savior will not then come in glory."[2] At that same conference, the Church voted to approve Woodruff's manifesto announcing the putative end of any more polygamous unions.

That manifesto sounded the doctrinal gavel on the 1891 question. Jesus' return was a long way off. If the Church was to survive, let alone grow to its professed destiny, the husks of its past had to flake off. And if Utah was to become one of the United States—however contrary to its original pretensions of independence—it had to show it was in step with U.S. norms. In marriage terms, that meant strict monogamy, an enormous shift in the Mormon community.

In musical terms, entering the mainstream meant full commitment to standard musical notation and a letting-go of the musical fad of Tonic sol-fa. The Sunday School Union took up the issue on 24 October 1890, less than three weeks after the manifesto vote. Its board met to discuss the respective merits of the Tonic sol-fa system versus "the old notation," notes on musical staves. That meeting ended with a resolve to invite Tonic sol-fa proponent Thomas McIntyre and "old-notation" champion Evan Stephens to come to their next meeting and make their cases. A week later, at 3 P.M., the two guests spoke "in favor of their respective methods of teaching music." Stephens began with a tone of compromise: "in his labors [he] depends a great deal on the inspiration of the moment, and generally blends the staff and Tonic sol-fa notations and finds the best results therefrom." McIntyre "uses the Tonic sol-fa system exclusively and thinks it far superior to the staff notation or a blending of the two." The discussion, Abraham Cannon noted, was "quite protracted."[3] The board selected staff notation. The next day, fortuitously, Stephens began a twenty-six-year stint as conductor of the Tabernacle Choir.

Stephens was already a legend in Salt Lake City, mostly for running massive singing schools for children and adolescents, who gave spectacular concerts awash in decorations and a flamboyance that even included Stephens appearing in drag. He had no formal training in Wales but had spent ten months in Boston in 1885 studying with George Whitefield Chadwick (who would eventually become the director of the New England Conservatory). Although Stephens touted that training in later years, he also claimed that he had quit studying with Chadwick because the latter drank liquor. Stephens apparently thought he had nothing to learn from a "gentile" who had not signed on to the Mormon health code that prohibited hard drinks.[4] But training had little to do with his conductorial appeal, which seems to have been based on charisma and fervor. One organist said that Stephens "led with up-beats, vigorously and inspiringly. It seemed impossible to sing flat; the singers were hypnotized."[5] Another observer simply said that "he is a conductor sui generis," whose prodigious accomplishments made him in fact "a young old man."[6]

For the conductorship of the Tabernacle Choir, the choice of Stephens had three clear benefits, each with its corresponding drawback. First, he could probably double the size of the Choir. He had been holding huge vocal classes and concerts for young people for years in Salt Lake City. Hundreds of students and former students would follow him into the Choir's ranks. The drawback was that these would be young singers, mostly teenagers. The second appeal was that not only was he a bachelor, and hence exempt from prosecutorial pursuit, but he had developed a large young male following. He could easily replenish the men's sections with bachelors immune to anti-polygamy laws. The drawback: the odds were that many of these young men would marry, leave to go on missions, or both. So their prospective tenure with the Choir would be short. Third, these new young singers could read music, which would allow him to pursue a more complex repertoire. The drawback: Stephens was a composer. That meant that many of the scores the Choir would learn might bear his name instead of better-known and possibly worthier masters.

One bonus advantage Stephens had was that he was Welsh. That would prove decisive in turning the municipal Mormon Choir into a national phenomenon.

Stephens seized his new job with gusto. Under his baton, discipline prevailed. He would lecture to the Choir on singing the words of the songs thoughtfully and forbid them from blank-faced mumbling. Soon he would insist that stake presidents and bishops relieve Choir members of any callings that would conflict with Tabernacle Choir rehearsals. In his first months as conductor, he urged his Church overseers to fund the purchase of scores—members would suffer no more handwritten parts as they had under Careless and Beesley. Some of the scores, of course, would be his own: within two months of assuming the conductorship, he had published two new anthems. One, "Let the Mountains Shout for Joy," would become the Choir's signature piece for decades.[7]

One year after his appointment, Stephens wrote a letter to the *Deseret Weekly* reviewing his achievements and laying down plans for the future. He had added over four hundred singers, bringing the rolls to 550 (though the average attendance was only "a little over 300 for the past year"). He had also created a new thousand-voice youth choir to train future members of the adult Choir. The youth choir had already had about sixty rehearsals, while the adult Choir, the Tabernacle Choir proper, had nearly 150 rehearsals and performed at around 125 church services or other assemblies. They also had performed in nine concerts: one with the Sunday School Union, one with a group of ward choirs, one with the Mendelssohn Quintette Club, two with the youth choir, two with the Salt Lake Choral Society and Gilmore's Band, and two by themselves.[8]

Stephens held the purse strings, too, about which he reported in the same letter. The Choir had amassed nearly three thousand dollars from its concerts, from tuition for the required new member classes—which Stephens taught—and from accrued interest. They had spent just over two thousand dollars on scores, classroom rentals, a blackboard, a new choral platform and seats, as well as fees paid to Stephens. The financial books, he added, were open for anyone to examine.

He then laid out his aims:

First, to bring and keep together a large choir corresponding with the size of the building and congregations meeting therein. Second, to keep ourselves in a supply of funds that will enable this large body of singers to receive such training free of charge to them, as will make their artistic status equal to their numerical; also to supply them with the very best and most suitable music to be found, in fact to remove all obstacles in the way of improvement and perfect work. We are now in a condition to give fifteen hundred people free class training in the following branches, so important not only to our improvement as a choir, but as a community: Sight reading, effective chorus singing, voice culture, conducting, harmony and composition, and pipe organ playing. Each of these studies will be taught to all members who desire them, provided they are willing to devote sufficient time and energy to the studies, and, in the latter studies, show sufficient talent and adaptability for the special branches to justify their taking them, and give a pledge that the choir will have the benefit of their services in return whenever desired and within reason. These I believe are privileges which no body of singers have heretofore enjoyed, and is brought about without hardship to any one, without even placing any one under obligations to any one.

All he requested from the Church, he said, was "simply a continuation of past patronage" and a list of improvements to the Tabernacle organ. He seemed confident he would get whatever he asked for: "The hearty support and practical encouragement I have received in the past assures me that all improvements necessary to our future growth and success within a reasonable time [will] be provided." Although his aims were unprecedented, he knew that the Church leaders needed this Choir to thrive if they wanted it to help polish their image in the eyes of the nation.

The United States was also entering its own age of self-consciousness—even, arguably, self-absorption—that achieved a kind of coronation in Chicago at the World's Columbian Exposition of 1893, the World's Fair organized to commemorate the quadricentennial of Columbus's arrival in the Western Hemisphere. While ostensibly opening this fair to the world, the country was actually pulling up its welcome mats. Hostility toward immigrants, most recently immigrants from Ireland, abounded. In 1892, the Congress extended the Chinese Exclusion Act, which suspended the immigration of Chinese laborers into the United States. And, of course, huge tracts of land continued to be taken from Native Americans by the federal government.

The Church and the Utah Territorial Legislature decided to use the Columbian Exposition to recalibrate their status with the country at large. Mormons and Utahns were indeed foreigners of a kind, self-exiled expatriates posing as new prospective immigrants. In *Exhibiting Mormonism*, Reid L. Neilson analyses how Mormons tried to use the Columbian Exposition to salve their ruined image.[9] Every fair—county, state, national or, now "world"—is built on exhibits of accomplishments. The main exhibit of the Church at this fair was the Tabernacle Choir. Its nearest ancestor, of course, had inhabited Illinois, the state from which the Church had fled the United States almost half a century earlier. The Choir now returned to Illinois as a quasi-Welsh contestant in a high-stakes sing-off for cash and, more important, for national bragging rights.

This showcase event was essentially a national eisteddfod, organized by a committee of Welsh choraliers wanting to showcase the choral competition of their immigrant communities on a grand stage. The eisteddfod would feature several singing competitions, including one for large mixed chorus with a first-prize purse of five thousand dollars, the second-place winner taking a thousand dollars.

Taking immediate notice of the event, two choirs in the Welsh-American hub of Scranton, Pennsylvania, were counting on it to certify which of the two was the superior group. The Scranton Choral Union and the Cymmrodorion Choral Society had long contended for preeminence in their region. Each felt that impartial national judges would now settle the matter.[10]

But during 1891, Stephens's whirlwind first year with the Choir, William D. Davies, Welsh cultural ambassador from the New York newspaper *Y Drych*, toured Utah, heard Stephens's Choir and pronounced it the best choir in the world. In May of that year, Davies wrote to Stephens to invite him and the Choir to the Chicago World's Fair eisteddfod. At first, Stephens demurred. His Choir was too new and too young to vie with established masters, he felt. And his choral plate was full, not only with the assorted conferences and concerts he had planned, but also with the Salt Lake Temple's completion (after forty years of construction) and its various dedication events scheduled throughout 1892 and 1893.[11]

But the Church President and Apostles saw the Chicago eisteddfod as a chance to garner massive goodwill with outsiders. They directed Stephens to accept the offer, which he did. Then he changed his mind and backed out again. That not only prompted the eisteddfod sponsors to make a special plea for him to reconsider, but also provoked local newspapers to editorialize on the virtues of daring to compete in Chicago. Through it all, Stephens maintained a coyness that would typify his career. Only when he had amassed huge popular and ecclesiastical clamor did he fully consent and commit. Once he did, he began to drill the Choir more than before to ready it for the contest. Thomas Griggs, now only a singer in the Choir, wrote that Stephens was working them "hard but intelligently industriously interestingly and successfully."[12]

While Stephens publicly vacillated about his Choir's worthiness to compete, the two main Scranton choirs upped their rivalry. Some choir members called for the two to join forces, take the best of each choir and create an unbeatable super-choir. But some felt that too much was at stake: the purity of the Welsh-language-based Cymmrodorion society versus the ecumenical open membership of the Choral Union. So both choirs dug in their heels. Stephens, of course, needed to best no one except perhaps his predecessors at the Tabernacle. Yet, even though he had swollen the Choir rolls with his acolytes, he now had to trim the Choir to compete: the size limit for choirs in the contest was 250. More pressing, he also had to raise funds for the trip to Chicago. For that, he held benefit concerts, including a large one in the Tabernacle the Sunday before their departure—an event that disgruntled some of the more pious Choir members, who considered any ticketed events on Sunday to be profane. Griggs wrote in his diary that the concert was "a grand mistake. Enquiries are made as to when we will have a sacred baseball game &c."[13]

When, even after all their fund-raising, the Choir came up short, Woodruff rummaged through Church bank accounts in England and Hawaii and found fifteen thousand dollars to commit to the trip.[14] The move must have raised eyebrows. The Church was in severe deficit and the national economy bleak. The crash of 1893 had just decimated bank accounts across the nation. So Woodruff's bankrolling the Choir revealed an almost desperate faith that the trip would pay off, if not in cash, at least in goodwill to the Church.

The Choir booked additional concerts in Denver and St. Louis. Although it had not been an option a generation earlier, travel by rail was now essential. Indeed the decision to allow the iron horse to invade Utah's tranquility and self-containment had split the territory into camps. On the one hand, self-reliance and self-sufficiency had defined the Church since at least the Nauvoo period. In Utah, "homemade" goods (even "homemade music") helped affirm sainthood. But some supplies, for both thrift and quality, best came from outside. Even musical type and sheet music had to be imported if the culture was to thrive. So, at the risk of pollution from the "gentiles," Brigham Young and his circle had allowed, even promoted, the railroad to ride not only through but straight into the heart of Deseret. Now, thirty years after the fact of its coming, the railroad carried the Church's prize Choir as its cargo, exporting it and all it represented from Utah into the heart of the industrial Midwest—Illinois, the land from which they had fled in the late 1840s.

As Choir members boarded Pullman cars, many for the first time in their lives, they felt at ease sharing space, since the unspoken code of Zion had always insisted on putting community above self. Too, since they were musical, the Choir members turned the cars into ad hoc musical soirees, from hymning to folk song to parlor tunes to opera. But the damp weather and crowds spread colds among the singers, leaving some unable to speak above a whisper. Woodruff went from coach to coach blessing them to be healed. But for the time being, health languished.[15]

If railroading had its adventure and sense of liberation, the variety and unreliability of changing venues night after night had its own sense of adventure. How much room on the stage would there be? Which members might have to sit out a concert for lack of space? Would there be risers or something allowing all the singers to see their conductor? What was the lighting? These questions and more faced any touring choir of the day.[16]

At Chicago, after five days en route, the Choir hustled into hotels, sharing rooms. They continued their ad hoc singing and playing, but also observed the other choirs competing. After hearing the superb Welsh male choruses, Stephens told the Choir: "That is worth more to us than a prize! That is perfection! Remember it, boys, and let us work up to it!"[17]

For the mixed-chorus competition, all the choirs had to sing the same three pieces, all drawn from Bible-based oratorios, two of them quite renowned and often sung: "Worthy Is the Lamb" (from Handel's *Messiah*), "Blessed Are the Men Who Fear Him" (from Mendelssohn's *Elijah*), and "Now the Impetuous Torrents Rise" (from David Jenkins's *David and Saul*). The middle piece would be the most impressive for the Choir, perhaps: it consisted almost entirely of *tutti* block chords. The opening of the Handel would give them a similar opportunity for sonorous display, then tax their contrapuntal powers in its second half

("Blessing and honor power and glory be unto him . . ."). The latter piece had the dual disadvantage of the unfamiliarity of the music and the lingering sickness of the singers. In the end, four choirs made it through the preliminary rounds: the two Scranton choirs, the Western Reserve Choir, and the Tabernacle Choir—the last entered as the Salt Lake City Choir for this competition. Some in the Choir claimed that heavenly voices had augmented their own in the performance. And one listener said, "Your choir looked and sang like a chorus of Angels."[18]

After the finals, the judges had to write a joint final report to justify their awards. It read in part:

> the adjudicators naturally looked for a standard of excellence befitting the event, but in this they were disappointed, for whilst the singing of some numbers showed very careful and persistent training, yet on the whole there was lack of refinement, musicianship, and artistic feeling so inseparable with first class singing. . . . The Cymmrodorion society of Scranton, which sang first, was, to our mind, less satisfactory than any of their rivals. . . . The Salt Lake City choir sang next and the impression they made upon us at the start was that they would probably make a hard fight for the prize. . . . As the awarding of the prize proved, the best work was done by the Scranton Choral Union—their superiority in all points was very discernable. They sang well together, kept well in tune throughout, and their general conception and interpretation of the pieces were good. . . . We admire much the singing of the Western Reserve, and considered that they gave the best performance of the second piece— "Blessed are the Men that Fear Him" . . . however, they were a little rough (in tone quality). They sang well in tune, and ran the Salt Lake City choir a very close race for second prize. Indeed, the adjudicators were some time discussing the questions before their final decision was given [to Salt Lake City].[19]

Pennsylvanians rejoiced. "The Keystone State bears the palm in music . . . thanks, not to herself, but to Wales!"[20] Amazingly, the neophyte Mormon Choir had taken second place, beating out the old-school ultra-Welsh singers of the Cymmrodorion.

For their part, given the persecution complex Mormons had acquired over the years, Woodruff and his cohorts in the highest levels of Church leadership thought their Choir had been cheated. They should have taken first place, but anti-Mormon prejudice and pro-Welsh bias, they said, disallowed that result. Apostle Abraham Cannon wrote in his diary that "it is said by those who are thought to be competent to judge that [our Choir] should really have been awarded the first prize." Woodruff, suspicious of the judges' motives, was more blunt: "The Welsh furnished the Money And it Could hardly be Expected that they would give it to a Mormon Quire."[21]

When the accusation got out, Stephens publicly refuted it: "It is my duty to correct through the press an error into which, however innocently, many of our friends have fallen, because it is nevertheless a gross injustice to a committee and a nation, both of whom are above reproach and deserving our highest gratitude rather than suspicion."[22] He noted that the three judges' credentials were impeccable, they were "most free of prejudice" and utterly just. He surveyed the judges' backgrounds and achievements. One of the three was Welsh, of course, he said, but Stephens turned the tables: at least one judge needed to be Welsh because the preponderance of Welsh choirs competing had to know they were not being discriminated against. "If national prejudice could play any part in their adjudication there were two against one against the Welsh. And to suppose that any unfair influence could be brought to bear on this committee's judgment by the Welsh people is a worse reflection upon the Americans and the Englishmen than upon the Welsh."

He concluded: "It is to be regretted that there should be any room for doubt about the justice of the verdict." His own adjudication of the post-eisteddfod Mormon critique of alleged unfairness had two effects. First, it showed that Stephens had grace. He came off as the more generous soul than those who had scorned the judges. Second, and more important, his response showed he was his own man, that he was not so beholden to his Church overseers as to support their views without debate. They had faulted the judges. But Stephens would not come along.

For its part, the Chicago journal *Music* gave its own critical review of the event. The reviewer called Stephens "a young man of more than ordinary musical ability," but noted the youthfulness of the Choir, "many of them under twenty years of age, good, hearty boys and girls, full of spirit and determination." They sang "mostly forte and without delicacy. In the soft passage at the end of the last chorus the voices fell from the pitch very much—a sure proof of imperfect training and forcing in the forte passages."[23]

At the one-year anniversary of the contest, Stephens passed the medal around at Choir rehearsal and mounted a commemorative concert, while Mormons in Salt Lake City threw anniversary parties and revisited the event in the press. An anonymous writer published an honest, though defensive memoir in the *Deseret Weekly*. Five things worked against the Choir at the eisteddfod, the author argued.

1. It was not fair to limit their size to 250, given all of the fine singers available in Salt Lake City.
2. They had only ten weeks' notice of the competition repertoire.
3. They had so many immigrant nationalities in the Choir that it was hard for them to blend.
4. The Choir had no experience competing at lower, nonnational levels.
5. The accompaniment for the competition was two pianos, while this Choir was used to a fine organ.

The writer conceded, though, that the Choir was "scarcely able to command that calmness necessary" for "Blessed Are the Men" and went "perceptibly" flat in "Now the Torrents Rise." But he invoked a new excuse for the Choir's mild shortcomings at the World's Fair. The main problem for the Tabernacle Choir, he said, was "the damp, raw climate of Chicago, to which we from the high altitude dry, pure air were thoroughly unaccustomed." Even so, the writer hoped the Choir would undertake a world tour.[24]

What seems to have eluded the leadership of the Mormon Church was how astonishing a second-place finish actually was, given the extraordinary competition of choirs from across the country struggling even to make it to the finals. The Tabernacle Choir's showing probably shocked most outside observers. But even if he was surprised himself at how well his group had performed, Stephens took the second-place finish as leverage to boost his personal musical empire. Within two years of the Choir's triumph at the fair, he threatened to resign because he was "unappreciated." The Presidency talked him out of it on the promise they would give him "all the aid in their power to continue the success of this musical organization." First order of business: they doubled Stephens's salary to two thousand dollars a year.[25] Under Stephens's leadership, as First Presidency Counselor Joseph F. Smith said, the singers of this Choir "were doing much to remove the prejudices that have existed against us."[26]

On 11 February 1895, the three-man First Presidency wrote a public letter to Stephens and members of the Choir. It began with four memoranda that would define the Choir's place, in some regards, for the rest of its existence.

1. "Members of the Tabernacle Choir are really acting as missionaries, called for their special work, their duties being to give the necessary time for training and practice, and their services on the Sabbath, and on other occasions as required by their Conductors."

2. "Being called especially to this work, all other duties of a public nature should be secondary. None should be under obligations to perform any other public duty which would conflict with their duties in this choir, unless first released from the choir."

3. "All those called to this work should be faithful in their attendance, and should give hearty and cheerful aid to their conductors; complying, as far as possible with the plans and movements deemed necessary to the Choir's proper advancement towards perfection in the 'Divine Art,' which cannot be attained without united effort in perfect discipline."

4. "The members may feel assured that any and all movements of any importance will only be taken with the full sanction, approval and encouragement of the proper authorities of the Church, by whom you are called to this labor."[27]

The letter indicated that the Presidency wanted the Choir not only to keep its post-eisteddfod reputation but to become "the highest exponent of [choral music] in all the land," not to mention the exemplar for all other choirs in the Church, "inspiring musicians and poets with purest sentiment and song and harmony, until its light shall shine forth to the world undimmed, and nations shall be charmed with its music." The Presidency then conceded that this was not a purely aesthetic ambition, but a means to an end. The Choir's success would "unstop the ears of thousands now deaf to the truth, soften their stony hearts, and inspire precious souls with a love for that which is divine. Thus removing prejudice, dispelling ignorance and shedding forth the precious light of heaven to tens of thousands who have been, and are still, misled concerning us." The Mormon Tabernacle Choir would be the musical Trojan Horse that would steal its way into the enclaves of the Church's former enemies.

In both the lore and the historiography of the Tabernacle Choir, the 1893 eisteddfod is the great threshold. Even the second-place win represented a sudden acknowledgment and acceptance of Mormons as a people of high culture. It was the only time for decades that the Choir would place in a national choral contest. But that hardly seemed to matter. The 1893 triumph provided the staging area for an elaborate superstructure yet to be built.

What is not so well recognized is the import of Stephens's 1895 threat to resign and the First Presidency letter it provoked. The threat was a gauntlet thrown down, the letter an attempt to appease. Neither move succeeded for long. Stephens renewed his threat to quit repeatedly thereafter, and the Church kept trying to meet his demands for the Choir's primacy in its members' lives. Significantly, however, the 1895 episode revealed a larger contest: was the Choir a missionary enterprise or an artistic one? Many members of the Choir, including its conductor, leaned toward the latter. They saw beauty as an end in itself, not a means to an end. But not all shared that view. Was the Church serving music, or was music serving the Church? From that question flowed all of the essential tensions that would vex the Tabernacle Choir for the next century.

The 1893 trip to Chicago proved the possibility and even necessity of two things: contests and touring. The former they could mount in their native West. The latter meant new fund-raising, booking, railroading, and promoting.

Almost immediately after the First Presidency's 1895 letter, Stephens helped plan a huge eisteddfod in Salt Lake City. It was putatively "national," but, as one would expect, leaned heavily toward regional artists and groups in nearby states and territories. Competing in the choral category were, among others, the Denver Choir (which had been very kind to Stephens and his Choir at the 1893 event, he said) and a new Welsh choir led by C. J. Thomas. The October 1895 event, reputedly the largest on the continent since Chicago, drew thousands of spectators. But it fell short of expectations. For one thing, the Tabernacle Choir didn't compete, but, as the reigning local champion, simply did a concert at the festival's close. For another, Thomas's choir didn't even make third place. One judge wrote testily of its performance, suggesting perhaps a distaste for the heftiness of traditional Welsh choral sound: "Voices coarse, forcing plenty of voice, but more noise than anything. . . . the loudest sound isn't the best sound."[28]

But the event's greatest problem was the rumor-mongering and complaints of bias dredged up. What some Mormons had once used against the Chicago judges, they now used against each other. Suddenly, Stephens took the high road and complained about such contests altogether, how they "seem to be productive of 'sores.'" He told the Choir at rehearsal that he was sick at the "bickerings" and "uncharity" being displayed, especially against himself, since he had served as one of the judges. He claimed that now he "did not favor these [choral] contests." Instead, he argued, a choir should "set up an ideal and let all try to attain it."[29]

Still, the next national eisteddfod, the official sequel to Chicago's, would be held in Denver the following fall. And the Tabernacle Choir, of course, would take part. In the meantime, however, they made a summer 1896 tour to San Francisco, a place to which Stephens had recently taken a liking for vacations with male friends. In some ways, this trip, compared with the trip East in 1893, proved more valuable to the Choir. They had no one to compete with and they were, given the West Coast's distance from the East, the proverbial "only game in town" for huge, classical choruses. They played to crowds in a motley list of venues and got the best press of their career so far.

The reviews tumbled with superlatives. Many noted the huge size of the Choir (175 voices, the ranks trimmed for travel), but also the precision of its attacks and releases, its elegant phrasing, balance, and blend. It was like "a regiment of organs," one reviewer wrote. The *San Francisco Call* correspondent aptly pointed out that it was not so much the "musical perfection" of the group that impressed him, but its humble, even despised, origins. In the 1890s, the idea of "sensation" often relied on the *unlikeliness* of an artist's achievement. In that regard, the Tabernacle Choir had a veritable tinge of the miraculous since they were not from "back east," but from the isolated frontier. And their religion was alien, cut off from "normal" U.S. Christianity.[30]

The pieces they sang were high-toned, some of them sacred and even secular warhorses—choruses from Verdi's *Traviata* and *Lombardi*, alongside, of course, Handel's *Messiah*—some slighter fare (e.g., Wilce and Bishop's singing school staple "Sleep, While the Soft Evening Breezes"), and that fanfare of national validity, "The Star-Spangled Banner," which the Choir had increasingly featured to show its commitment to the federal government. One crowd favorite was a version of Eliza R. Snow's "O My Father" set to the tune of James McGranahan's gospel hymn "My Redeemer."

They brought their repertoire—and notably formal attire—to the Denver eisteddfod in September. But after the competition, which Stephens had ostensibly shunned as of a year earlier, they came up empty-handed. Other eisteddfods followed every other year or so. Stephens's critique of musical competitions gave way to the need to enhance the Choir's visibility. This was, after all, a missionary choir. So they made an occasional appearance. But Stephens's heart wasn't in it.

Utah had applied for statehood in some form or another in each decade from the late 1840s through the 1880s. The biggest obstacle in almost every failed attempt was polygamy. The stratagem of the Manifesto put the territory on a winning track, and in January 1896 it finally won statehood. Stephens wrote a prospective state song, "Utah, We Love Thee"—a song he had imagined on the 1893 trip to the World's Fair—and performed it with the Tabernacle Choir at statehood celebrations. Though the Choir did not overtly factor in the Mormon territory's bid for statehood, it had come to symbolize the kind of cosmopolitanism a state needed. Their status at Denver as the reigning champions of choral music stood for the kind of civilization Utah needed. More than any other institution, one could well argue, the Tabernacle Choir had domesticated the image of Mormonism. The *Millennial Star* championed the thought in its 1896 article "Musical Progress in Utah," which observed, "if the civilization of a people is indicated by its advancement in the arts and sciences, Utah is by no means behind the rest of the country." And the Tabernacle Choir was the showcase of Mormon advancement as the Church tried to summarize itself to the world.[31]

With his state song, Stephens asserted himself as Utah's court composer. He saw himself as leading a mission to redeem Mormon music from the easy vernacularisms of gospel song style and define it as optimistic, distinguished, and, of course, self-reliant. He increasingly had programmed his own music with the Choir and was amassing an oeuvre that included over five hundred works (including hymns).[32] To what extent his music aided or stymied the reputation of the Choir is hard to say, though at its best it had both charm and sturdiness. Both of those traits summarized the personality that had come to dominate Mormon musical culture and turn the Tabernacle Choir fully into a nationally renowned institution. Indeed, it was now his choir—as he called it in a letter of recommendation for one of its members, it was "my Tabernacle 'Mormon' choir."[33]

Yet, to understand how avidly the Choir continued its mission of public visibility without even leaving Salt Lake City, consider just the main events they performed there in July 1897:

- they entertained representatives of the TransMississippi Congress (to be held in 1898)
- they entertained Christian Endeavor excursionists passing through the territory on the way to their convention in San Francisco
- they sang two concerts—with newly composed music—for the fiftieth anniversary of the pioneers' arrival in Utah
- they sang for the unveiling of the Brigham Young monument in downtown Salt Lake City

With such a prodigious schedule, Stephens did his best to outlaw slacking: he now charged Choir members fifty cents for each absence from rehearsal.[34]

As the Choir broadened its own reputation for skill and zeal, it also imported big-name performers to sing with them in the Tabernacle. These visits netted them not only territorial bragging rights but also a handful of compliments from their guests, blurbs and anecdotes that the Choir could recycle in their promotional materials for more tours. John Philip Sousa's band played with the Choir for the first time in May 1894. Sousa called the Choir "the best trained of any" of the choirs in the nation. Ignace Paderewski called the Choir "magnificent," "imposing," and "wonderful."[35] But it was Nellie Melba, one of the country's most renowned singers, who during her 1898 visit left the Choir some of the most colorful stories. Stephens poured on the charm when she arrived. As Choir secretary Mary Jack recalled it, when Melba arrived at the Tabernacle door she asked Stephens how many wives he had—a common inquiry of male Mormons, even for decades thereafter.

"Not so many, Madame Melba, but what I could take one more," the lifelong bachelor said. He took her to the front of the hall to listen to the Choir sing one of his anthems. "Mr. Stephens, I'll listen to it because it's yours, not because it's Mormon." He led the Choir in his signature piece, "Let the Mountains Shout for Joy." When it finished, Melba ran up and said, "Mr. Stephens, you've touched me to the depths of my very soul." All Melba mentioned of the trip in her autobiography, though, was how a Union Pacific man kept ringing the huge bell on her train while she was trying to relax. He promised to stop only on condition of her giving him free passes for her performance at the Tabernacle.[36]

For its part, the Choir found her in equal parts a wonderfully soaring vocalist and insufferable diva. One Choir member wrote in her journal, "Mme Melba seemed to have the ability to sing just as clearly and accurately as a flute could be played [but] perhaps she had no soul to express, for her language and actions behind the scenes showed her to be anything but a pure woman—greatly to the chagrin of choir people who heard her." Thomas Griggs wrote in his diary that "Melba is a grand singer but she and her company were full of professional haughtiness and she is a 'terror,' vulgar in language." The following week, "Stephens gave his critique of Melba & company. Her upper notes brilliant as Jewels, her manner not attracting."[37]

A landmark for the Choir and the two-year-old state capital, Melba's visit lingered in the memory as a vivid culture clash. The Choir was prepared for anti-Mormon bias but not quite for Melba's seeming disregard for the values of her hosts. Her visit confirmed to them both the world's need for their piety and some celebrities' face-to-face contempt for it.

But within six months, the Choir was under fire by an Apostle for its members' own moral conduct. On 8 October 1898, the Church opened its first session of General Conference with the Choir singing, as was the custom. President Joseph F. Smith then spoke, followed by the somewhat brash but charismatic namesake son of former Church President John Taylor. John W. Taylor spoke first about living a saintly social life, then moved to the status of sexual morality in the state. He mentioned his disgust at the open solicitation of prostitutes in Salt Lake City, mentioned sexual dalliances he had heard about in other cities (which he named, one by one) urging that such activities be stamped out. He then made the shocking accusation that "after the close of practices by the Tabernacle choir, several members come to [a local] rooming house for immoral purposes." He went on to say that Choir members of both sexes "had been seen in many places at times that would suggest acts of immorality." As he finished his talk, people saw Stephens in "earnest conversation" with President Smith's Counselor George Cannon (who had also been a Counselor to Taylor's father). When Taylor sat down, Cannon rose to chastise the young Apostle for his comments, wondering aloud how the parents of young people in the Choir would feel about what they had just heard from Taylor, one of the highest officers in the Church.[38]

What they felt became clear even before the Conference was over. Some Choir members and others voted against the continuance of Taylor as an Apostle. One member of the Salt Lake Sixth Ward said she knew about twenty female members of the Choir from her ward alone and knew that, if he had them in mind, "then Apostle Taylor lied." A father with two daughters in the Choir insisted they quit because of the Apostle's insult. At least one other member quit on her own. The community as a whole rejected any imputation against the Tabernacle Choir, for which Stephens gave public thanks.

Stung by the reaction, Taylor made a public apology. "The farthest thing from my heart would be to believe that this body known as the Salt Lake Tabernacle choir is impure. I realize with very great sorrow and regret how unwise it was to mention a rumor, and humbly ask your pardon for it." The Choir, for the most part, forgave him vocally then and there. But Taylor went on in strikingly obsequious words: "I feel like a criminal at a bar. . . . Brother Stephens, if he will remember, if he values my correspondence enough to remember it, has a letter in his possession giving my opinion—and I may say it has not changed one iota—giving my opinion of the labors of the Salt Lake Tabernacle choir and the effects of your Eastern and Western trips among the people with whom you have labored; and I will only repeat here one sentiment that I expressed in that letter, and that was that the Tabernacle choir was doing as much labor as any 500 elders there were in the church. . . . why, I would just as soon think that an angel was impure as the great body of the Salt Lake Tabernacle choir. If there is any one that has been indiscreet, it would be when the choir voted almost unanimously to sustain [me]." The Choir received no pay for what they do, he added, "and I may say in regard to the character of this Salt Lake Tabernacle choir that if my life will correspond with that of the average member of this choir, I will be satisfied."

He had been initially indiscreet, yes. But his apology showed not only how dramatically unpopular it could be to impugn the Choir, but also the lengths to which an Apostle would double back in his apologies, even putting the Choir's worthiness above his own. Stephens, following up on Taylor's remarks, seemed to raise the stakes of his own enterprise, insisting he would not get into "a frenzy about this matter. The choir is no more likely to go to pieces than the church is likely to go to pieces. The choir is here to stay." Thus, what began as chipping away at the Tabernacle Choir by an Apostle ended up as a solidification of the ecclesiastical preeminence of that Choir. Elder Taylor accused the singers, but then had to fight his own way back into people's hearts for having done so.

As the prestige of the Choir grew, so did Stephens's "czarlike autocracy," which sharpened as one century closed and a new one opened. He seemed more irritated at Choir members' tardiness, lack of mental focus, poor facial expressions, and chattiness. In 1901 he denounced popular musical settings, including two audience favorites. One was "The Seer," a paean to Joseph Smith set to an old whaling tune, which he attacked, in Griggs's words, "giving [the matter] such a grotesque coloring as to have a damaging effect upon thoughtless minds." Hearing of this, Apostle Abraham Cannon said that "if [Stephens] didn't like it himself[,] have it given for the satisfaction of those who did." He even scorned the McGranahan tune for "O My Father," which he had inadvertently made the standard setting for the Church. He "warned [the Choir] of the growing taste for wishy-washy 'Cheese-cloth' style of music such as the Moody-Sankey class" of gospel songs. He even told the Choir he didn't like older singers and that "it takes 'cheek'" for a singer over forty to remain with the group. Cannon said the Choir had now become simply "Stephens' Tabernacle Choir."[39]

Stephens's threats to resign persisted. In May 1899 he said he would quit after one more year and then "go abroad for years." In January 1901 he said he would step down when he was fifty (1904). When 1904 arrived, he threatened to resign yet again.[40] But in reality, there was not a chance of that. With no spouse or children of his own, Stephens had adopted the Choir as his family, and vice versa, with a mutual possessiveness not seen before with the Choir and probably not since.

The sudden swelling of the Choir's population when Stephens took the reins had given it an imposing look and a thick, somewhat unwieldy sonority. One logistical problem with its size was that, with many more singers per section sur-rounding any one singer, hearing the other sections became almost impossible. The rich acoustic of the Tabernacle helped a little, though the massed sound one heard was largely reflective, which made it harder to coordinate attacks and releases. Compounding the problem was the monolithic organ behind the singers, many of whom now had to sit inordinately close to the massive ranks of pipes. Stephens and his Choir had learned to manage. But when the demanding Tabernacle organ virtuoso John McClellan arranged for a bigger organ to be installed in 1901, Stephens had a very public tantrum that earned him a severe rebuke from Church leaders and the press.

At the Thursday night rehearsal, 18 April 1901, Stephens gave a brief speech about the refurbished Tabernacle organ, which, given all its replaced parts, add-ons, and retuning was essentially a new instrument. It was now too loud and lacked the subtle timbre it once had, Stephens complained. It should be restored to its earlier form if the Choir was to continue singing with it. Having gotten wind of his comments, the *Salt Lake Tribune* sent a reporter to Stephens's house for more late-night griping about the organ, which they published the next day. The *Deseret News* used its front page to outflank the *Tribune* by getting three people to write about the organ: Stephens, who had the chance (if he would take it) to recant or qualify his remarks, and two others who favored the "new" instru-ment—organist McClellan, of course, and Kimball Organ technician Frederick Hedgehall, who had overseen the rebuild. They printed these statements, said the *News*, "in order that all the facts may be known." But their deeper motivation would only become clear on the editorial page.[41]

In his front-page statement, McClellan praised the new organ in detail, enumerating its virtues and assuring readers that it would publicly prove its superiority in coming months. Hedgehall used his statement to take down Ste-phens more directly, accusing him of "defaming the historic reputation of the Tabernacle for acoustics" and mounting "a direct attack on the builders of the reconstructed organ."

As one might expect of him, though, Stephens did not back down. He con-firmed that reports of what he had said were essentially correct, though was not "in mourning" or "worked up" about the organ rebuild, "provided it doesn't mar the choir's work"—a clear suggestion that he thought it well might. The Choir had to sing with the organ, Stephens said, and he looked forward to any improvement in the relationship between voices and instrument that the organ's completion would accomplish. But though he had not sought to publicize his feelings outside the Choir, he felt "in no way under obligation to desist from freely expressing my views on the matter to the choir in my charge." He had actually held back for a long time, he said, but could no longer. He had asked for improvement in the organ for ten years. But the new organ tone was to the old one as an apple to a peach. The organ was supposed to be "an efficient aid and accompaniment to the choir," but "if it impairs or ruins our musical efforts, so long as it is my duty to attend to this matter, in justice to myself and the five hundred or more who labor with me, I shall not be content with the judgment of others, interested or disinterested, who think of the organ and certain effects it produces only, rather than the effect of the whole."

Stephens seemed not to realize that his insistence on speaking his mind was the real problem the newspaper had with him. In its editorial in the same issue, the paper's editors agreed with McClellan and Hedgehall, and they noted that Stephens had actually maligned the current President of the Church, Lorenzo Snow, who was not only a prophet, they asserted, but a skilled businessman. Stephens made a "grave mistake" in suggesting that Snow would have wasted twelve thousand dollars for a bad rebuild. "All this is startling to the public and injurious to all parties involved." The paper urged everyone to work together in harmony. But it then launched another salvo against Stephens, this time on sonic grounds:

> As to the power of the instrument and the probability that the choir will be drowned by the volume of its sound. Is that a fault in the organ? Will not the loudness and softness of the tone be regulated by the organist? We noticed in listening to it some notes [that were too] soft and delicate. Who that is rational would blame the instrument instead of the player? There should be perfect harmony between the choir leader and the organist, or there cannot be full harmony in our musical services. And surely the instrument, however powerful, can be so regulated as to suit both choir and congregation.

In the end, "We all appreciate the splendid talents and achievements of the choir and its noted leader, and we all want to keep up the reputation of both organ and choir."

The one advantage the Choir had over the organist, though, the paper failed to mention: the Choir, though far larger than the organ loft, was in fact portable. Only they could actually do what real missionaries do—travel.

Soon after this tussle, Snow died and a new First Presidency took charge, with the namesake nephew of the Church's founder, Joseph F. Smith, at the helm.

Smith almost immediately tried to rein Stephens in, having the Presiding Bishopric—the Church's fiduciary regulatory arm—appoint a finance committee for the Choir. Stephens resisted and blustered, writing to the First Presidency "for a reconsideration of the question."

Again, Stephens seemed to win the battle: his overseers backed off, dumping the old committee and reorganizing the Choir with a standard Mormon three-man presidency. The new president of the Tabernacle Choir? Evan Stephens. He and his two presidential counselors were to report finances quarterly to the Presiding Bishopric, just like any other Mormon ecclesiastical presidency or bishopric.[42]

This change of administrative fortunes was bookended by two trips to the San Francisco Bay Area, one a concert tour, the second a "pleasure tour" for the Choir's best singers. Press estimates of the Choir's size on this first tour varied from 150 to 550, though the numbers were skewed by the soloists and extra Church members who came along for the ride. One newspaper review gave a precise count: 45 sopranos, 35 altos, 30 tenors, and 35 basses, though conceded a few members had not been able to get to the choir loft because of the bustling audience. The Choir gained praise for its musicality, though what distinguished the group, wrote one reviewer, was its sheer "massiveness." Between concerts the members were objects of head-scratching curiosity, all of them wearing Mormon Choir badges as they rode streetcars, roamed the shopping districts, and dined in restaurants and cafés.[43]

After the 1903 tour, the Presiding Bishopric inserted itself further into Choir affairs by suggesting and even helping plan tours they thought advantageous to the Church. But Stephens always held the upper hand, not just as Choir President but as the conductor, who could determine if and when the Choir was ready to foray outside its comfortable precincts. One planned trip to the St. Louis Exposition, for example—where the Choir would compete for a $4,500 prize—seemed, as far as the Presiding Bishopric was concerned, ready to go. But then they met with Stephens. He had them consider that "the contest takes place in June when the weather is insufferably hot in St. Louis." And all conceded this would be an expensive trip: 250 members of the Choir would need fifty dollars apiece, and Stephens could not guarantee return receipts of fifteen dollars apiece. So, jointly, they decided that, "if the way opened up, the choir should go to St. Louis in Sep. or Oct.," skipping the competition, which Stephens disliked anyway. But that excursion never happened. Instead, the Choir blanketed its hometown with appearances designed to lure more and better singers into its ranks.[44]

During 1904–8, the Choir also remained close to home, perhaps because of a resurgence of anti-Mormonism stemming from the notorious Reed Smoot hearings. These U.S. senatorial hearings about whether Smoot, a Mormon Apostle, could retain the Senate seat to which he had been elected, garnered headlines and enflamed many across the country with the revelation that polygamy had *not* stopped in the Church as Woodruff's manifesto and subsequent official declarations had promised. Most shocking, perhaps, was President Smith's admission that he had not only continued to cohabit with many women who had been "sealed" to him as wives, but that he had vowed never to stop. He claimed he was, as Mormons had long been accused of asserting, accountable to God's law over man's.[45]

Even in the midst of the hearings, though, Smith worked hard to buck up the Choir, reassuring Stephens and his singers that God needed them to spread his word and salvage the Church's image. He also helped them recruit, notably in a 29 April 1905 letter to the president of the Salt Lake Stake. He wrote "especially in the interest of our chief choral organization, the Tabernacle Choir" that the stake choristers of the city be appointed as "aids to the conductor of the Tabernacle Choir, that they may in every way possible help him in securing as regularly attending members, the best available singers from these four stakes, also by their own personal attendance and that of the various ward and organization choir leaders throughout the city reach a closer harmony of action for the uplifting of all together." He went on to concede that securing musicians to any task in the Church proved taxing. But good singers had a gift that should reorient their lives to the needs of the Tabernacle Choir. And releasing them from other callings in the Church would provide more opportunity for nonmusical people to serve in those callings. That is, singers should sing, not merely administer. The President of the Church now publicly said that the Tabernacle Choir "should be full to over-flowing with the brightest, most talented young singers our community affords, and while we feel that it is the duty of the leader and trainer of that choir with his aids to select and train those to the highest artistic point possible, we feel that it remains for you and the local ward officers under you to so arrange the duties of these that there need be no conflict of duties standing in their way to receive this training." Stephens could do his job, but had to rely on priesthood leaders' support.[46]

That same month, the Choir flexed its ecclesiastical muscles—or priesthood leaders flexed theirs on the Choir's behalf. Edna Dyer reported that in April 1905, the Liberty Stake Choir, over 250 members strong, had worked up excellent numbers for their stake conference, but at the last minute their stake president told them that "unless they could sing as well, or better, than the Tabernacle Choir, the latter would be preferred." The stake choir backed off, the Tabernacle Choir interloped, and word hit the street that all stake choirs might be under threat of being displaced by Stephens's group. Of that eventuality, Dyer wrote, "I foresee rebellion in no small dimensions."[47]

Stephens, apparently with President Smith's blessing, also tightened his grip on Choir members. In October, Dyer reported, "Bishop Parry told me he had received a list of names from which the official roll of pledged Tabernacle Choir members is to be made and asked if I [a Choir member] desired to be checked off. . . . Under the new order, each member binds themselves to forsake all else and cleave only unto the Tabernacle Choir—no matter what other notable event may be taking place on choir nights." She hesitated to be tied down that way, because "frequently musical events of great moment to me happen on rehearsal nights, and if I were pledged to the choir I would have to deprive myself." But the other side of the question was that "the choir is a means of assisting myself musically and financially as many notable concerts are free to choir members in the Tabernacle. I am much perplexed, and have left the decision for papa."

In 1908, the Smoot hearings ended and Reed Smoot, rough testimony notwithstanding, remained in his Senate seat. But in 1910–11, a "magazine crusade" took aim at the Church.[48] So, for Mormons, national damage control had to begin in earnest. The Tabernacle Choir had made major pushes in three successive years: a tour of the Northwest in 1909; the Choir's first commercial recordings in 1910; and a tour of the east coast, including Washington, D.C., the site of the Church's most recent public bludgeoning, in 1911.

The late summer 1909 Northwest tour began with some of the Choir's most glowing reviews yet. One Oregon reviewer said he was "stunned" by the "avalanche of music" the Choir provided. Then he changed the metaphor: "Picture in your mind's eye an intricate but perfect and well oiled machine, increasing its speed, diminishing again, starting with terrible velocity, all at the beck and call of a master hand at the levers, and you have a rough prospectus of the masterly power and control which Conductor Stephens has over the 200 voices. . . . Without physical contortion, merely beckoning with a finger or a barely visible uplift of the baton, Mr. Stephens brought forth a mixture of staccato, pianissimo, pianoforte and ritard that was truly marvelous."[49] Similarly, in Tacoma, the Choir thrilled its audiences, and most people predicted an easy prize for the Utahns at the eisteddfod at the Alaska-Yukon-Pacific Exposition in Seattle.

What no one predicted was that the Choir would refuse to sing in the Seattle contest. They had signed up and arrived in good faith, when the organizers told Stephens and new Choir President David Smith (from the Presiding Bishopric) that each singer would have to pay a seventy-five-cent ticket price to get in. To ensure they would make their money back, the eisteddfod sponsors had taken this unexpected, unique step to charge the players in the contest as though they were the audience, too. When Stephens and Smith refused, a local "gentleman" stepped in and offered to pay for the 250-voice Choir to enter. The Choir leaders refused the offer—this was about principle, not money, even though, admittedly, they had already laid out ten thousand dollars to make the trip at all. The sponsors upped the tension by accusing the Choir not only of trying to create a disturbance to distract the other contestants, but of actually using the entrance price as a pretense to avoid competing and getting beat. So the Choir walked away from the prospect of a thousand-dollar prize, leaving in its wake a controversy that undoubtedly perked up ticket sales for their Seattle concert the next night. Critics again swooned, and the Choir returned to Salt Lake City without the prize but triumphant. After all, they not only had turned a profit on the tour, but had done the more important work of post–Reed Smoot image reclamation.

In 1877, the year Brigham Young died, Thomas Edison had invented his "phonograph," which would inscribe sound vibrations on a cylinder that sat like a cuff on a rotating horizontal post. The following year, the *Deseret News* announced that Edison's invention was now "among us." Not surprisingly, the Tabernacle Choir tried an ad hoc recording of itself doing "Open Ye Portals" as early as March 1900. But the recording didn't take.[50]

It was not until September 1910 that the Columbia Talking Machine Company, one of the two largest commercial recording labels of the day, decided it wanted the Choir on its roster. The label had recorded large ensembles before, but never a large choir. From the 1890s through the early 1900s, the label had focused on novelty acts, comic songs, political speakers, and marching bands. In 1907, Columbia switched from manufacturing single-sided to double-sided discs, necessitating a massive increase in recordings to fill its inventory. By 1909, the label boasted a raft of singers—operatic, art-song, and comic soloists, along with duos, trios, and even Chicago's well-known Paulist Choir. The Tabernacle Choir had two appeals: it was the largest choir, and it had the novelty of Mormon origins.

The distance from New York to Salt Lake City had initially been prohibitive, since the bulk and weight of Columbia's direct-to-disc master recording equipment made it too expensive to ship to Salt Lake City. But when they were able to get it from five hundred pounds down to a mere hundred, Columbia recording engineers and executives made the trip. Stephens insisted that, to represent the Choir fully, he needed four hundred singers to sing into the mechanical cone. But this process, and the paltry cylinders they used to record, badly imbalanced the sections of the Choir, cut the bass, and, worst of all, funneled the rich acoustics of the Tabernacle into a foot-wide, wire-and-fabric horn. So the experiment had failure written in its stars from the beginning.[51]

The engineers scrambled to figure out where to place the machinery, an intricate assembly of nearly five hundred parts. But they got some good test takes of the organ and then the Choir. The final recording sessions captured over a dozen potentially usable tracks, giving the Tabernacle Choir and organ their greatest "concert" ever—singing for the whole world, Stephens told the Choir. They listened to the proofs in October, at the end of which they had the final records, ready for a Christmas audience. The main tracks, Stephens's "Let the Mountains Shout for Joy" backed with the McGranahan setting of "O My Father" (i.e., the one Stephens disliked), had the artist name printed on the label as "Mormon Tabernacle Choir." But a separate record came out under the phonied-up name of "The Handelian Chorus." That record contained "Hallelujah" (from *Messiah*), split into two parts, one per side. Whether Columbia thought the pseudonym would give the Choir a market boost is hard to say. "Mormon" anything could still prove a liability to a national brand.

It is unclear how many of these records sold, though at least one Mormon scholar suggests that residual anti-Mormonism might have warded buyers away from the recordings. But another explanation for poor sales—if they were poor—lies in the inherent sonic contradiction the recordings exemplified. The Choir was known and promoted for its gargantuan size. It was a massive, overwhelming force in concert, especially in the Tabernacle. These records provided a thin, decidedly underwhelming sound. One heard only the raw, almost skeletal remains of the real sound. All sense of scale, one of the Choir's chief selling points, gave way to the mere novelty of what was still widely called simply a "talking machine," fit for crude documentation of sound but hardly for the tidal wave of sound that "the world's largest choir" could give. Although anti-Mormonism did linger, anyone who breached it to listen to the early records would have reaped aesthetic disappointment indeed.

Alongside these recordings, the Choir pursued a massive new tour, its first transoceanic excursion. It issued a pamphlet with a four-page supplement headed by this direct appeal: "SHALL THE CHOIR GO TO WALES IN 1911?"[52] In the pages before the supplement appeared reprints of the best reviews of the Choir from 1893 to 1909. The supplement then argued the case for a trip to Wales under three headings:

1st—Is the project feasible and practicable?
2nd—Is it worth while?
3rd—Will it pay?[53]

The questions, of course, were mainly rhetorical. Three local newspapers as well as the Native Sons of Wales Organization had endorsed the project and stood ready to give aid.

The cost would be at least fifty thousand dollars, which between Church, Choir, and community resources, could be handled easily. "The question is not, can we afford it. But the slogan should be, 'Can we afford to miss it?'" Using Chicago as the template of worth, the pamphlet insisted that the value of a European trip anchored in Wales could be incalculable. Here was an opportunity to appear in the "greatest of all Eisteddfods to be held at the very citadel or birthplace of the ancient and historic institution—not only to represent the city and state, but the NATION as well. Nay, more than that: A chorus chosen from, taken out of and made to represent, before the nations of the earth a CHURCH that is distinctively American." America's choir, indeed.

This dream project failed, replaced by a far more modest return to the East Coast. On 28 March 1911, Gilbert McClurg, general manager of the American Land and Irrigation Exposition, wrote to Eli Pierce (as tour manager of the Choir), offering the Choir (190 singers and ten instrumentalists) two thousand dollars and a free night's concert rental of Madison Square Garden if they would appear as part of the exposition, singing for a half-hour twice each day of the exposition for free, and including in their program the "Irrigation Ode" written by organist McClellan and Mrs. McClurg for the 1909 Irrigation Congress in Ogden, Utah. In April 1911, the Presiding Bishopric deliberated on the trip, with its leader initially saying he "thought that it looked bad to exploit our Tab. Choir as if it were a common troupe of minstrels." But they agreed to the trip and wrote to George Pyper, manager of the Salt Lake Theater, telling him he was their pick to manage a tour centered around the exposition.[54]

By May, Pyper's audacious embrace of the assignment was in full swing. He had letterhead designed and printed up that said "Tour of Mormon Tabernacle Choir, Largest Regular Church Choir in the World, Engaged for American Land and Irrigation Exposition." He wrote to the Steinway piano company, notifying them that the Choir would be appearing in twenty-five to thirty major cities on the way to Madison Square Garden and asking if Steinway would place free loaner pianos at each venue. Some negotiation ensued, until Steinway declined outright. Pyper continued unabashedly selling the Choir as a novelty. "It is universally agreed in the cities so far visited by me that on account of its 'uniqueness,' at least, the Choir will draw the crowds." Dozens of agents began vying for the Tabernacle Choir to appear in their venues. But some cities turned him down: "The Mormon Tabernacle choir is not in the least known in this section [Albany-Troy area] for a concert proposition and I do not believe that it would be a drawing card."

Once the Choir was on tour, Pyper broadcast its success to his friends in Utah. After they sang for President Taft himself, Pyper telegrammed the Salt Lake Bureau of Information: "auspicious occasion [at the White House] worth all our losses well received and refreshments served to choir." But the exposition performances themselves drew tough criticism from the *Chicago Daily Tribune*, which thought Stephens's tempi far too slow and the Choir slack in its response to his conducting—faults partly attributable, perhaps, to performing away from the Tabernacle.[55] Meanwhile, even with the Choir's name in lights ("Mormon Choir 200") in New York, some newspapers boycotted the exposition, mostly for political reasons. Overall, ticket sales for all concerts faltered.

By the end of the tour, which spanned October and November 1911, the Choir showed a net loss of twenty thousand dollars. Pyper thought the good impression they had made on many listeners was worth the loss. On the other hand, the tour kicked up residual anti-Mormonism. The Choir was banned in Boston for its religious subversiveness. And in Richmond, Virginia, the Union Theological Seminary students and faculty complained in a petition that the tour was "rank Mormon propaganda that will propitiate favor for Mormonism with the uninformed and thoughtless." The petition asked its signers to "give up fine music rather than lead your fellowman toward standards of Joseph Smith. Your home will be invaded within a short time by the agents of the Salt Lake organization."

Back at home, the Choir's essential mission, General Conference, continued to evolve from the simple affairs of Beesley's days. Consider the opening day of October General Conference, 1914. Church growth necessitated two concurrent morning sessions, one in the Tabernacle and the other in the Assembly Hall a stone's throw away—different speakers, different music, but taking place in the same timeframe. Stephens's Choir sang in the Tabernacle, of course (a hymn and two anthems with an additional vocal solo completing the musical fare). The Emerson Ward Choir sang in the Assembly Hall (a hymn and three anthems).

The afternoon had concurrent sessions in the Tabernacle, in the Assembly Hall, and on the grounds spanning the two buildings. The Tabernacle Choir sang a hymn and two anthems (one of them featuring a duet), and again, a solo filled the bill. The Waterloo Ward Choir—with string quartet accompanying it—sang a hymn and three anthems in the Assembly Hall. Outdoors the Twentieth Ward Choir sang two hymns. None of the musical numbers was duplicated all day among the various locations, whose afternoon attendance numbered 10,000, 2,500, and 1,000 in the respective locations.

When the leaders of the Church were voted on in this conference, the Tabernacle Choir was now, for the first time, on the list for the Church to "sustain" (pledge to uphold): two conductors (Evan Stephens and his assistant Horace S. Ensign), three organists (John McClellan and his assistants, Ed Kimball and Tracy Cannon), the Choir secretary and treasurer (George C. Smith), the librarian (Stephens's live-in "chum," as he called him, Noel S. Pratt), and, as a group, "all the members." Noticeably absent from the list was the Choir's actual President, David A. Smith, who still worked behind the scenes as a member of the Presiding Bishopric.

By 1915, the Mormon Tabernacle Choir was a brand name in choral music. Exploiting that fact, Joseph Ballantyne, conductor of the superb Ogden Tabernacle Choir began making plans for a July trip to the West Coast, where the Salt Lake Tabernacle Choir had played to packed houses and great reviews a few years earlier. For the Panama-Pacific International Exposition in San Francisco, Ballantyne planned a three-day, four-concert extravaganza, largely based on operatic arias, secular showstoppers, and sacred anthems, with no hymns but Dudley Buck's "Hymn to Music."

The program's title page clearly headlined the 200-voice group as "The Mormon Tabernacle Choir" in bold print, with "of Ogden" in fine print beneath. Whether local promoters or Ballantyne himself masterminded this bait-and-switch, one thing was clear: the Mormon Tabernacle Choir had the name recognition to sell tickets, no matter what residual anti-Mormon sentiment lingered in the more pious subcultures of evangelical churches.[56]

But the brand name mix-up coincided with an imminent, drastic change: the "resignation"—this one not a threat, but a forced retirement—of the conductor that George Pyper called a "musical Mussolini."[57]

CHAPTER 4

THE POWER
OF THE AIR

IN OCTOBER 1915, the *Salt Lake Telegram* broke the story that Evan Stephens was being fired. A high Church committee, it said, had reported to the First Presidency that it was time for Stephens to go in favor of a younger and presumably more flexible, less autocratic man. "Many of the members and former members of the internationally famous choir had become wearied of the music they were presenting at the regular services and at special performances and had not been assigned enough new music to sustain their interest."[1] Specifically, these singers had grown tired of having to sing so many pieces written by their conductor.

Stephens countered that charge of neglecting new music in a letter to the *Telegram*. He insisted that the spottiness of attendance he had complained about for years, along with local Church leaders' failure to defer to the Choir, made it impossible to perform anything but the most common pieces. Choir members with assignments in wards and stakes had to skip Sunday rehearsals and services at the Tabernacle. Members who had Church meetings in the mornings and evenings didn't want to go into the city between meetings, preferring to lounge at home or gather with friends. So the Choir took a back seat in the lives of many of its members.

Stephens then presented two lists to his newspaper audience. The first tallied six new pieces the Choir had worked up that summer, with composers ranging from Handel to Elgar to—naturally—himself. The second list named six of the "stock pieces" they had drilled in the preceding months: one by Handel, two by Mendelssohn, two by Gounod, and, again, one by himself—the "Hosannah" temple anthem he had written for the Salt Lake Temple dedication in 1893 (and which, it turned out, would be sung at almost every temple dedication thereafter).

He then made this challenge: "I freely invite the judgment of musicians at home and abroad as to whether or not the material given this choir ought to serve to have singers of merit get 'wearied of the music they were presenting' or to complain that they had not been assigned enough 'new music' to sustain their interest. Is it not far more likely that owing to the causes I have enumerated above, they have lost interest through absenting themselves, while the regulars are wearied of having to put up with their general absence and their irregular presence?"

But Stephens was indeed on his way out. Although he had conducted the Choir for twenty-five impressive years, the First Presidency already had narrowed the field to two possible replacements. One was Brigham Cecil Gates. Known as Pete by his friends and family, and Cecil professionally, Gates had studied at the New England Conservatory, graduated with honors from the Scharwenka Conservatory in Berlin in 1913, and now headed the music department of LDS University (later renamed the LDS Business College). Joseph F. Smith described him in 1916 as "a boy of clean life, good faith, modest and retiring in his ways and of a genial disposition." Gates's strongest credential in Utah, though, may have been that he was Brigham Young's grandson, a son of Susa Young Gates, one of the leading Utah women of letters and politics at the time.[2]

The second contender seemed both more and less plausible than Gates. Anthony (Tony) Lund was trained in Germany, France, and England, had already guest conducted the Tabernacle Choir, frequently sung solos with them, and had been a favorite teacher and conductor for twenty-one years at Brigham Young University (formerly Brigham Young Academy). On the negative side were his marital status, his social life, and even his physique. Lund and his first wife had somewhat bitterly divorced in 1901. He drank beer—still allowable in the Church at that time, but mostly frowned upon—and was well-known for his off-color storytelling, gambling, and short temper. Moreover, given his weight—285 pounds—some may have wondered if he could keep up the pace that Stephens had established.[3]

Both in his favor and against it was that he was the son of the first counselor in the First Presidency, Anthon Lund—a plus because he had inside knowledge and relationships with the highest Church authorities, a minus because the appointment would reek of nepotism. Any objection to the latter, though, could be countered by two facts. First, family favoritism had ruled in Church politics since Joseph Smith himself, who appointed his father and brothers to the highest positions in the Church beside his own. Brigham Young had appointed Brigham Young Jr. to the Twelve Apostles, and even Joseph F. Smith—nephew of Joseph the Prophet—had named his own namesake son to the Twelve. And as for qualifications, no one could dispute Lund's reputation as a musician, and a charismatic one at that. Many people felt there was simply no more able and renowned musician in the state. His opera productions had cast a spell on the cultural elite of Utah. And his following at Brigham Young University (BYU) was legendary, if esoteric.

One former student, William Driggs, wrote of it. Lund led a kind of "Bohemian" cohort at BYU, he wrote, and "was one of the few teachers in the entire country for whom his pupils would wait. The rule was that the class would disband if the teacher was more than fifteen minutes late. Not so with Lund's students, who would wait all fifty minutes of the class period just "to hear one of his jokes or chuckles." Driggs, like several of his smitten colleagues, devoted his academic life to emulating Lund and his methods. "I immediately fell under the spell of [his] magnetic personality. In fact, I thought he was some sort of a god."[4]

When Lund ended up getting the conductorship, the *Salt Lake Tribune* said that he had been quietly offered the job "many times" before.[5] If so, the official offer did not come until after 13 July 1916, when the Twelve met to consider who should replace Stephens. Senior Apostle Heber Grant—ever the cautious businessman—said they should table the decision. The third Apostle in line, David McKay, recommended Lund as the "most proficient" conductor in the state, most of whose other conductors had at one time been Lund's student. The second Apostle in line, George Albert Smith, then formally proposed Lund take the baton. The quorum unanimously voted yes.[6]

Six days later, the First Presidency wrote a long letter of dismissal to Stephens. They denied his requests to shore up Choir membership against other Church responsibilities. They then said that "a committee of investigation" had twice discussed his conductorship and both times the verdict was to replace him. Tony Lund would now take over. Stephens could either offer to resign or request an "honorable release, which we could grant freely under existing circumstances, and with full recognition of your claims upon our continued regard, and the hold you justly have upon the admiration, respect and affection of the entire Church as well as the tender memories of the Choir over which you have presided for more than a quarter of a century."[7]

Three weeks later, Joseph F. Smith named Cecil Gates as Lund's assistant conductor. And in another few weeks, Edward Kimball joined the staff as an organist—though he worried that Lund "is a little inclined to ignore me."[8]

A few weeks after accepting the post, Lund finally asked what he would be paid for this job. Smith proposed two hundred and fifty dollars a month, which Lund accepted.[9] He could augment it with many hours a week of teaching privately at the McCune School of Music and Art, a training center in Salt Lake City operated by the Church. But he would have to quit his BYU job. The university's president, George Brimhall, released Lund from the faculty with support but regret. "The school will be weakened by the absence of Professor Lund more than by the absence of any other member of the faculty—the President not excepted."[10]

Privately, Stephens assessed this turn of events. Since his leaders could not meet his demands, he and they had "agreed to try the 'new broom' idea and see if it will help." He had given up his "life's work," he said, though he felt the relief of a burden being lifted. At his last rehearsal, he handed the reins to Lund—after an hourlong speech to the Tabernacle audience and a forty-minute one to the Choir. Lund made his own, briefer remarks to the Choir, after which most singers approached to shake his hand.[11]

Stephens wrote an open letter of resignation and sent it to the newspapers. Because his proposals had been turned down, he wrote, he had asked for an honorable release. He referred to his previous "offers" (i.e., threats) to resign, which Joseph F. Smith had kept for twelve years. Now the time was right for Smith to accept them. Reviewing the "love and loyalty of thousands of my singers," he wished his successor equal devotion. "I shall continue to hope that the great musical progress of our people—with the tabernacle choir ever at the front—may continue."[12]

We know little of Tony Lund's early work with the Choir. Like Stephens, he had no minutes taken of Choir rehearsals. He kept no journal. He wrote few letters. His Choir concert schedule was slim and perfunctory, especially since his debut as conductor came in the midst of the First World War and a year and a half before the flu epidemic that ravaged the nation and state, even making Church leaders postpone General Conference in 1918—the last year Joseph F. Smith was President before he died and Heber Grant took charge. Lund went ten years before taking the Choir on tour. He had no ambition for musical empire. The Choir was not his life, as it had been Stephens's: he taught countless private lessons, sang solo in events throughout the state, lived it up socially, and hiked the mountain ranges of Utah.

We do know, though, that Lund dismissed all Choir members who had not already left when Stephens did. He offered eight free vocal lessons to anyone who wanted to join. He then auditioned prospective members until he filled enough seats in all the sections.[13] Late in 1916, Stephens dropped in on a rehearsal where Lund led the new group in a movement from the *Messiah* that they had never sung under Stephens. After rehearsal, "the members clapped their hands to see [Stephens]. He spoke about 15 min. He said he would neither commend nor criticize the choir, but he thought they showed some hesitancy at the beginning of the lines."[14]

For years Stephens remained bitter over his severance from the Choir. He privately said that his successor was not up to snuff and that audiences were now getting used to mediocre musical work, which Lund was allowing. Soon Stephens added the complaint that the Choir had gobbled up too much of his own assets when he was conductor—he would have done better professionally without having that job, he said. He also winced to discover that one of his "boys"—young male devotees, of which he had many in and out of the Choir—turned out to be on the committee that had recommended Stephens be dropped from the Choir in favor of "a younger man."[15]

Stephens's criticism aside, Lund took a harder aesthetic line than his predecessor. In a talk given after becoming conductor of the Choir, Lund proposed a new "supervision" or even a "censorship" of Church music that would "strike a well aimed blow at the frivolous unorthodox trash" one sometimes found in Mormon services. The Tabernacle Choir should lead out in a broad coalition of Mormon choirs who would share good repertoire that had a union of "simplicity and sublimity." Coordination meetings could take place at LDS General Conferences, using criteria he outlined. This should be done, he said, "all for the uplift of the cause." And what was "the cause"? Musical quality, not popular appeal.[16]

By the time Lund took over the Choir, the General Conferences of his Church had continued to blossom in size and musical scope. The Tabernacle Choir was still the featured group, but other choirs and soloists, both vocal and instrumental, also performed between the long sermons in the three-day event, which invariably filled the Tabernacle, the Assembly Hall, and the grounds between them. The musical numbers ranged from Mendelssohn songs to bombastic, homegrown anthems, some by Lund himself, and even more by Cecil Gates. Hymns were generally sung only by the Choir and congregation jointly.

By this time, anthologies of sacred anthems filled the racks of music stores across the nation or were delivered to choir directors through quarterly subscriptions. Some choristers thrived on this seeming godsend of repertoire. Not so Lund. He chided these collections, complaining that of about five hundred anthems he had examined in them, he found only about ten to be "meritorious." Anyone sorting through such alleged sacred choral music should consult "the most competent authorities on text and music." Without careful control, "mere jingles & frivolous poetry" could have a "pernicious influence" on congregations who heard them.[17]

Still, Stephens remained the best-loved composer of homemade music. After the flu epidemic subsided, his cantata "The Vision" was premiered, performed around the region, and published by the Church. In 1921 he won the new LDS General Music Committee's churchwide prize for a new sacrament hymn. In 1922 the Church subvented the publication of his next cantata, "The Martyrs." The Music Committee that year also authorized publication of a book of six Stephens anthems. And they continued to work on a new hymnbook that would contain over seventy hymns by Stephens. (He would die three years after the hymnbook came out.)[18]

Inspired or provoked by Stephens's classical pretensions and one-man dynasty, Cecil Gates worked up the premiere of an oratorio he had written eight years earlier, *The Restoration*, which Lund and David Smith approved for a Tabernacle Choir rendition. Some non-Mormon critics who examined the score considered parts of it "worthy of Chopin." A staff member at *Musical America* even claimed the work had "the best counterpoint and fugal work I have seen in any contemporary composers." But more to the point, President Heber Grant loved the work and pronounced it superior to Stephens's "Vision." One attendee at a meeting of the Twelve cited Grant as saying that some listeners had called *The Restoration* "a plagiarism of the masters." But Grant responded thus: "I taught George Pyper to write and for a time he copied my handwriting, but what of it? He got his own style after awhile and he was not harmed by copying at first after a better penman."[19] Any criticism of Gates or other Mormon composers should cease, he said. Grant "wanted all his Brethren to hold up our struggling artists—not to cast them down with cool criticism. . . . There was a general chorus of amens to all that he said—only one opposing voice, cautioning for more moderation."[20]

In preparing a report on Gates's piece after its premiere, the Music Committee held a meeting that was a veritable summit of Tabernacle Choir icons.

George Pyper, presiding, asked Gates for his opinion about his own work. Gates smartly declined. Tony Lund said "some lukewarm things" about the piece. Evan Stephens piped up and said that he had studied the score and originally thought some of it "would not sound right," but that he felt otherwise after hearing it. George Careless praised Lund's conducting technique at length but had nothing to say about the composition itself.

Although what Careless favored in Lund's technique is unknown, the recordings that Lund made with Victor in 1925 and 1927 ably show off the Choir's sound.[21] And they show even more vividly the break from Stephens's dynasty that Lund had accomplished. Of the eight sacred pieces the Choir recorded, none are by Stephens or Lund—no homemade music. The recordings targeted an audience who would value the Choir as the interpreter of things that Mormons had not concocted themselves. Victor spokeswoman Madeline Davis boasted that the recordings of so large a choir had been "felt by some to be an impossible feat," but now these records would "help advertise Utah more than any other means."[22]

What distinguished these recordings from the Columbia recordings of 1910 was the sheer sonority. Electrical recording had superseded mechanical record making. The Choir did not need to huddle around the speaker cone and sing into it. They could sit in their normal seats, letting the electrical microphones pick up not only the singers but the acoustics of the building.

Although the Choir recorded ten pieces in all during two separate sessions, Victor chose to release only four of them. The first record contained "By the Waters of Minnetonka," a popular pseudo-Native American song, which seemed either logical or ironic, given Mormons' historic devotion to Native Americans as Israelites. On its flip side was the anthem "Devotion," adapted from Mascagni's *Cavalleria Rusticana*. Of the two sides, "Waters" outshines "Devotion": the Choir delivers the relatively simple setting with confidence and a schmaltzy enthusiasm. More important, the Tabernacle audibly resonates, giving the phonograph speakers through which the songs play a lively sense of imaginary space. The Tabernacle itself actually becomes the star of this track.

The second record is the more ambitious, containing two difficult oratorio movements: on one side Handel's "Worthy Is the Lamb"—a staple of the Choir—and on the other side, "He Watching Over Israel" from Mendelssohn's *Elijah*. These two actually come off as more amateurish than the other recordings. The sheer mass of the Choir lends power to the tutti block chords. But the counterpoint, especially in the fugato sections of the Handel, gets ragged as the Choir attempts rapid sixteenth note runs but drags and falters again and again (especially among the tenors). In both pieces, the voices noticeably strain for the high notes. The renditions never get beyond rehearsal level. No polish, mostly bombast, but hints here and there of the Choir at its best: good intonation (in the low- to mid-ranges), moderately expressive phrasing, and the overall authority—and novelty—of its size.

In the months between recording sessions, Lund and David Smith accepted an invitation for the Choir to sing at the Hollywood Bowl on 28 July 1926. So they laid out a tour of stops in California and Reno, the first tour under Lund's baton. The Choir and soloists prepared eighteen numbers, a mix of short sacred and secular pieces, most of them longtime Tabernacle favorites, including "Waters of Minnetonka," Stephens's "Let the Mountains Shout for Joy," and "The Star-Spangled Banner," alongside works by European composers such as Schubert, Rossini, Wagner, Verdi, Elgar, and Massenet, and U.S. composers Arthur Farwell, Dudley Buck, and Charles Wakefield Cadman, who was one of the founders of the Hollywood Bowl Orchestra.

The 206 Choir members, eight soloists, and assorted guests (including Presiding Bishop Charles Nibley) arrived first in Sacramento. Members of the chamber of commerce and the Firemen Band marched with them nine blocks to the capitol, where David Smith and the mayors of Sacramento and Salt Lake City gave speeches, between which the Choir sang. They headed next to San Bernardino for a concert—featuring a speech by Reed Smoot—and then to the Hollywood Bowl, where they drew a crowd four-fifths the capacity of the 25,000-seat amphitheater. Concerts in San Diego, Pomona, and Reno, Nevada, followed.[23]

The Choir now boasted the most improbable command of choral literature in the Southwest. In 1928, Charles Boyd of the Music Teachers National Association took note of Lund in the organization's annual survey of "preeminent choirmasters," praising the Utah choir's mastery under Lund's baton. "While the Churches of the East were fretting over the introduction of the vested choir, progress was being made in the West," Boyd said. But the only choir he mentioned to back up that claim was the Salt Lake Tabernacle Choir, whose "repertory includes choruses of Haydn, Handel, Schubert, Beethoven, Mendelssohn; many works written for this choir; and of late choruses by Russian composers."[24]

Lund's reputation also spread into the corporate world of music. His name, image, and signature appeared on a brochure for the Steger phonograph, an ornate floor console with which, it said, he had spent "many pleasant hours." While he is credited for the boilerplate ad copy as the "Tabernacle Choir Conductor"—with both "Salt Lake" and "Mormon" noticeably absent in the name—it is not clear if he actually wrote the copy. The brochure makes eight points in favor of the Steger, quoting Lund as saying that "careful study and investigation" convinced him that this model was "unquestionably the finest reproducing phonograph," the "supreme" home record player. Among the eight attributes glowingly cited in the brochure are these: The reproduction was so perfect you could almost think the recording artist was there in person. The Steger played any sort of music. The tone arm was balanced, the sound chamber beautiful and all wood. The machinery was well-constructed, easy to play. And, of course, the machine bore a well-known brand name.[25]

Still, it would take a newer technological marvel to show off the essence of a choir's sound. That marvel was radio.

In a 1936 novel, Rudolf Arnheim illustrated radio's spectral powers with this vignette:

> Now there is silence except for slight noises and cracklings, the reader closes the book and gets ready to go out, and suddenly an entirely different voice from the loudspeaker announces that he will now hear Beethoven's 8th Symphony. The reader puts on his coat and cuts off Beethoven's introductory bars in the middle by a pressure of his finger. But the music persists, though more distant and raucous, drifting up the stair from the hall-porter's room. The reader nods to him as he goes past, bangs the front door, but Beethoven follows him down the street, loud and strident from the shoemaker's back room, softly from the second floor of a villa, and braying across the market-place from a little café—an acoustic relay race carried on from house to house, everywhere, inescapable.
>
> Busy and idle, rich and poor, young and old, healthy and sick—they all hear the same thing.[26]

That is, radio had at last fulfilled Paul Valéry's vision of "the conquest of ubiq-uity."[27] Now an individual or group—even a choir—could be everywhere. A choir in an auditorium had to sound polished. But a radio choir now enjoyed the mystique of "reception." Even the ebbing and flowing static that sometimes surrounded the sound provided a sonic halo. As a Mormon magazine observed in 1925, "Many an indifferent person has openly admitted that radio has done more to convince him of the immortality of things and of the existence of Deity than any other intermediary."[28]

Heber Grant instantly saw both the spiritual meaning and the practical benefit of radio. He helped launch the first Salt Lake City station, KZN on 6 May 1922.

He opened the first broadcast by quoting scripture about the "voice out of the heavens" proclaiming the gospel. His wife, Augusta, soon spoke, musing that "I would not be surprised if we were talking to the planets before many years."[29] Two years later the Church terminated its overflow sessions at General Conference, instead broadcasting the Tabernacle meetings to the outside grounds and Assembly Hall, though not to the public at large—almost no one had a radio yet.

But as the 1920s ensued, radio sales skyrocketed and the U.S. secretary of the interior began to debate the educational possibilities of the new medium. At the same time, KZN (renamed KFPT in 1924) stocked its schedule with broadcasts of religious programming from all manner of churches in and out of Salt Lake City. In November 1924, the Church station began a Sunday evening hour-long broadcast of a Mormon sermon and sacred music. The show evolved into a series with rotating themes. Soon the station itself mutated, adding huge wattage—with a loan from the Church that guaranteed it a controlling interest—and changing its call letters again, this time to KSL.[30]

In 1927 Congress passed the Radio Act, which required stations to offer a quota of noncommercial programs in the "public interest," a term radio entrepreneurs interpreted broadly. In that vein, Earl Glade, KSL's general manager, proposed to the National Broadcasting Company a weekly live half-hour broadcast from the Tabernacle, which would include numbers by the Tabernacle Choir and organists. The timing of Glade's pitch fit perfectly with both the Church's and the network's needs. The Church, still climbing its way out of the dim reputation it had acquired, was about to celebrate its centennial. It yearned to use that anniversary as an occasion to show the nation its own progress, much as the nation had tried to show the world its progress in Chicago in 1893. Meanwhile, NBC needed low-cost but appealing public interest content. So Glade's proposal seemed worth a try, especially since all of the production would be done in-house at the Tabernacle, with the grateful complicity of its landlord.[31]

On 11 July 1929, the Choir used its Thursday evening rehearsal time to set up and run through the program order of its first network show. First tasks: hang heavy drapes in front of the Choir and cover their seats with carpet scraps to dampen the acoustics; next, pull up the podium microphone as high as it could go and perch organist Ed Kimball's son Ted on a stepladder so he could announce the numbers. When all that was done, Glade and NBC engineer A. V. Saxton listened to a run-through, the format and content of which the KSL team had crystallized in the previous seven years of local broadcasts—except that now they had to time things more carefully to fit the network specs, on the staggering promise of up to ten million listeners. Lund and Kimball picked well-known numbers from their repertoire: three choir pieces and three organ pieces, alternating through the half-hour show, choruses from Wagner's *Meistersinger* and *Tannhäuser*, a hymn by George Careless, the finale from Mendelssohn's *Elijah*, an organ sonata movement by Boslip, and a folk arrangement by Kimball.[32]

Days later, NBC aired the as-yet-untitled show live, not on Sunday, but on Monday afternoon from 3:00 to 3:30, the time slot the show would occupy for the next three years. That slot, of course, posed a problem for the singers, all of them volunteers and mostly day workers or homemakers. But local businesses pitched in, giving their employees time off, while neighbors and extended families contributed their effort by tending children. This was one of the biggest cultural feats Utahns' culture had yet mounted. And nine months shy of the Church's centennial, it seemed a birthday gift from above.

The earliest shows had the blandest of boilerplate introductions: "greetings" from Salt Lake City, the network call letters, and an introduction of the players, beginning with "the L.D.S. Tabernacle Choir under the direction of Anthony C. Lund." The broadcasts included no sermonettes, instead running continuous music, with the organists playing accompaniments, solos, and modulations between the choral pieces.

The miking at the Tabernacle ran through telephone wires to station WJZ in New York, which then broadcast the signal to thirty other stations, including KSL. Because of a mysterious hum in the signal, some of the eastern stations had their audio feed cut midway through that first broadcast, leaving listeners only a teasing taste of this unprecedented program. For four months the same hum intermittently plagued the transfer signal from WJZ, but the network stopped cutting the feed to its secondary stations. For some of the audience, at least, the hum's aural barrier actually made the show a kind of half-forbidden pleasure: one had to work to get a sonic glimpse of the fabled Choir from the mysterious West.[33]

Other glitches in the new show cropped up, too, as was common in the fledgling broadcast industry. One Choir member recalled that a former soloist who had moved away made a surprise visit to the Choir while it was on the air. After one number was done, Lund saw her, put down his baton, and made a beeline to greet her. The organ played, finished its solo, and "it was time for the Choir again, and there he was up there talking, and some of the Choir had to go up and bring him down. . . . The organist [kept] them interested until he got back, and then the Choir went along as usual."

The stock market crashed just three months after the first Tabernacle broadcast. Soon the Tabernacle show started to feel like a spiritual outpost for a nation stumbling into the Great Depression. Newspaper critics praised the program. The *Albany Times* wrote that the show was "an interlude of amazing beauty— something different, unique, inspiring. . . . If you can listen to that magnificent choir and not get a thrill, something is decidedly wrong." One New Jersey newspaper advised people not to be scared off by a potential surfeit of churchy music: although some sacred music was on the broadcast, "there is much from the library of folk music, ballads and opera included"—even Stephen Foster songs, it noted. A New York paper opined that "somewhere in the world there may be more than one brilliant choral organization other than the Mormon Tabernacle Choir, but there is no broadcasting in America today to equal [this]. . . . Nothing with more majestic inspiration has been heard since broadcasting began." By the end of the show's first year, NBC accepted Glade's offer to have the Tabernacle Choir provide the network's annual radio performance of the *Messiah*. "The company was glad," Glade wrote, "to localize this responsibility on Salt Lake City."[34] The Mormons, in this at least, had become the putative spokespeople for mainstream U.S. Christendom in music.

But the Church was not only bringing goodwill to itself through its broadcasts. It felt it was providing an alternative to the pervasive Tin Pan Alley tunes and syncopated jazz of the era. At least, that was what Earl Glade hoped, noting that the shows were part of a trend that radio had the power to shape: "The country over, tastes in music are improving. People aren't leaning over backwards affectedly pretending that they like certain kinds of music when actually they almost suffer agonies while hearing it. Both the program selectors and the audience are getting together. The result is real progress and radio is the biggest single factor in this forward march."

Yet from the practical side, Lund and the Tabernacle organists had to spend more and more time seeking out new repertoire to fill a weekly half-hour without too much repetition. Moreover, they had to plan numbers that, with a little transitional patter, added up to the correct clock time. If Lund neared the end of a show and needed to fill more time, he had to slow down the tempo of whatever he was conducting; if time ran short, he had to speed up. The Choir had plenty of existing pieces to choose from, of course, though within a year of the first broadcast Lund began publishing many new compositions or arrangements of his own, typically ones he had featured on the air. Still, the Choir's repertoire never kept pace with the weekly demands. One heard the same pieces reappear in the broadcasts a little too often. It was part of the great radio readjustment: a touring choir could do the same small set of works over and over to a different audience in each new venue. Now the Choir had to sing new works each week to the same audience.

For a sense of Lund and his organists' choices, as well as the format they had settled into, consider three consecutive programs in 1930, filled with European classics, a few American works, and hymns:

I
Choir: Glorious Things are Sung of Zion (hymn)
Organ: Entrée du Cortege (Nuptial Mass) (Dubois)
Choir: My Lark My Love (Lieurence)
Organ: Gavotte Pastorale (Annette et Lubin) (Durand)
Organ: Angelus (from "Scenes Pittoresque") (Massenet)
Choir: Psalm 46 (Buck)
II
Choir: Author of Faith (hymn)
Organ: Prelude to Lohengrin (Wagner)
Choir: The Prodigal Son (Parks)
Organ: A Vesper Prayer (Diggle)
Organ: Suite Gothique Chorale Toccata (Boellmann)
Choir: The Heavens are Telling (Haydn)
III
Choir: Hail Bright Millennial Day (hymn)
Organ: In the Garden (Goodwin)
Choir: Psalm 19 (Beethoven)
Organ: Last Spring (Grieg)
Organ: Lans Deo (Messe de Marriage) (Dubois)
Choir: Gloria from 12th Mass (Mozart)[35]

Some fan letters approved of the choices. Others suggested changes. In January 1930, for example, W. C. Holt of Santa Rosa, California, wrote to the "Tabernacle Choir Leader" these lines:

I have just listened to your most entertaining program. Every syllable of every word was distinctly heard, and as clear as a bell. It is the first choir singing over the air of which that could be said. There is very little chorus singing where all the words can be clearly understood, even in the same building. Your choir is most evenly balanced as to parts. The tenor was fine in quality, but not quite heavy enough for a good balance with the other parts. Pardon this suggestion.

Sing old familiar, immortal hymns, including "negro spirituals." Radio listeners become over-tired with operatic and classic music, and long for soul stirring singing.[36]

Holt, of course, failed to mention the program's announcer, a post that resembled more an emcee than a preacher, and whose assignment passed through several men after Ted Kimball. Within three months of Holt's letter, though, a new announcer joined the show, a twenty-four-year-old KSL employee named Richard Evans. With his formal, journalist-cum-orator's elocution, Evans would not only become the official voice of the broadcast for the next forty-one years but, with his nonparochial sermonettes, would infuse the nation with a particularly noble image of Mormonness.

On 19 January 1931, Evans gave an elaborate, slightly overwrought introduction, from which decades of introductions would derive. It laid down the Mormonistic premise of the show in clear terms: "Greeting, ladies and gentlemen. The changing of a mid-nineteenth century sagebrush waste to a cultural outpost of the West was evidenced by the erection of one of the world's largest auditoriums, the Mormon Tabernacle, from which unique structure we bring to you weekly at this hour sacred and secular master-works of music presented by a choir of 300 voices, with accompaniments and solo presentations from the great Tabernacle organ, world-famed for its mellow majesty." In the sign-off, he surreptitiously used a paraphrase and trope of Mormon scripture ("men are that they might have joy"): "As the last notes of the great Tabernacle organ fade, may we leave you with a thought: Man is that he might have joy—joy in living—joy in art and music."[37]

He used this intro through April, then, perhaps at the urging of NBC, revamped his opening statement in a way that soft-pedaled the Mormon angle: "Those who live in the tops of the western mountains take pleasure in presenting for the nation's entertainment Salt Lake's Tabernacle Choir, with matchless music from Salt Lake's world-famed Tabernacle organ." The sign-off similarly pulled back, though wished listeners "peace and joy in living until we greet you at this same hour next week."

Amid the shifting name changes and patter, the Choir's network show had acquired one constancy: the singing and humming of "Gently Raise the Sacred Strain" before the announcer began speaking. For the older Choir members, this theme song must have had a special ring. Its music was composed by Thomas Griggs, the only person ever appointed to be the Choir's conductor who had never actually served in the position, but who had been a constant presence in and around the group for decades until his death in 1903 at the age of fifty-eight. At Griggs's funeral, Elder Charles Savage said that Griggs had now joined "the choir invisible" in heaven. Now, a quarter century later, his hymn introduced the Tabernacle Choir to the nation each week, a "choir invisible" to its listeners but omnipresent in the newly tamed radio waves above the Earth.[38]

The earthly sound of the Tabernacle, meanwhile, was attracting scientists. In January 1930, the *Journal of the Acoustical Society of America* published an analysis of the Tabernacle's acoustics. The author noted that the acoustic space had five seconds of reverberation when the building was empty but only one second when it was full. That latter time proved sonically ideal for a musical group, though still too long for a speaker at the pulpit to be understood. At different spots in the room, a listener got lots of interference from variously reflecting sound waves. Adding some strategic wall covering would cut down the interference. But then listeners in the back of the hall would lose some of what emanated from the choir loft. So, "it is doubtful that anything could be gained" by such a move.[39]

People who worked and worshipped at the Tabernacle, of course, had an unscientific but savvy awareness of its traits. Guides treated tourists to the famous Tabernacle "pin drop," in which one could stand at the back of the hall while a pin was dropped at the pulpit in front and hear a tinny clang via the reflected sound of the sloping ceiling. But however startling that acoustic feat was, the building's unusual acoustics would actually dog the Choir as it now pursued its mission through radio and recordings.

The Choir's new media life overlapped with other enormous commitments. In late 1929, the First Presidency had called a huge committee of musicians and thespians to mount an epic indoor pageant, *The Message of the Ages*, for the Church's centennial the following year. The Tabernacle Choir anchored the pageant's music with hymns, anthems—many by Careless and Stephens—and excerpts from Handel's *Messiah*, Haydn's *Creation*, and Gates's *Restoration*. Frank Asper (yet another Tabernacle organist) conducted a pick-up orchestra that played instrumental excerpts from Mendelssohn's *St. Paul*, Saint-Saens's *March Heroique*, and many other works. Instrumental and vocal soloists, along with dramatic readers and large-cast set pieces—representing scenes from the Egyptian exodus to the pioneer trek—filled up the program, which played thirty straight nights, beginning on the Church's actual birthday, 6 April 1930. Every night's performance sold out its six thousand available tickets. Thirty thousand additional ticket requests could not be filled. The zeal and quality of the pageant dazzled Church members and curious outsiders. But the spectacle almost ruined the fledgling radio broadcasts for almost four months: the sets, platforms, and curtains for *Message of the Ages* remained at least partially intact from March until June, undoing the carefully arrayed broadcast acoustics.[40] Still, for such a heady occasion, the hometown celebration had to trump the radio outreach.

On the heels of *The Message of the Ages*, David Smith gave permission for the Choir to perform in the soundtrack for the first Mormon-produced movie, *Corianton*. It was a tepid, ungainly would-be epic based on a Broadway play that had, in turn, been based on a novella by Mormon intellectual and General Authority B. H. Roberts. The choice of this entrée into film seemed both puzzling and inevitable. Anti-Mormon movies or scary Mormon villains had mildly infested the movie industry. Mormons wanted to fight back, even with as weak a melodrama as this one. David Smith, though, actually found the film impressive, explaining to an interviewer that *Corianton* had met "the highest standard to present day motion picture art," and therefore he was happy to sign a contract with the producers of the movie for "the first and exclusive right to feature the Choir and organ in motion pictures." Indeed, "Many previous proposals had been made for filming the Choir and organ since the advent of sound on the screen," said Smith, "but I have refused to get hasty. I have felt the keenest responsibility not only to the members of the Choir [and] the Church, but also that vast audience throughout the world—men and women of intelligent discrimination who in one way or another have become acquainted and favorably impressed with the work we are doing."[41]

Smith saw this performance as a media triumph parallel to the Choir's successes in touring, recording, and broadcasting. His optimism was nearly infectious, though overblown. The movie had, he said, "a whale of a ready-made audience." Beyond the Mormons themselves, there was an interested fan base, the size of which the movie's screenwriter weirdly calculated: "If during the past ten years, an average of 50,000 people each year, or 500,000 for the ten year period, have attended the free noon-day organ recitals in the Tabernacle, and each of these 500,000 people have talked with their neighbors and friends and have interested at least ten others," which "would make an appreciable public interested in the choir and organ of 35,000,000 people." Smith believed that the composer of the *Corianton* soundtrack, Edgar Stillman Kelly, had a huge fan base who would come out to hear what Stillman Kelly considered the "'crowning achievement' of his life's work." Finally, Smith noted, "there is the great Jewish population throughout New York City—interested enthusiastic theatre-goers—especially when any theatrical production tends to glorify a Jewish character or present a favorable sidelight on the Hebrew people." But even with so large a prospective audience, the show—which ended up being more risqué than the Church had bargained for—tanked at the box office.

By the middle of 1931, Lund was nearly spent. Amid the broadcast schedule, the recordings, the General Music Committee and General Conference commitments, along with a heavy schedule of private teaching, Lund's heart weakened and kidney disease flared up. His obesity no doubt aggravated his illnesses. But the stresses were about to intensify.

CBS, like its rival network NBC, had an assortment of live religious programs on its schedule. In spring 1932, one of those programs had to cancel its 10 A.M. Sunday episode for the week. CBS's manager of construction and building operations in New York, Stan McAllister, was asked by his boss to put together a one-shot filler program for that time slot. McAllister, who was Mormon, arranged for musicians from the Manhattan and Brooklyn branches of the Church to pinch-hit. The hastily assembled show succeeded so well that McAllister's boss asked him to come up with a regular show along the same lines. McAllister decided to try luring the Tabernacle Choir program, along with KSL, away from NBC. After about five months of negotiations, he forged a contract with KSL to switch networks and bring the Tabernacle show with it. This would also put the Tabernacle musicians and announcer in the loop for CBS's *Church of the Air* series, a Sunday show that rotated among denominations that agreed to present a nondenominational message and, of course, lots of music.[42]

On Sunday, 4 September 1932, KSL began broadcasting on CBS, with the Tabernacle show, now titled *The Hour Harmonious*, during prime Sabbath time, 10 to 10:30 Sunday mornings. Since the show had been recruited to the network by a Mormon, Evans may have felt licensed to return the show to its overtly Mormon branding: "Once more we beckon you through the portals of the Great Mormon Tabernacle, shadowed by the six-spired Temple and surrounded by the everlasting hills of the rugged open West." He then explained the show's name: "the hour harmonious when nature—art—science—music are tuned to sweet accord." Religion did not make the list.

And within a month, the word *Mormon* vanished from the introduction again. The show came simply from "the Great Tabernacle" in the West.

For the next year and a half, the weekly introduction would vary slightly—Evans seemed to resist pat repetition—as did the quick "thought" at the sign-off. Then, on 26 March 1933, the show expanded to one hour (9:30 to 10:30 A.M.). The expansion suddenly doubled the musicians' workload. To lighten their burden, and perhaps satisfy his own literary pretensions, Evans started to introduce longer inspirational musings before and after some musical selections. On 16 July, they dropped the *Hour Harmonious* name in favor of *The Thoughtful Sabbath Hour*—the adjective being added perhaps to distinguish this show from a number of local radio "Sabbath hours" that might rival it for potential audiences.

To understand the performers' new burden and how they carried it, consider two program schedules from December 1933, with Lund directing the Choir and Frank Asper at the organ—more hymns and simple classical organ pieces and transcriptions.

I
Choir: Hail Bright Millennial Day (hymn)
Organ: Cantabile (Franck)
Choir: Daybreak (Chopin)
Organ: Volga Boatman (Traditional)
Choir: Come Thou Glorious Day of Promise (hymn)
Organ: Loure (Bach)
Choir: Prayer (Beethoven)
Organ: A Cheerful Fire, and the Kettle Boils (Clolsey)
Choir: Come Let Us Anew (hymn)
Organ: Toccata (Dubois)
Organ: Prelude (Clerambault)
Choir: Unfold Ye Portals (Gounod)
Choir: Lead Kindly Light (hymn)
Organ: Nocturne in E Flat Major (Chopin)
Choir: Hallelujah (Beethoven)
II
Choir: Go Ye Messengers of Glory (hymn)
Organ: Meditation (Massenet)
Choir: O Isis & Osiris (Mozart)
Organ: Fugue in A Minor (Bach)
Choir: O Awake My Slumbering Minstrels (hymn)

Organ: Largo (Handel)
Choir: Come Unto Me (hymn)
Choir: O Worship the King (Haydn)
Organ: Symphonesque (Spencer)
Choir: How Lovely are the Messengers (Mendelssohn)
Organ: Londonderry Air (Organ)
Choir: I Need Thee Every Hour (Lowry)
Organ: Andantino in G Minor (Franck)
Choir: And the Glory of the Lord (Handel)[43]

Clearly the milestone of the Church's centennial had marked a new era for the Choir's prestige. In December 1932, for example, the Scranton-based Welsh American paper the *Druid* named the Tabernacle Choir the "Best All American Choir," an ensemble "beautifully and authentically trained in mass singing, voices always under control and extreme attention given to diction and phrasing, with the intonation at all times clear and true." The paper went on, increasingly colorful and verbose, in what might have been the best review of the Choir yet—and from the pulpit of the Welsh at that. This was the kind of endorsement the recently deceased Stephens had craved, only now given to the Scandinavian Lund.[44]

Alongside the Choir, the Church's prestige also blossomed. Who could have imagined ten years earlier that the Mormons' music and rhetoric—however diluted in doctrine—would be pouring into the nations' homes every Sunday morning for an hour? Yet, not only had the Church stepped over the wall that had barred it from "acceptable" America, it had welcomed U.S. technological progress into its own house. The physics expertise of Mormon Harvey Fletcher was helping guide Bell Labs in New York. The inventive prowess of Mormon Philo Farnsworth was leading to the creation of television. Two Apostles now had doctorates and were full-fledged scientists (James Talmage and John Widtsoe). Far from the "old-time religion" that might push back at science in the name of biblical literalism, many in the Church leadership embraced new technology on the premise that God inspired it for the benefit of his true Church and the spreading of its message. The Church had even begun to embrace psychology and intellection in its lessons, as in this definition of faith from a 1934 priesthood handbook: "What is faith? Faith is rationalized impulse."[45]

Mormonism had not become scientism, to be sure. But it had embraced the worship of innovation. Perhaps the best evidence of that was in the title of its official magazine, a trope on the name of its youth organization, the Mutual

Improvement Association. That organizational name bespoke fraternity and communal uplift, but the title of the magazine went further: *The Improvement Era*. That moniker forecast a new, forward-thinking age. And in a time of national Depression, the implicit rallying cry of that name suited the mood of the times.

All this intellectual ferment combined with the Mormon ideals of industry and cooperation. That combination struck none other than national hero Henry Ford, who invited the Tabernacle Choir to sing in the Ford Symphony Gardens at the 1933–34 Century of Progress Fair in Chicago, a sequel to the fair at which the Choir had won its first big prize forty years earlier.

In the second week of September 1934, the group opened its run at the fair with a survey of Choir favorites, greatest radio hits, and all the sorts of "respectable, taste-elevating" works that Lund favored:

Choral from *Die Meistersinger* (Wagner)
How Lovely are the Messengers (Mendelssohn)
For the Strength of the Hills (Hymn by Stephens)
Longing (Tchaikovsky)
Fly, Singing Bird, Fly (Elgar)
Build the More Stately Mansions (Farwell)
Sweet and Low (Barnby)
Before Jehovah's Glorious Throne (Handel)
God is Our Refuge (Buck)[46]

To those who had followed the Choir of Evan Stephens's day, though, the essential transformation in repertoire was astonishing: as the week proceeded, two hundred Mormon choral singers delivered numbers like the "Kiss Waltz" and "From the Land of Sky Blue Waters" as they stood under a giant archway with the Ford logo as a crown over their heads.

The Choir was now a radio choir. But as with any media stars, the public wanted a live glimpse. The Choir had sixteen differently programmed concerts, most of which consisted of light classical or parlor fare. Missionaries swarmed and hovered around those who walked over to the Mormon exhibit booth, presided over by a sculptural showpiece created by Avard Fairbanks. It depicted a foundation marked "Eternal Progress," on which an angel stood, arms outstretched to display the "Spiritual Guidance and Activities of The Church of Jesus Christ of Latter-Day Saints." Those were: Benevolence, Science, Priesthood of God, The Home Culture, and Creative Recreation. Within the relief image itself one found three principles: Health, Truth, and Love. Except for the obligatory—and not the first—principle, "Priesthood of God," the words offered only holistic values to which any fair-goer would assent. The image was attractive, polished, classical, reverential, but not overtly religious, except in the vein of the U.S. religion that united the country in the midst of the Great Depression, in which the brotherhood of man was the new savior.

That sculpture—pictured in the center of the pamphlet that missionaries passed out—perfectly complemented the vaguely nondenominational Salt Lake Tabernacle Choir and its statesmanlike spokesman, Richard Evans.[47] Paving the road for potential converts to come to its doors would be the Tabernacle team's mission for the remainder of the twentieth century.

The Choir and its entourage returned home from Chicago via a series of stops billed as "good-neighbor" appearances. Finally, at the train station in Salt Lake City, they were hailed as heroes of Church image redemption. The whole world had seen and heard a Mormonism vastly different from the insular, parochial one in the shadows of its past. David Smith quickly began talks with a New York promoter for a tour of Europe—a tour that would take twenty more years to accomplish.[48]

Meanwhile, the one-hour radio format had gradually begun to contain two sermonettes by Evans, each a one-paragraph inspirational message that often quoted Mormon scriptural passages, though these were never identified as such. Indeed, much of Evans's fan mail asked him where this or that scripture was found. He would reply that it was in, say, the Book of Mormon and then would send the listener a copy.

Four more events in 1933–35 converged to shape the "classic" Mormon Tabernacle Choir of the next generation. The first was the decisive subjugation of the Choir's conductor to the nonmusical Church hierarchy. Back in the April 1905 General Conference, the Choir's conductor, organists, *and all its members* had begun to be sustained (supported by vote) in General Conference. In October 1922, the sustaining expanded to include the secretary and treasurer of the Choir. In April 1925 the sustaining of the Choir's *members* was dropped from the vote. In October 1928 the *President* of the Choir was added to the vote for the first time—but after the conductor and organists. In April 1933, though, the order changed: the President was now listed ahead of the conductor. This change served public notice that the Tabernacle Choir was subject to the priesthood, less autonomous than its participants may have believed.

In February 1934, J. Reuben Clark, newly called as a counselor in Heber Grant's First Presidency, made a notation in his diary that suggested how closely the Presidency might be monitoring the Choir's work. The hour broadcast to which he listened was "not so good. The duet, trio, and solo work was poor. Asper's [organ] pieces were poor, and Richard Evan's [sic] announcements were not up to the standard: Richard was too precipitate, not deliberate enough."[49] The detail and rigor of his review suggest how closely the leadership intended to oversee the Tabernacle broadcast's "standard."

A second event was the 1934 realignment of the Church Music Committee, which subordinated Lund to a new member, Spencer Cornwall. President Grant had appointed new members for the committee—mostly to replace George Careless and Evan Stephens—and in the process "realigned" its subcommittees. At the head of the choristers and organists subcommittee was Cornwall, superintendent of music in Salt Lake City public schools, who had, like Evan Stephens, directed many youth choirs.[50] But Cornwall's choirs were under the auspices of the state itself. Lund, despite his choral reputation before and after his appointment to the Tabernacle, remained a committee member only, not the leader one would expect.

A third was Richard Evans's decision to stay with the broadcast, despite First Presidency coaxing to the contrary. In April 1934, Evans was considering returning to graduate school on the East Coast. President Heber Grant urged him to wait—something was coming up. That something was a First Presidency request for Evans to become the assistant editor of the *Improvement Era*. After days of deliberation, he accepted the job with the proviso that he remain as spokesman for the radio show. Whether he was swayed by the award he had received that January as *Radio Engineering*'s Radio Announcer of the Year is hard to say. But his decision to remain as the spokesman for the Spoken Word of Mormonism proved a bulwark in the show's long-term success.[51]

The fourth event was decisive: Lund's sudden death.

In the spring of 1935, Spencer Cornwall ran into Lund on Main Street, right in front of the Salt Lake Temple. Lund said, according to Cornwall, "Boy, I don't know how long I'm going to be leader of the Tabernacle Choir. I advise you to get your plate right side up." Cornwall had no interest in taking over the Choir. He was then directing a thousand-voice choir of children in the school district. After his encounter with Lund, a woman who didn't have a child in that district came to watch one of their rehearsals. Cornwall later learned she was the wife of Sylvester Cannon, first counselor in the Presiding Bishopric.[52]

Though the exact timetable is unclear, within a few weeks of that visit, Tony Lund had a heart attack. On 10 June 1935, Sylvester Cannon wrote to Cornwall that Cornwall would soon be officially asked by President Grant to take over the Choir as a guest conductor for at least two months until Lund recovered. He would also need to take the Choir on its planned trip to the San Diego Exposition that fall. "Terms can be arranged that will be satisfactory to you. This arrangement, it is hoped, will be the beginning of something more permanent."[53] The next day, Lund died.

President Grant immediately called Cornwall to his office, told him he had been appointed as the new conductor of the Tabernacle Choir and needed to quit his public-school job because this was a full-time position. Cornwall discussed it with his wife, with his city boss, and with his friend Hugh Brown (who would himself become a First Presidency counselor in a few years). Brown asked Cornwall how long he had been supervising in the schools. Twenty-two years, Cornwall told him. Brown replied, "You're treading the mill." That mild jab provoked Cornwall to accept the call. Grant laid hands on Cornwall's head, "set him apart" as the new conductor of the Choir, and called a press conference to announce the change.[54]

Cornwall would conduct the Choir for the next twenty-two years, leading it through two more U.S. wars, three Presidents of the Church, the Choir's first international tour, the first public demonstration of stereo sound, the first book about the Choir, two more movie soundtracks, hundreds more radio broadcasts, a presidential funeral, and a contract with the largest record company in the world.

A stereo view card of the "new" Salt Lake Tabernacle under construction in 1866, showing an outcrop of the elaborate wooden framing that supported the huge, tortoise-shaped structure. (Michael Hicks archives)

In the Choir's early decades, its members sang hymns from part books such as this: the individual musical part shown, but the text to be memorized or read from a separate, text-only hymnbook. (Michael Hicks archives)

Among the national celebrities who sang with the Choir in the 1890s was opera diva Nellie Melba, whose flamboyant and "worldly" language and behavior unnerved many Choir members. (Michael Hicks archives)

Evan Stephens (arm outstretched) on the train that carried the Choir across the continent on its controversial 1911 East Coast tour. (Michael Hicks archives)

The Choir eagerly bought up copies of the 1912 Schirmer edition of Handel's *Messiah*. Here the front cover with which the Church rebound it shows not only the name of the Choir, but the ecclesiastical authority that had now come to govern it. The stamped text reads: "This Book belongs to the PRESIDING BISHOPRIC and MUST NOT be loaned or taken off the premises without their permission." (Michael Hicks archives)

Festival Hall
Panama-Pacific International Exposition
San Francisco, Cal.

Four Grand Concerts
by the
Mormon Tabernacle Choir
of Ogden, Utah

200 Voices
and

Exposition Orchestra
of Eighty Musicians

Wednesday, Thursday and Friday Evenings
July, 21, 22, 23, at 8:30 P. M.
and Saturday Afternoon at 2:30 P. M.

The growing fame of the Mormon Tabernacle Choir led other groups to exploit the name, often subtly misleading the public—as in this 1915 instance, where only the fine print clarifies that this is not the famous Salt Lake City–based choir. (L. Tom Perry Special Collections, Harold B. Lee Library, Brigham Young University, Provo, Utah)

The corpulent Tony Lund, successor to Evan Stephens as the Choir's conductor, rests on the crest of Mount Timpanogos (near Brigham Young University) as his colleagues go ahead without him. (L. Tom Perry Special Collections, Harold B. Lee Library, Brigham Young University, Provo, Utah)

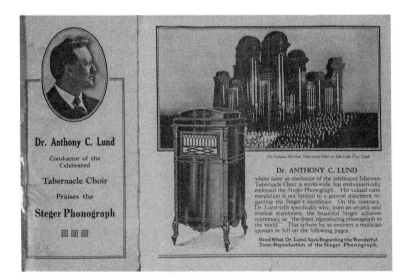

By the early 1920s, the Choir's reputation made its conductor a celebrity who, in this case, was worthy to endorse the popular Steger phonograph. (Scrapbook in Cornelia Sorenson Lund Papers, L. Tom Perry Special Collections, Harold B. Lee Library, Brigham Young University, Provo, Utah)

From the 1930s through the 1960s, the Choir's radio spokesman, Richard Evans, received hundreds of fan letters a year, most of them asking about the sources of quotations he used or the names of hymns the Choir sang. He and his assistants answered most of the letters, often at length. This photo shows the stack of correspondence from about two months in the 1930s. (Michael Hicks archives)

Via this striking image of the Choir (and Church leader Reuben Clark) spread from coast to coast, the Church newspaper exulted that CBS's *Church of the Air* broadcast would originate at the Mormon General Conference in April 1939. (Scrapbook in J. Spencer Cornwall Papers, L. Tom Perry Special Collections, Harold B. Lee Library, Brigham Young University, Provo, Utah)

The 1941 cast and musical personnel for Mendelssohn's *St. Paul* at the Salt Lake Tabernacle, one of several dramatized oratorios the Church and its official Choir staged in the 1930s to 1940s. (J. Spencer Cornwall Papers, L. Tom Perry Special Collections, Harold B. Lee Library, Brigham Young University, Provo, Utah)

On the eve of the Japanese attack on Pearl Harbor, Mormon President Heber Grant sent signed copies of a Mormon "hymnbook companion" (authored by the Choir's former tour manager) to all the Choir's members. The inscription above his signature thanks—note the order—the Choir's President, the Conductor and Assistant Conductor, the announcer (Richard Evans), the organists, "and each and all of the members of the Choir for the good work they are doing." (Michael Hicks archives)

CHURCH OF JESUS CHRIST OF LATTER DAY SAINTS
HEBER J. GRANT, PRESIDENT
SALT LAKE CITY, UTAH

August 15, 1941

Rea Malin

Dear Sister:

It gives me very much pleasure to hand you this copy of George D. Pyper's book, "Stories of Latter-day Saint Hymns." I am sure you will enjoy the contents of this book, and believe you would like to have the signature of the author, so I shall ask him to write in each, "Yours sincerely," and sign his name.

I am very grateful to the President, the Conductor, his Assistant, the Announcer, the Organists, and each and all of the members of the Choir for the good work they are doing.

Yours sincerely,

During the Choir's first European tour (1955), signs like this one in Cardiff aptly billed the group as "America's Most Famous Choir." (Scrapbook in J. Spencer Cornwall Papers, L. Tom Perry Special Collections, Harold B. Lee Library, Brigham Young University, Provo, Utah)

A 1955 poster in Denmark—illustrated with an image of the Utah pioneers—announces that the Choir's concert there is sold out. (Scrapbook in J. Spencer Cornwall Papers, L. Tom Perry Special Collections, Harold B. Lee Library, Brigham Young University, Provo, Utah)

In its ongoing quest for greater spectacle, the Choir performed Brahms's *German Requiem* with the Denver Symphony at the Red Rocks Music Festival, near Denver, July 1956. (Scrapbook in J. Spencer Cornwall Papers, L. Tom Perry Special Collections, Harold B. Lee Library, Brigham Young University, Provo, Utah)

One of the Choir's chief ongoing tasks has been to sing for Mormon General Conferences. Here Richard Condie—then considered only a temporary conductor—directs the assembled multitude at General Conference, flanked by the Choir, General Authorities of the Church below him (ca. 1958). (Richard Condie Papers, L. Tom Perry Special Collections, Harold B. Lee Library, Brigham Young University, Provo, Utah)

With curtains hung to dampen the Tabernacle's resonance, Richard Condie rehearses the Choir and the New York Philharmonic for the Leonard Bernstein–directed *Joy of Christmas* Columbia LP (1963). (Richard Condie Papers, L. Tom Perry Special Collections, Harold B. Lee Library, Brigham Young University, Provo, Utah)

In the summer of 1967, with the Church fending off charges of racism —and blacks still not allowed in the Choir—RCA published this Mormon Tabernacle–based advertisement in *Ebony* magazine. (Michael Hicks archives)

Richard Nixon raises the arm of Richard Condie on behalf of the Choir at the January 1969 presidential inaugural. (Richard Condie Papers, L. Tom Perry Special Collections, Harold B. Lee Library, Brigham Young University, Provo, Utah)

The Choir identification badge for the January 1989 inaugural of George Bush—with the Washington, D.C., Temple now replacing the standard image of the Salt Lake Temple. (Thomas Durham archives)

גירלד אוטלי, מנצח המקהלה

במשך 18 שנות כהונתו כמנהל מוסיקלי של מקהלת מורמון טאברנאקל, ניצח ד"ר ג'רולד אוטלי על יותר מ-900 קונצרטים שחלקן גדול מהם שודרו ברדיו CBC והוקלטו לחברות SONY ו-DECCA. כמו-כן הופיעה המקהלה, בניצוחו, בקונצרטים "חיים" בטלויזיה.

ד"ר אוטלי זכה להכרה בשל הפרשנויות המוסיקליות שלו לסגנונות המוסיקה השונים. חיפושיו המתמידים אחר הפרטים ויכולתו להשלים למיצבה גדול של צורה מוסיקלית, הפכוהו לאחד המנצחים המבוקשים באמריקה.

ב-1961 סיים ג'רולד אוטלי את לימודיו באוניברסיטת 'בריגהאם יאנג' וב-1967 קיבל תואר MA באוניברסיטת מאוניברסיטה יוטא. כמו-כן, הוענקה לו מילגת פולברייט ללימודי ניצוח, שאותם עשה בשנים 1968-69 באקדמיה למוסיקה בקלן, גרמניה. בשנת 1972 הוענק לו התואר ד"ר למוסיקה מטעם אוניברסיטת אורגן.

דונאלד ריפלינגר, מנצח מישנה

דונאלד ריפלינגר הוא בוגר אוניברסיטת 'בריגהאם יאנג' ובעל תואר MA ודוקטורט מאוניברסיטת יוטה. היה תלמידם של לרוי רוברטסון, קרופורד גייטס, פול סלמונוביצ'י ורונ'ר וונר של במקהלת רוברט שו.

ריפלינגר יזם ואירגן פסטיבלים למקהלות ברחבי ארצות הברית עם מנצחים אורחים בעלי שם עולמי. בשנת 1975 מונה מנצח מישנה במקהלת מורמון טאברנאקל.

מקהלת מורמון טאברנאקל, סולט לייק וחתמכת ע"י
כנסיית Jesus Christ of Latter-day Saints
וודל מ. סמוט, נשיא המקהלה
אודל א. פולסן, מנהל המקהלה
תרולד ל. גרגורי, עוזר למנהל
המשרדים:
50, East North Temple Street
Salt Lake City, Utah 84150

A page from the Hebrew program of a 1993 Choir concert in Jerusalem, featuring photos and biographies of conductors Jerold Ottley (right) and Don Ripplinger (left). (Thomas Durham archives)

A 2013 poster from the Chicago-based Ravinia Festival suggests how fully the Choir has been assimilated into U.S. popular music culture. (Courtesy of the Ravinia Festival)

The Tabernacle Choir and Orchestra at Temple Square as they assemble for a recording session of *Messiah* in May 2014. Note the quilts draped over the pews to dampen the building's over-resonance. (Photo by Luke Howard, used by permission.)

The Salt Lake Tabernacle in 2014, with the Salt Lake Temple and Zion's Bank visible at left and City Creek Condominiums at right. (Photo by Luke Howard, used by permission.)

CHAPTER 5

FROM WITHIN
THE SHADOW

AS WAS NOW THE CUSTOM, Spencer Cornwall began his conductorship by re-fashioning the Choir's sound. He summoned each Choir member to his office at the McCune School of Music for them to reaudition. All Choir members (or new prospective members) had to sing scales and "Drink to Me Only with Thine Eyes" or a similar song of his or her choosing. Beyond vocal ability, Cornwall also factored "character and personality" into the audition. He explained that "A person can't sing well in a group unless he feels he is wanted there." And he felt duty bound to uphold the moral rectitude of the group, since it was in many ways the face of the Church to the world. By the end of the auditions, Cornwall had cut the membership rolls by 187 from the levels at Lund's death. The new tally: 321 members total—206 female and 115 male—all assigned to one of not four, but eight parts, so singers would always know who was singing what in *divisi* passages.[1]

Cornwall brought not only new standards but a new set of ideals, attitudes, and rehearsal techniques. From Choir minutes, reminiscences, notes by Cornwall, and a few recorded performances, one can piece together what he aimed for. In the Choir's tone and delivery, Cornwall seemed to care most about dynamics, straight tone, and enunciation. He favored dramatic juxtapositions of dynamics and perhaps—it is hard to say, given the scant recorded evidence—used a wider range of dynamics than previous directors had. A devotee of the St. Olaf school of choral singing, he rejected vibrato, insisting his singers use straight tone only. And the tone should be bright, sung "in the mask," with lots of frontal resonance. He fastidiously attended to crisp enunciation. To keep the words intelligible, especially on radio, he actually charted the vocal musculature needed to form each phoneme, simplified it for ease of teaching, then drilled the members on the various types, on the premise that no other means could assure unity in so large a group.

As for the pacing and mood of rehearsals, Cornwall's public-school career guided his style. He had cut his teeth training public-school choirs, always looking for ways to ingratiate himself with young singers. Now, with a harried radio choir, he tried to start rehearsing each piece they would perform a full six weeks ahead of its performance, gradually phasing the music in, rather than drilling pieces during the week or two before a broadcast. He insisted on decorum, good dress, and punctuality. He also famously never lost his temper in rehearsals. Instead, he relied on what subsequent Choir conductor Jerold Ottley described as "gentlemanly wisdom" and "dignified wit," the latter of which Alexander Schreiner described as Cornwall's "unusual sense of humor." He had jokes at the ready, jotted or typed on slips of paper he kept in his pockets and rehearsal folder. He would deliver one to lighten the mood when a rehearsal got stuck on a thorny musical passage. For example: "A doctor had a patient who went deaf from too much drinking. When the man followed the doctor's advice and gave up alcohol his hearing returned, but soon he was back at the doctor's office again stone-deaf. 'You've been drinking,' accused the doctor. The patient nodded. 'I could hear fine,' he replied, 'but what I heard was so poor, I decided I could do without it better than without the whiskey.'" One longtime member put it simply: "J. Spencer Cornwall was cute."[2]

Cornwall told Grant that since what the Choir sang mattered at least as much as how they sang it, he wanted Grant to appoint a committee to review possible pieces for the broadcast. At this request, Cornwall says, Grant pounded his fist on the desk and retorted, "That is your job. You should put your ear to the ground and determine what you should sing." But Grant did enumerate some pieces he personally didn't want the Choir to sing, including "The Holy City" and "Sometime, Somewhere"—about which Grant said, "That isn't anyplace." Nevertheless, according to Cornwall, Grant added, "Who am I to impose my tastes on anyone?"—which made sense, given that Grant's own singing skills were notoriously bad.[3] So once Cornwall had dealt with membership, he called extra rehearsals to audition new pieces from the mounds of octavo scores and anthem books he had solicited from publishers.

He didn't need to solicit much. The Choir now had a reputation for quality, a pressing need for repertoire, and a huge population of singers. So, hoping for big sales, many choral publishers barraged Cornwall with complimentary scores. Cornwall, always systematic, adopted this method for evaluating submissions:

1. He made a first pass on any music sent him.
2. He let the music that made the first cut sit for several weeks, then made a second pass.
3. The music that made the second cut went into a folder to be reviewed by his own handpicked committee, who made its selection from that folder—though Cornwall still held final sway.

On 1 September 1935, Cornwall conducted his first hour-long *Thoughtful Sabbath Hour* broadcast. The sheet from which they worked listed the following works for that broadcast (organ selections appear with a bullet point):

"Come, Thou Glorious Day of Promise" (hymn by George Careless, one verse only)
- Fourth Concerto in C (Bach)
  "Happy and Blest Are They" (Mendelssohn)
- "If I Were a Bird" (Henselt)
  "How Can I Leave Thee?" (traditional, one verse only)
- Finale (Franck)
  "I Praise Thee O Lord" (Mendelssohn)
[station break]
  "O God We Pray" (Arensley)
- Allegro from Fourth Sonata (Guilmant)
  "They That Sow in Tears" (Parks)
- "Indian Flute Call" (Dillon)
  "Who Is Sylvia?" (Schubert)
- Toccata in F (Colby) [as is typical, the script says that this last organ piece should be cut if time is running short]
  "Hallelujah" (Handel)

Cornwall immediately learned how primitive the recording conditions were. KSL Radio, a block away from the Tabernacle, had only one microphone. To broadcast the Choir, engineers had to sign off the airwaves, carry the microphone to the Tabernacle, then sign back on with the Choir broadcast. Cornwall also discovered that he had no monitor and thus no idea how the Choir sounded on the air. The week after his radio debut, he arranged for a local studio to make a transcription disc of the show so he could hear it. After the broadcast, he, Cornwall, the technicians, and First Presidency counselor J. Reuben Clark went to the recording studio to hear it. What they heard shocked them. The levels kept going up and down, because the sound engineers responded to the louds and softs that the Choir sang by turning the inputs down at high points and up at low points, creating sudden or gradual overbalances or near-inaudibilities. This problem had apparently defined all Choir broadcasts since 1929. The solution? Scores marked by the Choir librarian to show the technicians when the musical dynamics would rise and fall. With these marked scores at hand, the engineers would not simply react to what they heard, but plan the levels ahead.[4]

To manipulate the sound of the Choir in the Tabernacle, Cornwall experimented with seating arrangements. He also repositioned the radio microphone in various ways, then added microphones and experimented with their placement. Soon, with Harvey Fletcher's guidance, he had sixteen mikes strategically placed throughout the Choir loft. Fletcher also helped Cornwall with the problem of the Choir not being able to hear itself. After a complaint from a listener that the Choir always sang flat, Cornwall consulted with Fletcher about the Tabernacle acoustics. The two men concluded that the Choir was hearing the organ accompaniment via its odd reverberation in the egg-shaped dome, matching their pitch to a distorted, slightly lower reflection from the back of the hall. Cornwall and Fletcher tried to remedy this with monitor speakers mounted on stands above eye level. After one of them fell on a soprano in the front row, sending her to the hospital, they designed a network of monitor speakers mounted under various choir seats.

Much of the power of radio itself came from a sense of intimacy, the feeling that the voice on the air, whether Bing Crosby's or Franklin Roosevelt's, was being delivered and received one person to another. *The Thoughtful Sabbath Hour* worked in the same way, crossing a sonic line about which the Church Music Committee had once warned. In June 1932 the committee—under the byline of Tabernacle organist Edward Kimball, no less—had published an article in the *Improvement Era* titled "A Reprehensible Practice." That practice was crooning, soft singing into a microphone to make the most intimate voice suddenly audible from a distance. The practice had "crept into" popular music, making listeners feel that the singer was within arm's length from them. The music committee called it "a reprehensible prostitution of art," a "hideous error," which Mormons "must keep out of our worship!"[5] This feigned intimacy crossed a line, transgressed the proper sonic space that should separate a singer's mouth from a stranger's ear.

Drapes hung around the Choir and seats covered with carpet scraps now combined with Fletcher's new miking arrangement to make the Choir sound clearer, more unified, and indeed closer to the ear of the radio listener. In later years, many studios would try to make small spaces sound like large ones, transform dead rooms through electronics into cavernous imaginary space. But here one heard the opposite: a cavernous space transformed through dampening and miking into a small room—a parlor where the listener could feel the Choir was singing just for him or her. In this way, the "reprehensible practice" had crept into the Church broadcasts. If a choir could croon, the Tabernacle Choir now did so, too.

While private in their tone, the broadcasts were also loose and spontaneous, not just for being live, but for Evans's subtle manipulation of the show's pace. "We often improvise on the air," Evans said. "We know when to whisper in the organist's ear, to tell him what to stretch and what to cut. We make no attempt at showmanship."[6] In these early years of Cornwall's conductorship, Evans also brought new phrases into the show's introduction, phrases that would gradually become standard. On 6 October 1936, for the first time, Evans began the broadcast thus: "Sunday morning on Temple Square in Salt Lake City finds us gathered once more within the shadow of the everlasting hills. . . . We welcome you to the cross-roads of the West." Soon Evans began to end his sign-off with a wish for "peace this day and always," a tag line that has continued to this day.[7]

On 30 August 1936, the show was cut back to the half-hour beginning at 9:30 on Sunday mornings (where it has remained ever since). A sense of relief set in for the musicians. And for Evans, the curtailing of the time block left room for only one full-blown sermonette. On 24 January 1937, he began using a new stock phrase in his introduction. He again welcomed the listener "from the cross-roads of the West" to Temple Square, where "we beckon your thoughts to the peace and quiet of another Sabbath, as music and the spoken word are blended on this day of rest and reverence." That phrase "music and the spoken word" (or sometimes "music blended with the spoken word") kept reappearing in the introduction throughout the year, just as he more frequently omitted the phrase "this thoughtful Sabbath Hour" from the sign-off. Within a year, with the length, time slot, and format settled, the show gradually became known simply as the generic *Music and the Spoken Word*, the current and presumably the last in a series of titles it would bear.

During this new phase of the show, Cornwall also realized he needed an assistant conductor to fill in for him from time to time. In 1937, thirty-year-old Richard Condie asked Cornwall to consider him for the job. Condie had been an occasional tenor soloist with the Tabernacle Choir and the star of the popular KSL radio show *Midnight Hour Sunday Evening on Temple Square* from 1932 to 1934. He had also studied with one of Cornwall's choral heroes, F. Melius Christensen (of St. Olaf's esteemed choral program), and had just assumed the directorship of the vocal and choral program at the University of Utah. Cornwall thought him a good fit. University administrators arranged to lessen Condie's load so he could join the Tabernacle Choir staff. Working both jobs, his combined pay was fifty dollars a month.[8] When Marvin Ashton learned of it, he called it a disgrace and upped the Church's portion. Well-regarded in some inner circles of Church leadership, Condie would be at the Choir's podium for most of the next four decades. But he described his duties under Cornwall brusquely: "I went to every rehearsal and every broadcast and I listened."[9]

The following year, David Smith was released as President of the Choir after thirty years at that post. Grant then inaugurated a new administrative era for the Choir by removing the position of president from the Presiding Bishopric and calling an independent businessman to be the new president. Lester Hewlett, who would oversee the shift of the Choir into a bona fide perpetual business concern, had one stunning credential: in the 1920s, his company, Hewlett Brothers, had made its fortune in Salt Lake City largely by processing, packaging, and selling coffee, a drink Mormons ostensibly shunned.[10] Only an entrepreneur with an eye for business could succeed like that.

And the Choir was indeed a national brand of its own, a radio show without commercials apart from the underlying commercial the Choir constituted for its sponsoring Church. A typical broadcast from October 1938 shows how the *Music and the Spoken Word* formula and stereotyped delivery now worked. The Choir opens by singing "Gently Raise the Sacred Strain," then, as the singing segues into humming, Evans begins: "Again we pause at the crossroads of the West as Columbia presents the Salt Lake Tabernacle Choir and Organ. On this day of rest and reverence, music and the spoken word are heard again from Temple Square in Salt Lake City, where thoughtful men still believe that the Lord is God, that truth is truth, and that principle transcends convenience." He then introduces the conductor, organist, and opening number in an eclectic set of pieces meant to reach almost every slice of the U.S. demographic. The opening "Listen to the

Lamb" (Dett) shows off the Choir's precise diction and enormous dynamic range. The organist then takes up Grieg's "Erotik," whose title Evans declines to mention. Evans briefly ruminates on the danger of the era and the Choir answers with a glacially paced "A Mighty Fortress Is Our God"—a single verse lasts two minutes. The organist follows with an African American spiritual, as many Tabernacle broadcasts now included (for this broadcast it was "Deep River"). Evans delivers a spoken message about various kinds of worth and worthiness in our lives. The Choir then ponderously sings a sacrament hymn composed by its former director, George Careless. Evans introduces an organ medley of "those hymns much cherished in the valley lands of the inland West"—that is, Mormon hymns. After a long, florid introduction by Evans—almost a second sermonette—the Choir shows off its bravado with a relentlessly chipper but ragged version of "And the Glory of the Lord" (from *Messiah*). It had been a staple of the Choir for more than half a century. But its sixteenth-note runs and soprano high notes remained as unforgiving as ever. "Gently Raise the Sacred Strain" then resumes and Evans proclaims that "this Sabbath Hour from the inland West" has ended.

Although this was now a radio choir, Cornwall insisted it keep its concert skills honed. He would sometimes tell the singers, for example, to imagine the microphones were gone and sing a true fortissimo—that is, with no distortion to worry about. As for large-scale repertoire the Choir might master, Grant himself almost offhandedly supplied the answer. As early as 1905, Grant had heard Mendelssohn's oratorio *Elijah* and avidly wished the Tabernacle Choir would mount "something of this kind."[11] That specific oratorio actually suited Cornwall well. He had previously been a director of the Mendelssohn Male Chorus of Salt Lake City. The Tabernacle Choir had by now often sung two numbers from *Elijah* ("He, watching over Israel" and "And then shall your light break forth") in concerts, on the air, and in the case of "He, watching over Israel," on both the 1925 and 1927 Victor recordings. The oratorio was a popular nineteenth-century successor to the eighteenth-century oratorios of Handel—and, indeed, *Elijah* was not *Messiah*, which, though endlessly popular, tended to be overprogrammed.

Perhaps most important, *Elijah* came with a particularly Mormon imprimatur. The resurrected Elijah had appeared to Joseph Smith and revealed temple ordinances for the living and the dead. The highest missions in the gospel, according to Smith, were first that of Messiah, and second, that of Elijah. "The spirit and power of Elijah," he said, precedes the Second Coming, "holding the keys of power, building the Temple to the capstone, placing the seals of the

Melchisedec Priesthood upon the house of Israel, and making all things ready; then Messiah comes to His Temple, which is last of all."[12]

In the fall of 1938, Cornwall mounted not just the music but a staged, costumed, pageant-like version of *Elijah*. He borrowed a dramatic script he had heard being used with the oratorio in Chicago, imported a fine baritone soloist to play the title role, had a stage built in front of choir seats and organ pipes, and scheduled three nights in the Tabernacle to coincide with October's General Conference. The performance included three hundred Choir members, 125 dancers, a fifty-member orchestra, and a hundred other players and staff both onstage and off. The performances made big news, attracted patrons back to repeat performances, provoked thunderous plaudits, and prompted a repeat run the following year.[13] But the *Deseret News* music critic, Gail Martin, focused less on the content of the oratorio and more on its composer and the current politics of playing his music. "Reading of the terror practiced upon defenseless Jews by the Nazis," she wrote, "one cannot help but thank God that Mendelssohn lived in an older and better time. Now his music is reviled and 'verboten,' say reports from Germany."[14] In other words, these performances were not just a Mormon act, proclaiming the mission of Elijah, but a political act.

The Church's national concerns still trumped local festivities. When it came to the Choir, it was their large "Gentile" audience that mattered to leaders more than the applause of local Saints. And for the nation, the Church's broadcasts had become a refuge from not only the Depression, but Europe's descent into the Great War's grotesque sequel. One fan letter embodied the solace that the broadcast provided its listeners in this awkward but powerful way: "Never have I been more disappointed and utterly disgusted with Radio than last Sunday morning when Columbia replaced your Tabernacle hour with war hysteria. Instead of the comforting sacredness of your music and words, our morning was spoiled. . . . I have not turned on my Radio since."[15]

At the same time, though, CBS's connection to the Choir had itself come under siege. Two months after *Elijah*, NBC tried to lure KSL back. Although the Church owned a controlling interest in the radio station, the other shareholders were pressuring it to take NBC's terms, which would have made them more money in the long run. Members of the First Presidency met with Frank Stanton. They wanted to stay with CBS, if for no other reason than its sturdy support of *Music and the Spoken Word*. But CBS would not only have to meet NBC's offer, Clark told Stanton, they would have to sweeten their arrangement by guaranteeing three things:

- the network would accept no alcohol advertisements on KSL
- the network would accept no tobacco advertisements on KSL *on Sundays*
- the network would reserve daily time spans for local advertisers, periods when the network could not bump local ads for more lucrative ones of its own.

Stanton agreed, not only because of his allegiance to the Church, but because KSL, with its market dominance and powerful signal, made good profits for the network—something NBC knew and hoped to rack up for itself. KSL, which would add a television signal in June 1949, remained with CBS for the rest of the century.[16]

The popularity of the broadcast also lured Alexander Schreiner back to the Tabernacle.[17] He had tentatively agreed to work there as an organist in 1932, discussed salary with the Presiding Bishopric, then balked and took two non-Mormon jobs in Los Angeles—a decision President Grant had said was "a very serious mistake."[18] Early in 1939, he told the First Presidency that he wanted to come back and play for the broadcast, though only under conditions that would beef up his personal portfolio. One condition was that Evans would announce his name before every number Schreiner played on the broadcast. Evans refused and Reuben Clark backed him up, calling such constant individual credits on the show "contrary to the spirit of the whole broadcast, which was a religious service." Clark went on to say that the radio show would fail if it exalted the reputations of its individual players. Even the fan mail that Evans got, Clark said, often spoke of how much people appreciated the collective effort, not the individual celebrities, of which Evans, of course, was chief.[19]

Schreiner had other ideas for "making some radical changes" in the radio program and, indeed, wanted to subject all Tabernacle music to his purview and guidance. The First Presidency rebuffed all such pretensions, with Clark even getting, in his own words, "unduly rough" with the organist, feeling Schreiner had succumbed to "great selfishness" and "acted very much like a child—a spoiled one at that." The organist could come back as the senior member of the "organists corps," yes. But the hierarchy of this musical venture was clear: "Your work with the Choir will be under the leader thereof, and the general supervision of all your work will be under the Presiding Bishopric."[20]

Clark also put Cornwall and the Choir on notice that they too served the Church, not vice versa. "Remember," Clark said, "you are a choir, not a choral group."[21] In other words, the Salt Lake Tabernacle Choir, whatever its celebrity, was only an appendage of its sponsoring church.

But it was a necessary appendage. Within weeks of the Schreiner flap, the First Presidency issued another official letter to bishops and stake presidents about the Choir's interactions with local ward callings and responsibilities. In the five-paragraph document, the presidency declared that bishops and stake presidents must not call Tabernacle Choir members to other assignments in the Church unless those assignments would not conflict in any way with their Choir service. No matter how talented in other church-bound ways a singer might be, "membership in the Tabernacle Choir will take precedence over any other assignment." This letter superseded earlier letters and statements on the subject. It would be cited and reissued to local leaders for decades thereafter.[22]

At the same time, the Presiding Bishopric took up the matter of the Tabernacle's acoustics. The First Presidency was worried that, if an earthquake hit Salt Lake City, the Tabernacle ceiling plaster might crack and fall on worshippers inside. So the leaders were "seriously considering" lining the whole ceiling with quarter-inch Celotex (a fiberboard insulation material) for safety. The question they had, and which the Presiding Bishopric posed to Harvey Fletcher on 12 August 1939, was simply this: if they installed the Celotex, could one still hear a pin drop in the back of the building? "The acoustics of the Tabernacle are paramount," counselor Marvin Ashton wrote, and if the pin-drop trick no longer worked, the presidency would drop the Celotex proposal. Fletcher diplomatically replied that the Tabernacle acoustics were not what he would call "good" to begin with. They were only "peculiar." But Celotex would wreck their peculiarity, and the pin-drop trick would fail. Perhaps wire netting over the plaster would work, or even some more advanced acoustic material as a covering. Still, he felt, "because of the traditions of the past, it would be wise to leave the acoustics peculiar as they have always been."[23]

But Fletcher had his own sonic plans for the Choir. In August 1939, he wrote to Clark to ask if the Tabernacle Choir and organists could make some records in October using a new process Fletcher had worked out at Bell Labs: three-channel stereo. He had made some orchestral recordings with Stokowski and Ormandy but thought the Choir would give a contrasting sound and, though he needn't say it, enhance the Church's image. Jumping at the offer, Clark alerted Cornwall, Hewlett, the Presiding Bishopric (to provide any needed funds), and KSL (to provide technical help). The recordings finally took place on the Thursday and Sunday of the first week in January 1940. Thursday night, the Choir recorded excerpts from *Elijah*. Sunday morning, before and after the live broadcast, they recorded two programs. Old warhorses constituted the first program: the *Pil-*

grim's *Chorus, Voix Celeste* (organ), "Come, Come Ye Saints" (arr. Cornwall), and "Worthy Is the Lamb." The second program was a mock version of the radio show (without the sermonette): a spoken introduction (over "Gently Raise the Sacred Strain"), five short pieces (including two hymns) alternating between Choir and organ, followed by a reprise of the opening hymn. Cornwall knew something special was afoot: "The recording device promises to be the most remarkable yet devised," he wrote in his diary. Two weeks later, he heard a rough dub of the recordings, and wrote simply: "High fidelity accomplished."[24]

Fletcher demonstrated the new lateral deployment of recorded sound in a widely publicized Carnegie Hall demonstration of the three-channel stereo records on 9 April 1940, almost thirty years before two-channel stereo became a standard format on consumer-grade record players. In so doing, he also unleashed the enormous volume levels now possible through amplification. New York headlines blared the news: "Sound Waves 'Rock' Carnegie Hall . . . Tones Near Limit That the Human Ear Can Endure"; "Super-Volume Concert Records Scare Audience . . . Listeners Stop Up Ears." The *New York Herald-Tribune* celebrated the spectacle, which "alternately astounded and scared the wits out of" its audience. The volume was loud, at its highest point when the chorus in *Elijah* roars, "which was enhanced until it sounded like a million banshees wailing at once." The volume was so high that "no home application of the recordings is believed possible." The *New York Times* lead was this: "The loudest music sounds ever created crashed and echoed through venerable Carnegie Hall last night as a socially invited audience listened, spellbound, and at times not a little terrified."[25] Unwittingly, Fletcher foreshadowed not just stereo but the powerful volume levels of a later generation's hard rock music. As music industry historian Greg Milner later put it, "Let history record that it was the Mormons, disciples of America's homegrown religion, who were the first emissaries of the sonic roar that America bequeathed to the world."[26]

On another technological front, the Church tried to fortify the Choir's radio presence by moving it onto European airwaves. In 1937, KSL applied to the Federal Communications Commission (FCC) to allow it to erect and operate a 50,000-watt international shortwave outlet that would, among other things, regularly beam General Conference and Tabernacle Choir broadcasts to other continents. On 22 June 1938, the FCC denied the request on the grounds that the station might cause "objectionable interference" with existing stations, and that the broadcast "will not serve public interest, convenience and necessity." In 1940, Apostle Albert Bowen took the matter up with Fletcher, who suggested some alternate technical means for getting a Mormon shortwave station into Europe, including a point-to-point shortwave system routed through Luxembourg. But after Fletcher warned of the likelihood of interference problems, the Church dropped its shortwave plans for the foreseeable future. The Tabernacle broadcasts would remain for now a strictly North American phenomenon.[27]

The staged performance of *Elijah* at the Tabernacle had succeeded beyond anyone's guess. But how to follow it? Cornwall returned to Mendelssohn for a staged version of another biblical character study, *St. Paul*, to be presented during General Conference evenings in April 1941. As often happens, the sequel did not live up to its forerunner. It did its job for local audiences, struck another implicit blow against Nazism, but lacked the spiritual resonance Elijah as a character possessed—and indeed, Mormonism was in doctrine quite far from the best-known grace-oriented theology of New Testament Paul. What the production did most, though, was draw the Church into one small vortex of the Depression's waning: the musicians' union.

Since 1940, the Church had awkwardly fended off the advances of the WPA-related Utah Symphony, making the puzzling argument that church and state should be kept separate—honored in Utah mostly in the breach. But since they wanted to use a full orchestra for *St. Paul*, they recruited the BYU student orchestra for the production. Hearing about this, the local chapter of the American Federation of Musicians (AFM) demanded that all union members withdraw from the production and possibly from all unpaid service in the Church. Choral singers, of course, were exempt; they had no stake in the union. But Tabernacle organist Frank Asper, an active union member slated to play in the oratorio, got caught in the crossfire.[28]

The Presiding Bishopric, the Church Music Committee, and eventually the First Presidency all got involved. Marvin Ashton (first counselor in the Presiding Bishopric) telephoned Asper on 7 March to warn him about the union's demands. If it came down to a fight, would Asper "stand emphatically with the Church, no matter what the cost?" Asper said he would. Twelve days later, Tracy Cannon met with Asper, Clark, and McKay, the last of whom insisted they go on with the oratorio "and see what happens." Finally, a week later, Asper met with Clark alone and asked for advice. Clark demurred, saying it was illegal for him to give legal advice. But he laid out the choices: Asper could leave the union, "reform" the union, or refuse to play in the oratorio. Asper then went from the top of the Church to the top of the union, Jim Petrillo, who ran the AFM from Chicago. Petrillo said to go ahead and play, Asper reported: it was a local matter, and Petrillo would stand aside. So the oratorio went on, Asper played in it, and nothing happened. In this standoff, at least, the Church had won.

That summer, Cornwall started feeling out of sorts, with pain in the abdomen so severe, he wrote, that, "at times it almost unbalanced me" during rehearsals and broadcasts.[29] The diagnosis: appendicitis. After he had the appendix removed, he wrote the Choir a comical letter from the hospital describing the operation as though it were one of their radio shows. Less than three weeks after his hospital release, he conducted the farewell concert for the Choir's California tour. The cover of that concert's program, 10 August 1941, shows both how much radio had defined the Choir and how Church authority now clearly circumscribed the group. The Choir's name is shown in its radio form, the Salt Lake Tabernacle Choir, even for a local LDS audience. And, revealingly, it lists the personnel this way:

Lester F. Hewlett, President of Choir
J. Spencer Cornwall, Director
Alexander Schreiner, Accompanist
Frank W. Asper, Accompanist
Richard L. Evans, Radio Commentator
Richard P. Condie, Assistant Director and Tenor Soloist
W. Jack Thomas, Business and Tour Manager[30]

Hewlett clearly presided over Cornwall, a paradigm shift that would endure.

Once more, the group booked an appearance at the Hollywood Bowl. The review by Isabel Morse Jones in the *Los Angeles Times* had a particularly elegant authoritativeness. Although the program was varied, she said, it all conveyed "a religious idealism, a challenge to modernists and an exhortation to the faithful." She noted, as many had, that the Choir's size blurred its individual lines. The Choir had "a harmonic rather than a polyphonic authority," as she put it. But "the singing of the whole Choir was so well balanced that the structure was firm and the climaxes were inevitable." Of their San Francisco concert, Alfred Frankenstein—soon to become one of the country's most esteemed music critics—was more measured, even cautionary. The Tabernacle Choir gave proof that choral music could still retain its "vitality and vividness." But the organ was overbearing and the hymns sometimes too sentimental. "One sensed that, because of its great success on the radio, the Choir has fallen victim to the fetish of giving the public what it wants, to the detriment of more significant values." The conductor and organists "are, one suspects, better musicians than their circumstances permit them to be. If so, they are neither the first nor the last to be in such a position."[31]

In December, the United States officially entered the World War. As under the Edmunds-Tucker Act of fifty-five years earlier, male members showed up less and less to Choir rehearsals as the new war summoned them. But unlike during the First World War, not only were men leaving the Choir, but women's duties at home and in the workplace drew down the Choir's female sections, as well. Absenteeism, the Choir's chronic bane, set in. In the midst of all this, the First Presidency revived its commitment to Cornwall in the form of a huge raise in salary. On 18 February 1942, Grant wrote to the conductor that they were increasing Cornwall's salary from three hundred dollars a month to four hundred. The increase, he explained, "comes to you without any solicitation whatever on your part and as a deserved recognition of your faithfulness and devotion to duty."[32]

Whether or not there was any connection to the raise, after over sixty years of no rehearsal minutes being taken, Cornwall suddenly started them up again. The minutes reveal that only about two-thirds to three-quarters of Choir members were showing up for rehearsal, although often still showing up for the Sunday broadcast. In April, one member suggested that singers from ward choirs be "drafted" into the Tabernacle Choir as a mission calling. But Cornwall insisted that the Tabernacle Choir should remain a purely voluntary choir, not one people were ordered to join. Meanwhile, to conserve energy, Tabernacle concerts were canceled and the building closed to the general public for the remainder of the war.[33]

The wartime Choir minutes show Cornwall's doggedness about two things: tone and appearance. Cornwall reminded his singers that his was "a desperate attempt for a straight-voiced choir." He gave them assignments such as singing every day from a leaflet of vocalises he gave them; or, "Strike note on piano and practice singing it sharp until you are out of tune with the piano." He even installed a recording machine in his office to review and evaluate auditions (old or new).[34] The reason for all this training had a higher purpose, he noted: this Choir had to meet the needs of radio audiences who now, more than ever, needed solace and a purpose for living. One listener, for example, wrote to thank the Choir for "the greatest music the earth has ever produced." He went on, though, "to encourage any part you can play in holding back the multiple-millionaire war mongers. They nauseated the national mental condition. I refuse to patronize any firm which sponsors our entrance in a foreign war."[35] The most important thing for Cornwall—and the raise seemed to confirm it—was to stay the course the radio show had mapped out. Keep promoting peace, unity, and brotherhood.

How listeners construed the message or tailored it to their religious opinions and allegiances was their own business.

With the Tabernacle closed to all but a few select visitors, one might think the appearance of singers would be less important. But Cornwall had two reasons to continue harping on it. One was sonic: women usually wore hats in the Tabernacle, which was well enough, but hats absorbed sound and needed to be removed for the broadcasts. After almost two years of attention to the matter, the minutes recorded that "the 'ladies hats' problem has been *nearly* solved" (emphasis added). And the restricted number of visitors actually argued, in Cornwall's mind, for more attention to appearance: "We are seeking tone not only in singing but in everything connected with the Choir. It is hard to tell who might be in the audience and how we will be judged. Only the choicest few get the opportunity to visit a broadcast now and we must always be on guard." The most egregious breach he named? A soprano combing her hair during the "Hallelujah Chorus."[36]

At the same time, more and more people listened to the broadcasts, both the Sunday program and the weekly nondenominational *Church of the Air* programs that the Church was responsible for once each quarter. (*Church of the Air* and *Music and the Spoken Word* were ranked first and second, respectively, among CBS stockholders.) The network did worry, though, even complain, when Church leaders seemed to use *Church of the Air* to promote their religion and particularly its founding prophet.[37] But *Music and the Spoken Word* impressed the George Foster Peabody Award Committee—essentially the radio medium's equivalent to the Oscars—so that in July 1944 the show received the award for Outstanding Entertainment in Music. Since the show's debut, the Committee said, the all-volunteer Choir had "maintained . . . the highest standard of choral singing."[38]

Despite the image of peace the Choir tried to embody, Cornwall felt that the Choir could not refuse any service to the war effort it could provide. So, without consulting Evans, Hewlett, or the First Presidency, he accepted a proposal for the Choir to perform background music for *The Battle of San Pietro*, a movie directed by John Huston and produced by the Army Signal Corps. A montage of images meant to commemorate the U.S. victory in Italy, the movie featured a bombastic new soundtrack by Dmitri Tiomkin. On 22 June 1944, Cornwall announced the recording at the regular Thursday night rehearsal. Cornwall noted with pride that there was "only one choir" in the nation that could do this job. And they were it. They recorded the Choir tracks in the Tabernacle, strictly timed to be matched with an orchestral score Tiomkin would conduct and record with the U.S. Air Force Orchestra later.[39]

Hewlett discovered the situation when, arriving at rehearsal, he found microphones and recording equipment set up and release forms being signed by Choir members. He reported this to Clark, who soon got wind of a new request from the Signal Corps, this time to sing in *The War Comes to America*, the seventh and final film of Frank Capra's *Why We Fight* series. Clark insisted that Cornwall was out of line and had no business making such a deal, not just because he had acted independently, but because of the nature of the project itself: "I talked with President McKay about it," Clark wrote in his journal, "and found that he thought about it just as I do, that it is most improper for our Tabernacle Choir to be singing a background while our boys were going in and being blown to pieces." Clark confronted Cornwall, who explained how he felt he had gotten permission through the Presiding Bishopric, and how the relevant scene in the *San Pietro* film had nothing to do with an actual battle. The orchestra played on the soundtrack throughout, but was joined by the Choir only at minute 26:55, as the film shows images of the townspeople who had been in hiding throughout the war now returning to their homes. The choral music is epic, with thick chordal harmony as though accompanying a processional. At minute 28:32, children appear, and the Choir suddenly shifts to light Italian folk songs. It then resumes the earlier style until the movie's end (minute 31:45).

Clark told Cornwall to consider if the film was propaganda, to which Cornwall said, of course not, because it was for the government. An opponent of the war, Clark retorted that "the Government was doing more propaganda business than any other agency in the United States." He, McKay, and Hewlett told Cornwall he could make no other film arrangements, even for the war effort, without going through the known channels—the Presidents of both the Choir and the Church.

The problem, of course, was not one of careful bureaucracy, but of the Choir's essential reputation. Cornwall saw the film proposal as a tribute to the Choir's musicality and national esteem. But Clark and McKay believed that the Choir needed to trade on its own broadcasts' pervasive theme of "peace this day and always." So at the end of that November, with the *Battle of San Pietro* in the can, they directed Hewlett to tell Signal Corps Major Bulton that "we feel the Church Choir ought not to participate in war pictures and that when peace comes and they are trying to build up the brotherhood of man—all of our facilities are at their disposal."[40]

Clark, however, did insist on a closer identification of the Choir with the Church when it came to the credits of the San Pietro film. The producers had credited the Choir with the name it went by on radio: the Salt Lake Tabernacle Choir. Clark saw the credit and insisted the name be changed to the *Mormon Tabernacle Choir*, which the Choir had used on all its earlier recordings and would always use on later recordings (sometimes with "of Salt Lake City" attached to "Choir"). President Clark's insistence that "Mormon" replace "Salt Lake" in the credits to *Battle of San Pietro* seemed a commentary on any pretensions the Choir had to representing the art of music per se. It was the Church's reputation at stake, not the Choir's.[41]

In August 1945, with the war officially over, the Tabernacle reopened to the public. The Church and Choir were already looking ahead for how to celebrate the centennial of the pioneers' entry into the Salt Lake Valley in 1847. Recalling the centennial of the Church, the First Presidency reprised *Message of the Ages*. Cornwall also decided to reprise *Elijah* and mount a new performance of an old Choir favorite, Haydn's *Creation*, accompanied by a BYU student orchestra. But the hit of the 1947 centennial was neither the pageant nor the classical warhorses, but a new musical, Crawford Gates's *Promised Valley*, in which the Tabernacle Choir took no part. No matter: that December, the First Presidency praised Cornwall for agreeing with them that the Choir's primary mission was to make good broadcasts that would "spread the gospel." To that end, they told Cornwall, "intensify the spirit which you are able to give to your listeners over the air."[42]

Postwar optimism ran high and good feelings abounded. Clark praised the Choir for "spreading good Christian Music so vital to the world in this post-war era."[43] In 1945, he and his colleagues in the First Presidency even decided to give five thousand dollars to the Utah Symphony, providing the orchestra would draw its members from throughout the state, perform around the state, and employ as few non-Utahns as possible. But two months after the gift, Clark heard that the thirty-seven symphony players were being imported from out of state. He complained not only of betrayal of trust but of the spirit of music making in Utah itself. The Tabernacle Choir was the ideal: all-volunteer community service conjured the true spirituality of music. The Utah Symphony showed that it was only interested in the best that money could buy. Clark nearly exploded. "This whole thing looks to me like somebody is taking all of us nit-wits for a ride." And so the walls between Choir and symphony went back up. The Utah Symphony was trying to use the Tabernacle Choir as a "catspaw," Clark said.[44]

This might have been a footnote in Tabernacle history, except for one thing: Leroy Robertson, the Church's most decorated living composer, had created a gigantic oratorio for the 1947 pioneer centennial. He wrote the *Oratorio from the Book of Mormon* specifically for the Tabernacle Choir. But they had no orchestra. And the wedge between them and the Utah Symphony could not yet be removed.

In 1948, though, the symphony's conductor, Maurice Abravanel, went straight to Cornwall to propose they collaborate on Beethoven's Ninth. Absolutely not, Cornwall told him—it would ruin his Choir's voices. Abravanel insisted that he knew better than to do that. After talking to an impasse, Cornwall returned to the argument that the Choir was Church and the symphony was state.[45] So the pattern began of major choral works being performed by the Utah Symphony and University of Utah choirs, while the Tabernacle Choir sang a capella, with organ, or with a BYU student orchestra. It would be many years before the two groups buried the musical hatchet.

On 17 October 1948, the Choir made its thousandth weekly broadcast. They held a special program afterward, with guests ranging from Earl Glade to the First Presidency giving testimonials. Cornwall himself laid out, perhaps for the first time publicly, his four aims for the Choir. They constituted a small manifesto. His first and foremost aim was to make a musical organization that other musicians would admire. Second, and "some would put this first," he knowingly said, "to be of value to the Church which sponsors us and under whose organization we work." Although that concession was necessary, demoting the primary goal of his ecclesiastical bosses to second place effectively laid down a gauntlet. Third, he wanted to make the Choir a true choral ensemble, not a group of soloists. Fourth, he wanted to expand the Choir's repertoire, although he needed to explain what he meant by that. He wanted to bring the best choral music to the Choir, of course, but not "get too far away from the Church." That is, the Choir would seek out and perform superior choral music but always "come back and sing the music of our Church people," trying to "satisfy all." In doing so, he noted, they would implicitly breach his first aim: "Some people find fault with us because we don't do master works all the time."[46]

Cornwall seemed more attuned to the Church Music Committee than his Church ecclesiastical overseers were. The committee had become more fastidious in its oversight of the Church's music, which it insisted be sophisticated and European-classical in its style and tone. In fall 1935, the First Presidency had asked Tracy Cannon to write up his thoughts on "opportunities for cultural development of Church members."[47] First on his list: the Tabernacle Choir, which, he said, had a sixfold role:

1. To be a model for all other Mormon choirs, "an ideal from which to pattern their own work."
2. To encourage "home composers" by performing their work so that they would "build music of a type that would fill the Church."
3. To sing music by the world's master composers.
4. To mount "great festivals of Church music" that would draw upon singers from all around the Church.
5. To keep close contact with local leaders by calling them to the Choir.
6. To recruit good singers for local ward and stake choirs.

The First Presidency had to have noted that the list nowhere mentioned the Choir's missionary assignment, which in their minds trumped all the others. Now Cornwall was moving in the same art-based direction.

Cornwall's aesthetic aims would compete for dominance when the Choir returned to record making almost a decade after their experimental stereo discs for Fletcher. During the last two and a half years of the war, the government had essentially shut down all commercial record making in the United States because of a ban on the nonmilitary use of shellac. After the war ended, Columbia had devised a new speed and a new disc material—vinyl. The combination of these two things would enable what was once called an "album"—a binder of short-playing discs needed to encompass a complete single classical work—to be consolidated into a single, larger (and less breakable), long-playing disc. These new long-playing "albums," also known as LPs, could also contain sets of shorter pieces.

The twentieth anniversary of the radio broadcast occurred in 1949. Looking forward to the anniversary, Frank Stanton, now president of CBS, had arranged for Columbia Masterworks to record two albums of the Choir doing, in effect, a "best-of" selection from their radio shows. The Choir recorded these sets 2 June to 4 June in the Tabernacle, using the Church's equipment, which was more accustomed to dealing with the unwieldy Tabernacle acoustics than the equipment Columbia had brought to the building. Under the simple title *The Mormon Tabernacle Choir of Salt Lake City*, Columbia issued the first album in October—twelve tracks opening with the Choir's two most popular radio hymns ("Come, Come Ye Saints" and "O My Father") followed by six more hymns and three anthems, ending with "Lift Thine Eyes" from *Elijah*. To be safe, the label issued this album in the three competing formats of the day: four 12-inch 78rpm discs, four 7-inch 45rpm discs, or one ten-inch 33⅓rpm LP.

The other nine tracks the Choir recorded were released the following March with a "Vol. II" attached to the original title. This time the label dropped the 7-inch format, whose use was veering toward popular music, but kept the other two formats. This new album displayed the Choir's showier, more pretentious side, all but one of its tracks being anthems, ranging from Evan Stephens's "Let the Mountains Shout for Joy" to the Wagner *Pilgrim's Chorus* to short works by Haydn, Mozart, Beethoven, and, of course, Mendelssohn (this time from *St. Paul*). The *Saturday Review* called the results "as fine choral recordings as have yet been done, in spite of the echo of the Tabernacle." The Tabernacle Choir, the magazine said, "sings circles around some plushier, less spontaneous groups." *High Fidelity* invoked familiar thoughts about the Choir, praising its "massive, homogeneous tone. . . . as long as it is dealing with nonpolyphonic music." At the same time, these records began to be used to train local choirs of all denominations. One non-Mormon choral director, for example, wrote to Cornwall that of the thirty-five members of his choir, only five could read music. So they had to learn new pieces by rote. These records allowed them not only to learn classical pieces well but also to cut rehearsal time in half. And at least one Presbyterian church actually began playing the records in their worship services.[48]

In some ways, the recordings misled listeners about one of the Choir's most impressive feats: its voracious consumption of new repertoire. Just as those recorded collections of old standbys were being released, Cornwall proudly announced to the Choir that they were adding to their repertoire fifty pieces per year—almost one new piece in their cache of performable works every week.[49] Many of these new pieces were, in fact, old masterworks. Cornwall kept ratcheting up the elitist standards of the music his Choir sang. "At one time," he said, "Evan Stephens music was the only music of our church—he was a lover of Italian opera and injected it into many of his songs." But Stephens's was "an idiom not for sacred music."[50] In 1949, Cornwall had the Choir begin an Easter tradition of singing Brahms's *Requiem*. He used these Easter concerts to present other large works as well, especially Bach motets and cantatas. Indeed, Bach became the poster child for the aesthetic aims he had for the Choir. On 22 February 1951, "Bro. Cornwall mentioned that we have received more 'fan mail' this week than any week since he came into the Choir. Some say 'you have gone highbrow'— 'too much Bach and Wagner'—but Bro. Cornwall explained that we must keep a high level at all times . . . and try to bring these people to our standard."[51] In February 1953, he winsomely quoted a fan letter that read "More Bach—less bunk." He soon told the Choir that he was "discouraged with the attitude Choir members are taking on better music, especially Bach—it shows lack of training or capacity." He asked Choir members to "get rid of this resentment."[52]

Highbrow repertoire was one problem. But other problems arose. As the Mormon origins of *Music and the Spoken Word* had become better understood in the 1940s, the show had taken sporadic heat. For more than five years, for example, the broadcast had been silent in the Boston market because the 70 percent Catholic demographic had snubbed it, according to Evans. At the same time, television was allegedly eroding the old radio market, especially among young people. In 1950, Cornwall warned the Choir that "people who have been enjoying TV are reluctant to turn to radio where there is nothing to 'see.'" Television, he said, was "geared to teenagers," while "our program [is] geared for serious people."[53]

But in the fall of 1951, with McKay now the President of the Church, the Choir faced a new obstacle: beer advertising. President Clark had dug in his heels about KSL taking beer ads, even though the station had always allowed cigarette ads (except on Sundays). Now, by refusing to air five network shows that were sponsored by breweries—including one of the most popular "family shows," *Amos and Andy*—KSL was losing ground in its market as competing stations in Salt Lake City picked up the shows they refused. Frank Stanton told the First Presidency that if KSL kept snubbing CBS and its sponsors, *Music and the Spoken Word* was at risk. Evans confirmed the threat: if KSL fell to second or third place in the market, he said, "whatever influence we have . . . nationwide may be in jeopardy." Clark retorted that "all my instinct is against" advertising beer, the consumption of which violated the Church's health code. But, for the sake of the Choir, having KSL be "paramount" in the Salt Lake market overrode his concerns. "We are in a practical world and we have to face the thing as it comes, and do the best we can." Upon saying that, Clark relented, and two weeks later the first beer ad popped up on the station. A few Mormons (and even non-Mormons) grumbled, demanding an explanation for KSL's breach. But both Evans and Clark's daughter Louise reassured Clark that the beer ads were "in far better taste" than the cigarette ads. And the national megaphone of Mormonism was again safe in CBS's hands.[54]

As though constructing a brilliant finale for his decades as tour manager of the Choir, Jack Thomas came up with the idea to have the group tour Europe—its first venture outside of the Western Hemisphere. Having imported their musical traditions from the British Isles, the Mormons would begin with a pilgrimage back to them. They would continue through as many nations as possible, representing not just themselves but the United States, whose empire had been confirmed and consolidated in the war years and the Marshall Plan aftermath. (Indeed, one European mission president for the Church asked that the Choir not bill itself as "Mormon" but as "a choir from western America.")[55] Most of all, of course, the tour would be the sequential invasion of multiple lands by gentle, nondoctrinaire missionaries. Thomas himself described it in his 277-page book about the tour: "Never has such a large group of missionaries left their homes in a body to storm into the great cities of the World and fill them with Love, Peace, and Good Will to all mankind."[56]

This would be a seismic move, of course, involving the coordination of steamships, railways, multiple languages and currencies, the renting of venues and lodging, hauling equipment (including twelve loudspeakers) from country to country—even the mere keeping track of over three hundred fellow travelers would daunt the keenest logician. But the First Presidency approved it, according to some observers, not just as Thomas's swan song, but as Cornwall's, too. Cornwall pushed back at the plan, citing the unprecedented rigors of the trip and his own inability to hold up under the stress. The antidote, his leaders told him, would be to let Condie conduct on the tour whenever possible. Adding to the musical demands—and Cornwall's growing feeling of ostracism from his bosses—Jack Thomas was leaning on the Choir to make a bigger impression by singing everything from memory.[57]

During the year and a half preparation, 1954 through early August 1955, the Choir continued its usual round of duties, earning more attention, and completing its twenty-fifth year on the air, which generated congratulations from leading artists. Rudolf Bing of the Metropolitan Opera noted that these western Mormons were "already a veteran of two years" when the Met began its storied broadcasts. Howard Hanson, director of the Eastman School of Music (and a composer whose work the Choir would later program), wished them "many more quarter centuries." George Crothers, director of network religious programming, called *Music and the Spoken Word* "one of the stars in the CBS crown." Edward R. Murrow featured the Choir on his *See It Now* show in April 1954. Even *Life* magazine devoted a half page to the Choir, emphasizing its longevity and Americanism. It ended with these lines: "It is a national institution to be proud of, but what matters more is that Americans can be linked from ocean to ocean and year to year by the same brief respite from the world's week, and by a great chord of common thoughts on God and love and the everlasting things." A listener gave a more homespun assessment: "If I never get to Heaven, I will always know how the Angels Sing."[58]

But the tour preparations ate at Cornwall. In April 1955, his son Allen wrote a four-page letter to Apostle Mark Petersen, one of the tour's overseers, passionately interceding for his father. This tour should be the climax of Cornwall's career. But now there was a "division at the head." Cornwall had been "cut and hurt very deeply" in the process, not so much by Condie's almost inevitable ascendancy, but by Cornwall's colleagues seemingly being turned against him and by Jack Thomas's being licensed to help select the Choir's tour repertoire—in direct violation, Allen Cornwall wrote, of the charge Grant gave his father to decide the music for himself. "Believe me, when I say my father is on the verge of breaking. He feels alone."[59]

Meanwhile, the Utah Symphony and the University of Utah choirs combined for a performance of Robertson's *Oratorio from the Book of Mormon* on 28 May 1955. Its program bore the inscription: "A Testimonial of Appreciation to the Tabernacle Choir on the occasion of its European Tour."[60]

When the Choir and its vast entourage—totaling over six hundred shipmates—landed in Glasgow, they began a nine-day stay in the United Kingdom. They knew that this was for Mormons a kind of homecoming: their musicianship flowed from the British Isles. And so much of Mormon demographics and genealogy branched off from the United Kingdom that Evans felt compelled to mention the fact whenever he spoke there on the tour. Nevertheless, wherever they appeared on the tour they had to confront a wide diversity of logistics. Then, as the Choir moved through Amsterdam, Scheveningen, Copenhagen, Berlin, Wiesbaden, Berne, Zurich, and Paris, they encountered all different sizes of halls (most without organs, only pianos), and diverse attitudes of audiences.

European journalists emphasized three mundane messages they got from the Choir's between-concerts demeanor and conversation.

1. Mormon women wore makeup.
2. Mormon men, generally, didn't wear beards. (McKay was the first clean-shaven Church President since Joseph Smith.)
3. Polygamy was dead and buried.

The music critics had three more salient responses.

1. The Choir had a warm tone, good balance, and general polish.
2. The accompaniment (whether piano or organ) was overbearing; the Choir should sing more a cappella.
3. The program repertoire was too shallow.[61]

McKay, though, whose opinion mattered most to the Choir's continuance, said of the Choir: "In all their experience they never have undertaken anything that has resulted in more good to the Church, to Utah, and to the country" than this tour. At the same time, from his perspective, the Lord Provost of Glasgow discerned the Choir's sly proselyting method: "You haven't come to convert us to your religion with words, but with singing, a psychological approach which I recommend."[62]

The Choir recorded portions of eleven concerts from the tour, distributing the resulting three-LP sets to Choir members for a pittance. The recordings reveal the deft and ingratiating non-parochial emceeing of Evans, the bright, almost over-cheery performance of the exuberant Choir—though with a discernible change in character (darker, more portentous) when Condie conducted it—and the fervent responses of the audiences, who seemed overcome with this non-parochial religious gift from the New World. It appeared to be a worthy sequel to the Marshall Plan, with broad-based but high-toned inspirational events being infused into Europe by unflappable volunteers. And the Church could not have wished for more.[63]

How monumental its leaders regarded this tour may be seen in one small but horrific coda to the tour. Deciding to separate from the main body of the group, six Choir members flew in a separate plane home. It crashed, killing all of them. Cornwall explained to the Choir that, as with every major threshold the Church had crossed in its persecuted history, this tour now had to have been "sealed in blood."[64]

Knowing that McKay had planned the 1955 tour to be Cornwall's finale with the Choir, Condie jockeyed hard to take over as conductor. Although Mormons are discouraged from coveting positions, Condie did covet this one: "I admit I sinned," he later said. Cornwall had balked at the tour, saying his health wasn't up to it. Knowing that, Condie labored to upstage Cornwall on the tour, partly with the encouragement of his friend, Mark Petersen, who saw Condie as the heir apparent.[65] Choir members, though, many of whom did not like Condie, began gossiping about his apparently less-than-dignified conduct both during and after the tour. Shortly after their return, Evans spoke on the radio broadcast about the dangers of rumormongering, which some Choir members took as a response to their complaints about Condie. At the next Thursday night's rehearsal, Adam Bennion excused Condie from the rehearsal so that Choir members could speak freely about him. Bennion reaffirmed that Condie was only an assistant and did not have equal billing with Cornwall. But Choir members who were closer to Condie than to Cornwall let Condie know about certain members' misgivings about him.[66]

On 8 September 1955, the Choir celebrated its twenty-fifth anniversary on CBS. Cornwall told the Choir after the broadcast that he continued to make up the programming "with fear and trembling," wondering if it would be accepted by his leaders. Thankfully, he noted, some listeners would always write him with thanks for this or that piece they had performed. Still, he said, "where the sword of Damocles will fall next time no one knows."[67]

A CULTURAL
NECESSITY

ACCORDING TO RICHARD CONDIE, President McKay "never liked" Cornwall.[1]
His aesthetically ambitious repertoire, his seeming self-containment—not answering to his overseers as much as they would like—and his subtle downplaying
of the Choir's proselyting role, all conspired to jeopardize Cornwall's conductorship. On 20 August 1957, the First Presidency met to discuss who should replace him. They decided on Newell Weight, a popular choral conductor at BYU.
Since Weight was on a two-year leave doing graduate work at the University of
Southern California, Condie should be called for now, they decided, although
with the understanding that the appointment was "limited."[2] On 6 September,
McKay called Cornwall to his office. He told Cornwall he was about to be let
go as the conductor. Cornwall asked if his work hadn't been satisfactory. "Yes,
very much so," McKay diplomatically said, "but it is a good time to change at
the high point of your success." Cornwall disagreed, saying the time wasn't right,
but then reversed himself and said it needed to happen right away. "What do
you mean?" McKay asked. Cornwall replied that, knowing what he now knew,
"I can't face the Choir any more."[3]

McKay called Condie to his office to tell him he could take charge of the Choir
"for a year or so." McKay gave him three options: stay on as assistant director
even though the director had been released; be called as acting director; or be

called as director and then, when released within two years, accept that people would be questioning why.

"Suppose during that two years I make a success of that Choir, is there a chance to be continued?" Condie asked.

"My answer to that will have to be no. I should rather be frank with you."

"I admire you for your frankness."

"Which would you rather do?"

"I would rather be the director, and I thank you very much for giving me that chance."

McKay discussed the ramifications of that. "Some of the members of the Choir may fall out."

Condie forcefully blurted out, "Brother Cornwall didn't even give me a chance to train the group going over on the tour."

"Well, undoubtedly there will be members of the Choir drop out now, and you have full authority to build up your choir."

They discussed the prospects of a tour to the Northwest and a few particulars about the upcoming General Conference. Then Condie left, no doubt with a spring in his step.

McKay reported the conversation to his First Counselor, Stephen Richards, wanting it to be on record that there was a "definite understanding" about the terms. Richards replied, "The more humility he [Condie] shows, the more he will build himself up with that group." Adding that he thought this was the right course, Richards said he hoped Cornwall would "get over his release and recognize it." He had done a great job, he should enjoy the rewards of that. But it was over.

When McKay went to the pre-broadcast Choir rehearsal on Sunday, 15 September, he told the Choir that a change in conductors had been contemplated for some time, that Cornwall had recently asked to be released right away and that he, the President of the Church, was simply complying with that request. He then praised Cornwall's reputation, conducting ability, and missionary success, but said nothing about the music he had chosen to infuse into Mormondom. After announcing Condie as the new "leader" of the Choir and making a few more general remarks—though not disclosing Condie's temporary status—McKay went back to his opening: "The fact that the change might seem somewhat precipitous is now explained by the fact that Brother Cornwall preferred immediate action." He added what by now had become obvious: "Leaders may come, leaders may go, but the Choir continues constantly."[4]

Three days later, McKay and his Counselor Stephen Richards tried to resolve a new wrinkle: the University of Utah did not allow moonlighting, which Condie now would be doing. He would have to resign his faculty position, jeopardizing his retirement for what McKay, his counselors, and Condie knew would be only a two-year position. So, as much as they wanted to keep Condie's short-term status secret, they realized they would have to disclose it to Ray Olpin, the university president. McKay did, and Olpin allowed Condie to take a two-year leave of absence. "That is probably necessary for his salvation," McKay quipped.[5]

Condie ended up directing the Choir for sixteen years.

Although his Church pay had grown gradually through the years to almost ten times its original amount under Cornwall, it now jumped up to $650 a month— the same as Cornwall's had been, though still slightly ($16.50) lower than Schreiner's as organist. It was a decent salary for a choral director in 1957, but hardly what one would expect for a de facto radio star: within three years, the Nielsen ratings showed that *Music and the Spoken Word* had 2 million people listening to all or part of the show in any given week and 5.6 million listeners each month.[6]

To get to that listenership, Condie had to do the usual surgery on the Choir rolls that every new conductor had performed. Three weeks after he took over the job, Condie began testing his singers' voices. On 15 January 1958, many members of the Choir arrived at rehearsal only to find that they had been cut (the notices hadn't been mailed yet). Condie said that he regretted having to "take the joy out of a person's life." But "a seat is worth working for." If you couldn't do that, "you must step out."[7] His all-business style, a contrast from that of the easygoing Cornwall, rankled some members.[8] The previous September, Lester Hewlett had publicly denied that either he or Evans had anything to do with Cornwall's termination and told the Choir that "those who cannot pledge support to Bro. Condie should ask for release."[9] "Blessed is he who is not offended," Condie genially told them.[10] By the end of January 1958, Hewlett told the Choir that releases were necessary because "this is to be a year of dedication"—presumably higher dedication to the Lord and the success of the Choir's divine work.

That April, rumors spread that Condie was dropping old members and installing in their places his University of Utah students. He was turning the Tabernacle Choir into "a university chorus." Condie rebuffed the charge: there were only twenty students in a 375-voice choir. But when President David O. McKay heard the concern, he simply asked, half rabbinically, "Why shouldn't they be in the Choir?"[11]

For many, Condie's apparent toughness suggested why Cornwall had kept him in the background, unable to dampen the geniality Cornwall worked toward. Cornwall had his bugaboos, of course—and, according to the Choir minutes, became increasingly irascible in the last year as conductor—but tried to keep things light. He befriended the Choir, preparing jokes for rehearsals and showing a joviality that made singers feel at ease with him, perhaps to a fault. He was also a compulsive organizer, seemingly making lists for everything in his life and conduct, especially with the Choir. By contrast, Condie seemed reserved and haphazard, sometimes even morose, though always the disciplinarian. And he could be hot-tempered.[12] (In describing their experiences with him, people sometimes mentioned him "yelling" and "screaming.") He courted loyalty and might suddenly drop people from the Choir if he thought them disloyal. He held grudges—eventually even against Church leaders. Cornwall was essentially a conductor and taught the Choir how to follow him. Condie was essentially a singer and taught the Choir how to sing well. Cornwall conducted precisely, confidently. Condie had no training in conducting—until Eugene Ormandy persuaded him to take lessons. Cornwall always used a baton. Condie began without one but after a few years picked one up.

Future director Jerry Ottley "took exception" to Condie's rehearsal methods: "There was a lot of time wasted." He tended to just run through whole pieces over and over, not often stopping to fix trouble spots.[13] Yet Condie transformed the Choir via a threefold method. First, he focused on rich vocal tone and the correct physical mechanisms for achieving it. Each rehearsal became a mass voice lesson. Second, he used romanticized rhetoric, wheedling the group into a swooning passion, no matter the actual "content" of the music. "All art," he said, "is exaggeration of the beautiful."[14] Third, he relied heavily on poetic and metaphorical imagery to shape the sound. This sometimes took the form of vernacular images to critique or assure the Choir: flat tires or basketball hoops, for example. More often, though, he drew on images from nature: flowing water, tall trees, wilted plants, and so forth. He even borrowed the perfect metaphor for the Choir itself. They were—and should be—"like an elephant dancing a ballet."[15] Condie's assistant conductor, Jay Welch, explained that, because the vocal chords are hidden, "you have to use analogy, you have to use poetry," and Condie, Welch said, was a master of both. "He would encourage, he would cajole, he would scold, he would compliment, he would illustrate." And in all these ways, the singer "taught them how to sing."

Condie altered seating arrangements, moving the taller singers to the back of their sections and stronger-voiced singers away from the microphones. The members of each section varied as much as twelve inches in height. "If the good Lord made you tall there is nothing we can do about it," he said. To those who complained the rear seats weren't very good, he retorted, "if they weren't[, we would] get rid of them."[16] As for moving some "powerful" singers away from the microphones, no explanation was needed.

In 1958, the Choir released two Columbia LPs under Condie's direction, *The Lord Is My Shepherd* and *The Beloved Choruses*. Although both albums were almost entirely sacred—only one strictly "secular" piece apiece—they already attempted to show off the Choir's enviable split repertorial personality, which would divide both their non-Mormon audiences and their ecclesiastical supervisors.[17] On the first record, the Choir, for the first time, *recorded* two spirituals ("My Lord, What a Morning" and "There Is a Balm in Gilead"). These foreshadowed the looser, quasi-popular side for which the Choir would soon become well-known. Still, the record had only organ for accompaniment. The critical response was mixed. *High Fidelity* magazine, for example, called *The Lord Is My Shepherd* "a hodgepodge of sacred music" that ranged from the commonplace to the dignified. "Musical gold there is here, but in minute quantities." Still, "no small pleasure is to be derived from [the Choir's] undiminished excellence."[18]

The second LP was all hard-core classical—again a first. No hymns, just shorter masterworks by Bach, Handel, Haydn, Schubert, Rimsky-Korsakov, and Sibelius. More important, though, it featured for the first time the accompaniment of the Philadelphia Orchestra, conducted by Eugene Ormandy. Ormandy and his orchestra were superb players but were overshadowed on the Columbia label by Leonard Bernstein and the New York Philharmonic, a conductor and orchestra whose fame had been climbing in the previous five years. It became clear that there was no point exhausting the same limited pool of orchestral "masterworks" with variant performances by the two orchestras in the label's classical stable. The strategy of aligning Ormandy's orchestra with the Tabernacle Choir to perform choral-orchestral masterworks solved not only the problem of what to program for Ormandy and his group, but also how to package the Tabernacle Choir, whose main recording rivals were the Roger Wagner Chorale (about half its size) and, through 1965, the Robert Shaw Chorale, which had anywhere between thirty and sixty voices.[19]

After hearing demo tapes of the Choir before their first recording session, Ormandy made three criticisms:

- The Choir tended to go flat.
- Their attacks were "not always clear or together."
- They needed bigger climaxes and more "variety of tone color."

Condie used these criticisms as leverage with the Choir. While they now had a deal with Columbia for two LPs a year, which included regular collaborations with Ormandy, only about half of the Choir could sing if the recordings were done in Columbia's New York studios, which could hold only about 150 singers. Thus, only the Choir's best singers might appear on record.[20]

The Beloved Choruses seemed almost a gauntlet thrown down, the Choir daring the classical world to take it more seriously. Ray Ericson, the same reviewer who had yawned at the previous LP, took notice. While the Bach choruses, especially, deserve a smaller choir, he wrote, "in *A Mighty Fortress*, the *Finlandia* arrangement, and the Rimsky Korsakov setting of *Slava*, musical purism matters less, and the massed sound, so clear and beautifully disciplined, becomes truly exciting, particularly in the perfectly balanced, spacious stereo version."[21]

In 1959, the Choir released its third album with Condie and second with Ormandy. Titled *The Lord's Prayer*, it contained the usual radio fare, hymns, small sacred pieces, and arranged folk songs. Some of the hymns were arranged by Leroy Robertson, whose *Oratorio from the Book of Mormon* had suffered amid the Choir—Utah Symphony skirmishes in the previous decade. One non-hymn track was "The Lord's Prayer" from that oratorio, which had become a favorite on the radio broadcasts. His unusual arrangement of the pioneer trail song "Come, Come Ye Saints" unsettled some listeners, including a Mormon General Authority who said that "Robertson really let us down this time."[22] The last track on the album, though, stood out: Peter Wilhousky's version of "The Battle Hymn of the Republic." It would appeal to the nationalist fervor in the nation, a self-promotional enthusiasm now fueled by *Sputnik* and the competitiveness between the Soviet Union and the United States. But a quirk in the popular music charts led Columbia to release the Choir's "Battle Hymn" as a 45rpm single—unheard of for a classically trained church choir.

In April 1959, RCA had released a comic military ballad, heavy with banjo, snare drums, and a chanting male chorus, that rose dramatically up the *Billboard* pop charts: "The Battle of New Orleans" by Johnny Horton. It quickly reached No. 1, where it stayed for six weeks. It was catchy and patriotic, utterly unlike the formulaic hits of rock 'n' roll or Brill Building pop. Soon, rival labels tried to mimic its success. One imitator was the overt parody by Homer and Jethro, "The

Battle of Kookamonga." Another attempt to cash in, a long shot indeed, was the Tabernacle Choir's "The Battle Hymn of the Republic." Both of those records entered the charts on 7 September (at numbers 76 and 78, respectively). Both climbed up the charts, although "The Battle Hymn" went higher, peaking at no. 13 on 26 October, just below hits like Bobby Darin's "Mack the Knife" (no. 1), Paul Anka's "Put Your Head on My Shoulder" (no. 3), "Poison Ivy" by the Coasters (no. 9), and "('Til) I Kissed You" by the Everly Brothers. That fall, it won the Grammy for "Best Performance by a Vocal Group or Chorus," beating out the Ames Brothers, the Kingston Trio, the Browns, and the Robert Shaw Chorale.

On 20 August, the First Presidency and the Twelve had met to consider the prearranged end of Condie's tenure. On 3 September, McKay had received news that sales of both *The Lord's Prayer* and "The Battle Hymn" were soaring. McKay decided that Condie would stay on indefinitely. He called the conductor to his office and said, "Your two years of acting are up, aren't they? Take that choir and go to it!" A month later, the Choir sang "The Battle Hymn of the Republic" at General Conference. During Conference, Condie announced to the Choir that sixty thousand copies of *The Lord's Prayer* and three hundred thousand of "Battle Hymn" had been sold.

While the single was an unexpected win for the Choir in popular music, another in classical music was about to match it. In the spring of 1958, the Choir began to organize a full-scale East Coast tour with a $330,000 budget—and another $80,000 to 100,000 for publicity—authorized by the First Presidency, and funded by recording royalties, concert receipts, and apparently by "two wealthy members."[23] It included twenty concerts and two prospective days of recording with the Philadelphia Orchestra, finally on Ormandy's own turf.

In 1953, newly elected President Eisenhower had named Mormon Apostle Ezra Taft Benson as his secretary of agriculture. Now, in the fall of 1958, Eisenhower had Benson proffer an invitation to the Tabernacle Choir—via McKay—to sing at the White House.[24]

Ormandy had assumed they would do a large-scale masterwork together. The Tabernacle team, at Schreiner's suggestion, narrowed the field to three works: Mendelssohn's *St. Paul* or *Elijah*, and Haydn's *Creation*, all of which the Choir had performed for more than fifty years. Never shy about making requests about repertoire, Richard Evans said it would be "splendid" if they did Handel's *Messiah*. The others tried to talk him out of it: *Messiah* was overdone and over-recorded. But Evans pressed his case and, now an Apostle in the Church, overrode the others' rejection. Evans sent the request to Ormandy, who phoned him back and explained that Columbia had just recorded a version with Bernstein and the New York Philharmonic to be issued in 1959, the same year as this new Tabernacle Choir collaboration would come out. Columbia would not issue a second version in competition with itself.

Nevertheless, Evans remained quietly adamant, explaining that some people were confusing "Mormon" with "Moslem" and he wanted to seize this chance to show the Church's Christianity. So Condie and Ormandy hired noted soloists and worked up *Messiah* for a concert on the tour, knowing a recording was out of the question. Fred Plaut, a senior Columbia recording engineer, happened to attend the Philadelphia performance. When it ended, he immediately called John McClure to insist they record this version, which, he said, was the best he had ever heard. McClure refused until Plaut finally said that he himself would put up the money for recording costs. So Plaut oversaw the recording and the label opted to issue Bernstein's version in spring 1959, for the Easter market, and Ormandy-Condie's version in the fall for Christmas.

Bernstein was by then a trusted brand name. But the Tabernacle Choir had its own massive name recognition from its radio broadcasts and, lately, "The Battle Hymn." According to Schreiner, who had opposed Evans's choice, the Tabernacle Choir version outsold Bernstein's ten to one. It also got strong reviews, especially for the quality of the recording—and, as always, criticism for the lumbering Choir's inability to sing rapid counterpoint. "A better engineered and more opulent sounding alternative to this Philadelphia Salt Lake City effort would be hard to find," *HiFi Review* magazine wrote. This was "a powerful, vital statement of the music, moving along at energetic yet unhurried tempi." The Choir and orchestra were "admirably balanced and the choral articulation reveals the steadiness and considerable virtuosity of the Tabernacle singers."[25]

In February 1960, Columbia gave the Church a check for the combined sale of 1,202,134 recordings of "Battle Hymn" and *Messiah*. In 1963, *Messiah* would earn a Gold Record—rare in the classical market—and continue to be reissued over the next five decades. In 2004, the Tabernacle Choir's *Messiah* was inducted into the National Recording Registry, which canonizes works that "are culturally, historically, or aesthetically important, and/or inform or reflect life in the United States." Condie and Ormandy had unwittingly won the gamble, but the biggest winner was Richard Evans, who gained more authority in matters of repertoire.

As for the rest of the 1958 tour, logistics complicated the plans. Carnegie Hall could accommodate only two hundred singers with the orchestra, even with seven rows of seating removed. Lester Hewlett suggested that half the Choir sing the first half of *Messiah* and that the rest of the singers replace them for the second half of the oratorio. Even fewer (150) singers could fit on the stage of the *Ed Sullivan Show*. Fortunately, the hall at the Academy of Music in Philadelphia could hold everyone. Midway through the tour, Condie told the Choir, "the past may be glorious but the future may be more interesting." Ten days later, CBS invited the Choir to tape its own half-hour Christmas television program. Although the Choir had performed on television before, this was its first complete telecast. But many in the Choir didn't yet have televisions and so could not watch the show when it aired on 21 December 1958.[26]

Before and after the tour, Hewlett had been in touch with George Romney, one of the most prominent Mormons east of the Mississippi. He explained to Romney the rationale of this and all other Choir tours: "our only reason for going out like this and spending several hundred thousand dollars is to break down prejudice so that our missionaries can get entrance into more homes." Choir tours would make people accept the Church's teachings faster and more efficiently than "just hammering doors like you and I did years ago."[27]

The broadcasts, of course, had the same intent. Approaching the thirtieth anniversary of the Tabernacle radio shows in 1959, the broadcast team (Condie, Evans, et al.) asked listeners to submit requests for pieces to be performed on the anniversary show. Avid replies flowed in, 4,199 suggestions, which, once tallied, yielded only 1,427 different titles. They ranged from classical favorites by Handel, Mendelssohn, and others to Stainer's "God So Loved the World," and even to "How Great Thou Art," the hymn the Billy Graham choir sang at the opening of his *Hour of Decision* shows.[28]

The Choir was also appearing more often on television shows, notably the NBC *Easter Hour Sunday Showcase* in April 1960, which featured four numbers by the Choir, along with sacred music by other artists, institutions, and groups. One thing vexed some Choir members, though: the show included dancing as part of the artistic interpretations of one of Christendom's most holy days. And while dancing had been more acceptable to Mormons than many, if not most, other denominations for over a century, this seemed to cross a line in the minds of some singers. Could dance be dignified in the same way as choral music? Some had their doubts.[29]

But a greater issue with television appearances was the nature of each show. A religious public-service program was fine. But if a show had a commercial sponsor, that changed the game. Less than six months after the *Easter Hour*, for example, the Utah Oil Refining Company requested that the Choir appear on shows it sponsored. While taking no stand on the company or the shows, McKay took a position that was half moral and half financial: the Church should not let television "launch the Choir toward a professional career, which would commercialize it and ultimately make demands upon the members of the Choir so great that it would necessitate compensating them for their services." How this related to the Choir's budding recording career he left vague.

That spring, Columbia Masterworks producer John McClure had visited the Tabernacle to evaluate its acoustics. Deciding the sound was too quirky to keep recording there, he suggested that the Choir fly to one of its coastal studios for future recordings with Ormandy and the orchestra. Evans countered that the Choir would sooner skip future recording projects "than try to explain why we didn't record in the Tabernacle in our own setting." McClure had a lot of clout, of course, but Evans argued that "we shouldn't let the personal preferences of one young man talk us out of a distinctive and significant recording in our own traditional and widely acclaimed building."[30]

If they were to stay in their venerable homestead, at least one aspect of the sound needed fixing. Although the speakers Cornwall had installed under the Tabernacle seats had improved and stabilized the Choir's intonation, the speaker cones had deteriorated, prey to silverfish and the desert air. By April 1960 Tabernacle engineer Paul Evans reported that, between the current decay and the motley ad hoc replacement of speakers over the years, the whole system was inconsistent and imbalanced. The Choir's pitch would go flat if the speakers weren't totally repaired or replaced.[31]

The Choir's popularity had two impacts on the Tabernacle itself. One is that the building became more and more of a media center. Consequently, the building had to be a better studio than ever. Another is that Tabernacle tourism grew. As a result, it had to be both more welcoming and functional for guests. Throughout the 1960s, newer and better equipment was procured and installed. And, as early as 1962, the staff added to the old needle-drop trick a recording of the Choir and the Philadelphia Orchestra, a simulation of a recording session that would feed tourists' imagination.[32]

As much as the First Presidency under David McKay craved the attention the Choir brought to the Church, they took pains to control more and more of its repertoire. They tried to prevent the Choir from becoming a group for hire—except for Columbia jobs—and kept it from political and commercial endorsements. They turned down sponsorships offered by businesses ranging from appliance companies to wax museums. The First Presidency had to approve all selections on every record as well as for performance at General Conference, for which McKay wanted more hymns, those and other works all composed by Mormons, if possible.[33] But for the rest of his tenure as conductor, Condie bristled at ecclesiastical attempts to shepherd his repertoire.

The record label was also trying to squeeze the Choir into new, possibly more formulaic recording projects. In April 1960, Schuyler Chapin and John McClure of Columbia Records wrote to new Choir President Isaac Stewart to explain the situation. The only albums that survived in the market anymore, they wrote, were those built "around a strong central idea." In Columbia's case, that meant laying out a pattern of theme-based LPs.[34] By 1960 that pattern had three main components: sacred music, Americana, and, its perennially best-selling genre, Christmas music. Columbia could see a market, though, for more secular non-Americanist inspirational albums. The first issue in that vein was *Hymns and Songs of Brotherhood* (1961), a slightly less religious trope on the earlier sacred collections. More adventurous was their *This Is My Country* (1963), which, despite the seemingly Americanist title, bore the subtitle "The *World's* Great Songs of Patriotism" (emphasis added). And, indeed, the tracks on this LP roamed from U.S. songs to European to the Israeli song "Hatikva." Worried that the last selection might imply Mormon support for Zionist causes, the First Presidency ruled that, if this song was included, the LP should "also include some such music from Arab sources." Meanwhile, the Presidency nixed one selection the Columbia team had made: the Russian song "Meadowland," with words from the perspective of a Red Army recruit who vows to defend his homeland. The rigorously anticommunist McKay said the song was "not approved for broadcast or recording."[35]

At least one Apostle disliked the way the Choir was veering into secular music. Twice widowed, Joseph F. Smith's son Joseph Fielding Smith had recently married again, this time to one of the Tabernacle Choir's most popular soloists: Jessie Evans. On 8 August 1961, the couple appeared on *After Hours*, a public affairs show on the University of Utah's television station KUED. The host, Rex Campbell, asked Apostle Smith what he thought of the Tabernacle Choir, in which Smith actually had sung under Stephens. He immediately harped on an old controversy: "although I'm not a music critic, they were the winners at the [1893] Fair." Campbell then asked about the Choir's current touring.

"I think they're traveling too much," Smith said. "The Salt Lake Tabernacle Choir was not organized to travel around the world."

Pressed about it, Smith conceded some travel was necessary but opined that "they are overdoing it."

"I know one man who takes the opposite view," Campbell replied. "A top-flight TV network official who was here just the other day. He said he had one objective: to see the Tabernacle Choir on Broadway singing Broadway tunes."

Apologizing in advance for his bluntness, Smith continued, "I don't think the Salt Lake Tabernacle Choir belongs on Broadway."[36]

Broadway was one thing, the space race another. On 9 July 1962, the first Telstar communications satellite went into orbit. Within a day, live television between New York and the Eurovision network began. Two weeks later, the three U.S. networks (ABC, CBS, and NBC) collaborated on a broadcast to Eurovision, a live show that included the Tabernacle Choir. The original plan was to have the Choir appear at the Tabernacle singing the choral finale of Beethoven's Ninth Symphony, with its assurance that "all men will become brothers" under the wings of universal joy. To negotiate a timely broadcast in both the United States and continental Europe, the live signal would have to be transmitted from New York at 10 A.M.—thus 7 A.M. in Utah—to feed seventeen major stations on both continents. Ted Cannon exulted in the Choir taking part in this "milestone in communications history," especially since it would "present tremendous opportunities for the Church, simultaneously reaching untold millions of people, without question the largest single television audience in all history."[37]

But an astute tiny-market TV executive in the Black Hills of South Dakota persuaded the networks to move the Choir to Mount Rushmore, where the symbolism of U.S. progress and implicit dominance could be made visible. He pulled strings with a friend—President Kennedy—and 312 members of the Choir flew to South Dakota, where they sang, not Beethoven, but "A Mighty Fortress Is Our God" and, no surprise, "The Battle Hymn of the Republic."[38]

All that year, Evans assiduously pursued more radio outlets. As of 1962, there were 202 radio stations in the CBS network. Of these, only thirty-five did not broadcast the Tabernacle program. Those that did ran it at all hours of the day and night, though always on Sunday. Some ran the show a week behind, but most broadcast it live. Trying to get all network stations to run the show, Evans began a one-man crusade of writing to mission Presidents who had a CBS station in their area that did not run his show, asking them to find and persuade "some influential member or non-Church friend" to lobby the station to pick up the show. They should emphasize that the show is "not . . . for proselyting purposes, but for music and a universal message." They should say that the request was not made for the Church's purposes, but because "here is a universally accepted broadcast with one of the world's greatest musical organizations to offer their listeners." Many mission Presidents complied, although some reported that more and more churches, especially in the South, were creating and pitching their own religious programs to fill the public-service time on their local stations. The campaign failed.[39]

In 1962, CBS proposed that *Music and the Spoken Word* prerecord its shows. If the Church wanted it to continue as a live broadcast, the network would require $7,000 to $8,000 a year for a separate line feed. "It's easier to do it on tape," Evans said, "but psychologically you miss something."[40] McKay was quick to concur: "Don't let this become merely a taped show." The discussion allowed McKay to weigh in on three more matters. First, the Choir should sing more on the show and the organ play less. The sung message, that is, should outweigh mere instrumental musicianship. Vocal music trumped instrumental. Second, the show should reclaim five minutes that the network had taken away and go from what was now a twenty-five-minute program (technically, 23 minutes and 45 seconds) back to a half hour.[41] (That, though, wouldn't happen until after McKay's death.) Third, the Church should get to approve what advertising preceded and followed its broadcast, "to see that it is in an appropriate mood with suitable subject matter." All told, the Choir should now be able to call some of the shots it would never have considered calling before it became a recording star.

In the summer of 1963, the First Presidency and the Tabernacle team had to face a new incursion on the Choir's brand name. The state of Israel had invited the "Mormon Choir of Southern California" to sing at a national choir festival in July 1964. Although the name of that California choir had been allowed years earlier by the Church, the popularity of the Tabernacle Choir had not only enhanced the cachet of the California choir, but other choirs who included the term "Mormon" in their name as a potential bait-and-switch ploy to unsuspecting listeners, who might have only vague notions of the Tabernacle Choir's specific name (which, indeed, had almost never been consistent).[42]

Evans suggested the Church try to trademark all permutations of the name "Salt Lake Mormon Tabernacle Choir." McKay suggested that the California choir be allowed to go to Israel on condition that all advertising had to omit the word "Mormon." Others suggested that the California choir simply remove the word "Mormon" from their name henceforth. Condie agreed that this California choir was trying to ride the coattails of the Tabernacle Choir, but they weren't really competitive, and he held no ill will against them. And indeed, Ike Stewart showed his colleagues, the California choir had used (or had allowed the use of) advertising in Las Vegas that clearly billed them as "The Mormon Choir—The World Famous Choir." The discussion intensified, especially when it was brought up that any implicit recognition of Israel by the Church could antagonize Arab neighbors in the region. The First Presidency drafted a letter "requesting" that all choirs but the Tabernacle Choir remove the word "Mormon" from their names.

Three months later, a three-man delegation from Southern California arrived with Apostle Howard Hunter, who was from that region, to meet with the First Presidency. The conductor of the Southern California choir explained that his choir was also helping missionary work, that they had been careful not to claim to be the Tabernacle Choir, and that they hadn't issued any records, as had another quasi-rival group, "the Mormon Choir of Los Altos." Hunter argued that this choir's members "consider themselves missionaries. They are raising the dignity of the Church to a very high level among the people who are at the top socially there." McKay decided that the group could continue if they switched the name to the "Southern California Mormon Choir," with the word "Mormon" in their publicity materials at least 40 to 50 percent smaller than the words "Southern California."

From 1960 through 1970, the Choir would record five Christmas albums, the most acclaimed and financially profitable being the only one that featured an orchestra—not the Philadelphia Orchestra, but the New York Philharmonic, conducted by Leonard Bernstein. The recording sessions for this 1963 LP provided some of the Choir's most enduring lore.[43]

On 1 and 2 September 1963, Bernstein and his orchestra recorded in the Tabernacle before an audience for which the Tabernacle had sold tickets. This piqued the conductor, who was shocked at the difficulty of coordinating attacks within the building's odd acoustic. The Choir, he said, was "like pulling seven Mack trucks." From the recording booth, John McClure told Bernstein the ensemble wasn't jelling. "Yes, John," he replied. "Write me a letter." The orchestra had gotten the error-ridden parts at the last minute, partly because Bernstein didn't want to rehearse before the sessions. He complained about wrong notes from his players, only to find they had the wrong written notes. The first night's session ended bitterly at ten minutes to midnight.

The second day's sessions went more smoothly. The stories differ as to why. McClure said Bernstein, a Jew, disliked recording Christmas music. He may also have been miffed at the Choir for declining to record the Berlioz *Requiem* with him the previous summer.[44] While everyone agreed that Bernstein used rougher, more vulgar language with the Choir than they were used to, why he stopped is unclear. Rumors spread (and persist) that McKay himself had summoned Bernstein out of the hall and told him if he didn't clean up his language he would have to leave and cancel the recording. But the best records show that it was Ike Stewart who confronted Bernstein, to argue not so much for greater propriety but for greater sympathy: these Choir members were all volunteers, he said, sacrificing their time, in effect paying to be in these sessions, and they didn't deserve the scolding one might give to professionals. Bernstein, stunned at this realization, toned down his speech. For decades thereafter, Stewart got a card from Bernstein each Christmas.[45]

On 22 November 1963, President John Kennedy was assassinated in Dallas. All the U.S. television networks scrambled for proper ways to cover the shooting's aftermath, more or less continuously for four days. For its Sunday programming, CBS turned to the *Music and the Spoken Word* team, who put together a ninety-minute program. CBS had aired half of it when the next news broke that Jack Ruby had shot Lee Harvey Oswald, Kennedy's alleged killer. So the nation never got to hear the Choir's full-scale attempt to console the nation. A year later, a CBS budget executive wrote the Choir asking what the network owed them for preparing the Kennedy tribute. Evans shrugged off the inquiry. This was a pro bono service that the Choir had been happy to perform.[46] But Kennedy's successor, Lyndon Johnson, would effectively make up for any service they had been denied by circumstance.

In February 1964, President Johnson asked McKay if the Choir could come to sing at the White House that summer. McKay jumped at the chance and, via his associates in the Church and Choir hierarchies, negotiated not only the date, but an East Coast tour to go with the Washington visit. In May, the Republican National Committee invited the Choir to sing at its national convention that fall in San Francisco. On July 23, the Choir sang at the White House, Johnson was reelected, and, before the year was up, they had been invited to return to Washington in January to sing at Johnson's inaugural—another breakthrough in the Church-via-Choir's pursuit of federal sanctity. McKay called this performance "the greatest single honor that has come to the Tabernacle Choir."

Johnson's inauguration in January 1965 lifted not only the Choir's reputation, but the marketability of Columbia's Tabernacle Choir catalog. Goddard Lieberson, president of Columbia Records, returned the favor. That year he released the seventh record in the deluxe *Columbia Legacy* series, this one called

The Mormon Pioneers. Handsomely packaged, with a silver gatefold cover into which was sewn a forty-eight-page booklet of essays and photos, the album included tracks by folk singers from Columbia and other labels, often with an unidentified "chorus," alongside readings from pioneer diaries and letters. The closing track, the hymn "Come, Come Ye Saints," was sung by the (attributed) Tabernacle Choir.

The *Pioneers* album had actually been in the works since the fall of 1962, when Columbia provided a preliminary version to Evans, Stewart, Condie, and others in the Tabernacle team to review. The team had problems with some of the references to the so-called Mormon War of 1857 as well as, of course, polygamy. Could they cut such things from the text? Beyond that, the songs themselves had "a bit of the 'hill billy' flavor" and weren't quite "in keeping with the dignity of the Church or the Choir." The music, in short, "doesn't convey the image we should have." If he could get some "concessions and modifications" in both the script and music, Evans thought the First Presidency would approve it—"especially," he wrote, "if we can get Joseph Smith's Prayer and Our Mountain Home included by the Choir."[47] Neither of those songs, however, fit the bill—although certainly about the religion and the state of Utah, they weren't really "pioneer" songs.

Lieberson wrote an introduction and dedication for the LP in which he admired Mormon values, especially Mormons' devotion to family, as well as to music and poetry. He dedicated the album, glowingly, to Church President David McKay. He also strikingly made the case that the Mormon pioneers were an example of the "flight from bigotry and intolerance." They may be mainstream citizens today, wrote Lieberson, but "perhaps the most poignant factor in [their] history was that they were truly—in this 'land of religious freedom'—the victims of prejudice." He likened the "brutality of bigotry" against Mormons to that experienced by other groups, including Native Americans, although he wisely did not mention blacks, since, indeed, Mormons were staving off criticism for their persistent denial of the priesthood and temple worship to African Americans.

The *Saturday Review* praised this deluxe Mormon package. It depicted real people, the magazine said, not Hollywood western mythology. It showed how Mormons lived by the motto, "Let the beginning and end of all your thoughts be utility." The *Journal of American Folklore* also thought the album "a significant contribution to Americana," but cryptically noted that "the choral heresy was not absent."[48]

Behind the scenes, 1965 brought renewed hand-wringing about authority, personnel, and repertoire. Three weeks after the Johnson inauguration, Evans,

Condie, Schreiner, and Stewart met with McKay to settle a dispute about what the Choir should sing. Evans had taken the stand that he by rights should have the ultimate say. Condie and Schreiner insisted it should always be their call, a position with which McKay agreed. In the same meeting, Condie brought up a problem in the organ loft. Schreiner, of course, was the star. But Frank Asper, who had been playing in the broadcasts virtually since they began, suffered by comparison. "He makes many mistakes, and letters are received from musicians all over the country from time to time complaining." McKay ruled that Asper should be released and Robert Cundick take his place as second organist, and Roy Darley continuing in the third spot.[49]

In April, though, another organ matter arose, this one the sticky matter of salaries. Schreiner, as it turned out, was not only making substantially more than the other organists, he was making more than Condie. After discussing the layout of salaries, the First Presidency decided to restructure the payments of Tabernacle musicians, giving all of them a raise, leveling out Condie and Schreiner—both now would make $1,000 a month—and even giving Asper an "emeritus" salary of $600 a month, with the other organists, Cundick and Darley, receiving $900 and $750, respectively.[50]

With everything seemingly settled, McKay was startled to learn in July that University of Utah Music Department Chairman Lowell Durham was telling people—including the university president—that he was the new assistant conductor of the Tabernacle Choir. McKay called several meetings on the matter, until the scenario became clear: Condie's current assistant conductor, Jay Welch, had told his boss, Durham, that he needed a leave of absence to guest conduct at the University of Washington.[51] Durham volunteered to temporarily replace Welch. He floated the idea to his friend Hugh Brown, a Counselor in the First Presidency, who tentatively approved it. Brown took the idea to Condie, who also approved it, though Durham had already construed Brown's encouragement as the completion of the deal. Not only did the episode tighten the procedure for hiring, it led McKay to bar Durham, one of the most conspicuous and avid promoters (and critics) of the Choir, from ever conducting it.[52]

This awkward incident overlapped with some heady discussions about the Choir's future. By August 1965, three Church-owned television stations in Washington, Idaho, and Louisiana had been showing *Music and the Spoken Word* occasionally "on an experimental basis." Now Isaac Stewart proposed to the First Presidency that they accept CBS network executive Frank Stanton's invitation to have a thirteen-week run of the show on two CBS TV stations, one in Los

Angeles, the other in Billings, Montana.[53] The Presidency approved, the series aired, and audiences loved it. From then on, more CBS television stations began adding the show to their schedules.

The shift to a visual medium, though, "would require some modifications," Stewart wrote.[54] Camera deployment, angles of vision, and so forth, all had to be mastered. And the drapes and ad hoc sound dampening had to go, if the camera was to show the Tabernacle in its spacious splendor. (Whether or not to have a camera on the audience, as most shows did, remained a question.) Evans could no longer roam around and direct the timing. Everything should be tightly laid out and choreographed before the cameras went on. Absenteeism became more damaging, because any empty choir seats would wreck the visual effect. The general appearance and demeanor of the Choir now mattered much more than before, when its broadcast spectators had only consisted of a relatively small crowd in the Tabernacle. Choir uniforms—especially dresses—had to be more eye-catching and varied. And individual facial expressions had to be more self-consciously controlled, since at any moment a camera could zoom in for a close-up. All told, the Church needed to dazzle, even with a choir.

By then the Choir's fan mail was matched by invitations, requests, and contracts to visit here, concertize there, collaborate, raise money for one cause or another, you name it. Policies steadily evolved, money and propriety guiding them. The Choir could not afford to run at a deficit, unless the First Presidency thought the loss was an oblique investment in missionary work. The Choir could not be seen as a shill for outside fund-raisers, no matter how worthy the cause.[55] And, for well-worn but still weak reasons, the Choir could not sing with the Utah Symphony.

At the same time, the Tabernacle itself had continual needs, provoked constant questions. Throughout the mid- to late-1960s, memos circulated about adjusting the furnace for warmth, fixing the noise the heating system made during recordings, improving the lighting for the Choir, patching leaks in the basement ceiling, improving the lettering on the granite panels outside the Tabernacle, and installing air-conditioning, new carpet, a teleprompter at the pulpit, warning lights in restrooms (to alert occupants the broadcast was about to begin), a trophy case (for Gold Records and other awards), bulletin boards, equipment cases for visiting orchestras, pay telephones, bigger cupboards, and more drinking fountains.

Right before October General Conference in 1964, Tabernacle recording engineer Paul Evans excitedly reported that scheduling of television coverage of conference sessions was up, largely because of the Choir's increasing involvement. In the past, he noted, the Choir usually sang about six numbers in the course of the conference. That October, with 150 television stations and many more radio stations carrying one or more sessions, they sang: six pieces on Saturday morning, three on Saturday evening, five on Sunday morning, and three on Sunday afternoon—and these do not include four more sung by the Choir with the congregation. None of the pieces were duplicated, and only five of the seventeen pieces sung without the congregation were hymns.

Paul Evans said that some media outlets wanted the Choir to sing after every speaker, which would have doubled the number of pieces. So the massive infusion of music into the conference ultimately was the result of a pragmatic compromise: McKay wanted less, the broadcasters wanted more, and the Choir simply had its limits.[56]

From the middle of the decade until its end, the Choir's multifarious LP issues with Columbia fell into four broad categories, each replenished from time to time with a new collection, though less than half of them featuring the Philadelphia Orchestra.[57] First were its bread-and-butter Christmas albums. Every label needed them and the Tabernacle Choir proved one of the most reliable factories for them. The 1963 *Joy of Christmas* album with Bernstein remained the bestseller in their Christmas cache (unless one includes the Choir's *Messiah* in this category). The Choir didn't release a Christmas album in 1966—something that Choir watchers would have noticed, although by then the Choir had plenty of back titles still available. To fill the one-year gap, Capitol Records released a 1966 Christmas album by the Southern California Mormon Choir.

A second category consisted of LPs that anthologized short sacred pieces— eight of these albums from 1960 to 1970, all with just the Choir and organ (except for 1962's "sequel" album, *The Lord's Prayer, Vol. 2*, which again included Ormandy's orchestra). These were, in effect, distillations designed to cash in on the free public-service broadcasts the Tabernacle team had been providing for decades: Choir and organ combining for uplifting radio-style music. These albums served as replayable, anytime versions of the Sunday shows—though without the voice of Richard Evans, who by now had a string of books; collections of his *Spoken Word* messages could now be read with or without the recordings for enhancement.

A third category was Americana: six LPs from 1961 to 1968 (half with the Philadelphia Orchestra). Starting with overtly patriotic songs, this series moved toward non-patriotic American songs, culminating in 1968's *Beautiful Dreamer*, a collection of Stephen Foster songs. The most interesting of the series, though, was *This Land Is Your Land* (1965), not so much for its content but for the effect that content had on one of the more obstreperous apostles, Ezra Benson, long departed from Washington but tightly aligned with John Birch Society politics.

After this quaint but stirring set of folk songs was released, Benson wrote to Stewart complaining about it because two of the songs, he said (including the title song), were by "two hard-core Communists," Woody Guthrie and Pete Seeger, the latter of whom he called "the pied-piper" of Communism. After describing both men's "insidious" influence on the United States and warning of the dangers of both communism and socialism, he opined that "The use of music by these Communist authors will be used to give aid and comfort for the Communists, their fellow-travelers and dupes, and can only bring difficulty to the Church."[58] If difficulty ensued, one wouldn't know it from the growth of the Church and the expanding fame of its official choir.

The fourth category was the only one that confidently qualified the Choir for the "classical" sales charts and reviews. Four releases in this category, 1960–70, were anthologies of shorter choral-orchestral works, some of which they had performed in other collections, with or without orchestra—*Beloved Choruses Vol. 2* (1964), *Anvil Chorus: Favorite Opera Choruses* (1967), *Hallelujah Chorus* (all Handel, 1969), and *Jesu, Joy of Man's Desiring* (all Bach, 1970). As early as 1963, Ormandy had pushed for the Choir to do Mahler's Eighth Symphony with his orchestra. But the Choir, for unclear reasons, wouldn't sign on. And the prospect of singing Catholic liturgy in Latin was enough for the Choir to nix Ormandy's second choice, the Berlioz *Requiem* (which they had already turned down with Bernstein). They did record the Brahms *Requiem* in English with Ormandy in 1963, though, a piece for which they would become known for the rest of their career. Reviews of the recording were mixed. Consider this from the same *High Fidelity* critic who had praised their *Messiah* three years earlier: "The oversized Mormon Tabernacle Choir . . . shouts its way through the score with lusty tone and a seeming unawareness of the meaning of such words as dolce and pianissimo. (What it does to the lovely little intermezzo movement, for example, must be heard to be believed.) . . . [They] sing the lines with a crudely accented vehemence which results in an evangelical sentimentalism to my ears even more offensive than the self-conscious 'reverence' of the traditional German reading."[59]

The later recordings in this decade-long string of choral-orchestral issues were generally "in the can" well before the decade ended. Indeed, Ormandy and his orchestra recorded thirty-two pieces in fourteen hours of recording sessions with the Choir in June 1967, after which Ormandy gave high public praise to his favorite choir in the world. "You don't have to play second fiddle to anybody. Utah is marvelous. Wonderful! You have the greatest choir; you have a beautiful hall . . . a wonderful conductor for the Choir, and a wonderful President [of the Choir]," all of which, he said, "stems from one of the greatest human beings I have ever had the honor to meet"—ninety-four-year-old David McKay.[60]

But five months later, RCA wooed Ormandy and the Philadelphia Orchestra from Columbia, strictly, the orchestra's trustee said, "for financial and business reasons."[61] Other than collaborations with the Tabernacle Choir—which were paying lots of the Masterworks bills—Ormandy's orchestra had little repertoire approved for recording against the main Columbia orchestra, the New York Philharmonic, whose reputation kept overshadowing Ormandy's. So, with this migration to a new, more hospitable label, the popular joint choral-orchestral Tabernacle recordings were now over. With what was already in the can, the Tabernacle Choir–Philadelphia Orchestra pairing would sputter to a halt over the next two years.

With Ormandy's departure from Columbia, the Choir put on its best stoic face. Stewart wrote to Condie that, despite losing their most valuable recording ally, "we will continue our recording, making new friends in the musical world, as well as performing our other assigned duties under the divine guidance of President McKay and his counselors."[62]

Just before Ormandy's flight to RCA, the Utah Symphony had again been trying to collaborate with the famous Choir up the street. But Stewart explained once more why they could not do that, using the same arguments Condie and Hewlett had used since 1960.[63] The difference between working with the Philadelphia Orchestra and the Utah Symphony, he said, was that the Choir worked with Ormandy's orchestra for the broad audience it gave them as well as the huge financial rewards. The Utah Symphony could offer neither.[64] But by 1970, one "new friend" it made in the recording world was the cryptically named Columbia Symphony that would back the Choir in several post-Ormandy recordings. No such entity existed, of course. In at least one case, this "symphony" was a pick-up group that, when recording with the Tabernacle Choir, consisted of local players in Salt Lake—individually contracted members of the Utah Symphony.

Among the other "assigned duties" of which Stewart spoke, of course, was General Conference. In 1967, Arch Madsen, director of KSL television, told McKay that Church members were increasingly requesting that the Tabernacle Choir sing more familiar hymns at General Conference. In response, McKay appointed a new Television-Radio Broadcast Music Coordinating Committee to deal with the new national exposure those conferences were getting: one or more sessions of General Conference would be broadcast on over 228 television stations that year, mostly because of the Choir's appearance at the conference. So someone besides Condie, McKay felt, should review what music the Choir would perform. The chairman of the committee, Apostle Mark Petersen, complained to Evans about his new assignment: "You should have been in charge of this not me," he wrote. Still Petersen had met with Condie and worked out the program, after which Condie "lost a night's sleep over it . . . and was ready to quit. I don't understand why we need to do things like this," Petersen wrote.[65]

Alongside General Conference and weekly shows—*Music and the Spoken Word* now appeared on 425 radio stations (many of them independents), thirteen TV stations, as well as short-wave and the Armed Forces Network—the Choir kept booking small-scale tours and appearances, often with only a third to a half of the Choir standing in for the whole group. The proselyting purpose for these appearances remained clear: after one 1967 concert, a local LDS Mission President wrote, "the names and addresses of those who attended were taken and catalogued for missionary follow-up."[66]

More milestones were reached in 1967 than in most years, including the Tabernacle's centennial, the 2,000th broadcast of *Music and the Spoken Word*, the 120th anniversary of the pioneers entering Utah, and the first *color* television broadcast of General Conference. But as the Tabernacle Choir's public stature grew, the Church increasingly had to confront opposition to its longtime denial of priesthood and temple privileges to African Americans. At some point, it became clear, the Choir had to deal with the issue. It had sung African American spirituals on its broadcasts for almost half a century. In December 1966, they sang backup for Mahalia Jackson on a televised holiday special. And in March 1967, RCA had even run an ad featuring the Tabernacle Choir in *Ebony* magazine. But in November 1967, a black woman asked to audition for the Choir. Condie felt he had to clear her prospective membership with the First Presidency, who balked at the request and created a new policy: no one could join the Choir who was not "temple worthy," which would proscribe blacks from the Choir only indirectly. Nevertheless, not wanting to address even this issue head on, one of McKay's counselors directed Condie to tell the woman that the Choir was not currently accepting applications.[67]

Far from signing on to the civil rights movement of the sixties, the Choir had increased its identification with conservative Americanism. In January 1969, the

Choir performed for its second Presidential inauguration, its first for a string of Republican presidents. Nixon's inaugural committee had second thoughts about using a choir that represented a church, especially one in the firing line on civil rights.[68] But by then, many radio and television stations opened their broadcast day with a recording of the Tabernacle Choir singing "The Star-Spangled Banner." John McClure summed up the situation from Columbia's point of view in a letter to Stewart in March 1968: "Thanks to the unique collaboration of our two organizations, you become increasingly each year a cultural necessity in millions of American homes." Nixon himself wrote to Stewart after the inaugural, thanking the Choir "for what you have come to mean to our country and for the sake of our country. Continue on."[69] Requests for Choir appearances at patriotic events or for commercial and political usage of their recordings increased. Pleased at the notoriety, Evans still tried to put the brakes on: "if we were to permit ourselves to be over-exposed or try to play two roles, we have reason to believe that we could lose what we have been building for over 40 years."[70]

But not everyone agreed on what they had been building. By 1969, the fortieth anniversary of the Tabernacle Choir's radio show, Condie, Evans, and Stewart seemed to be locked in an administrative contest: the conductor, with his own musical agenda and professional connections; the emcee, also an Apostle, who had been machinating Choir affairs from the broadcasts to the recordings to General Conference; and the strong-willed Choir President caught between them, constantly trying to test his authority. Beneath them, the organists, the engineers, and the tour officers constantly had to speculate about who answered to whom. And the Church Music Committee had been subverted by the new media committee that overshadowed them. The one man who could set things in order, President McKay, was failing, mentally and physically. Faced with widespread murmuring and inefficiency, McKay's Counselor Hugh Brown asked his old friend Lowell Durham for advice. Durham prepared a dismal report on the structure and dynamics of the Church's musical organization.

Condie should be let go, he urged, with assistant Jay Welch taking over (both men still employed by the University of Utah music department that Durham oversaw). Since the departure of Ormandy from the recordings, Condie had shown his inability to conduct ensembles—painfully evident in his conducting of the Philadelphia Brass (players from the Philadelphia Orchestra) on their recent *God of Our Fathers* album. Stewart, too, Durham advised, should be replaced with new blood. Stewart not only had pushed his personal vision too hard with his colleagues, but he had also started pushing his own picks for repertoire and bullying Tom Frost, McClure's counterpart at Columbia Masterworks. And, in any case, argued Durham, everyone from the Church Music Committee to the Choir's wardrobe seamstresses should accept Evans as the man in charge, by virtue of both his apostleship and his competence.

Whatever the remedies, the Choir's reputation was dwindling, Durham wrote. Where they had once sung at "elite concert halls," they now sang to "mobs adjacent to the circus calliope, as at Toronto two months ago." When Stewart was questioned about it, according to Durham, Stewart said: "Why sing to 2,000 when we can sing to 20,000? This is what the brethren want us to do!" What Durham strikingly pointed out was the ongoing tension about the Choir's aims and functions. And that went deeper than any short-term realignment of leadership.[71]

Unfortunately, nothing happened. McKay died in January 1970, four months after Durham's report. Joseph Fielding Smith succeeded McKay as President. But, nearly as old as McKay and less mentally able, he was unlikely to take on big changes with the Choir of which his wife, Jessie Evans, had once been a star soloist.

One change of the Choir's image, though, did take place: during McKay's final weeks of life the policy prohibiting blacks in the Choir succumbed to public pressure. A few weeks after the Reverend Roy Flourney in Denver called for a boycott of Tabernacle Choir records until the Church's policy on blacks changed, Marilyn Yuille was allowed to join and ended up singing at McKay's funeral in January 1970. Before January ended, another black woman, Wynetta Martin, joined; a black tenor was also poised to audition. Suddenly the Choir was ostensibly integrated—a fact the television cameras would point out for decades, almost comically giving disproportionate airtime to close-ups of black members.[72]

Nevertheless, the "colored problem," as Apostle Harold Lee called it, remained sensitive for the Choir. In mid-July 1970, Lee wrote to Stewart about that problem because he had heard rumors that the Choir, on its recent visit to Columbia, South Carolina, had not been as enthusiastically received as it should have been, perhaps because black audience members resented the Church's racial policies. Stewart denied that, assuring Lee that many "colored people" had been present in the audiences and had showed no sign of dislike, verbal or otherwise. When the concert ended, they excitedly rushed the stage alongside their white counterparts to get autographs from Evans, Condie, and Schreiner. As for "the two colored members of the Choir," Stewart wrote, they seemed happy, were well treated, and got "no indication whatever that their color made any difference. We all had a sacred mission to perform and did so to the best of our ability."[73]

The first Sunday in 1971, CBS finally gave *Music and the Spoken Word* back the five minutes it had taken for advertisements in 1960, returning it to its full "half-hour" (i.e., 28:55). Condie alerted the Choir that that extra five minutes of broadcast would mean fifteen minutes more rehearsal. At the same time, the network and the Church both worried that the change would mean a loss of stations who carried the show. That proved unfounded. In fact, the increased time was met by an increase in stations that carried the broadcast—in just the first two months, fifteen new stations began to air *Music and the Spoken Word.*[74]

Within three weeks of the time extension, Evans wrote a long letter to Condie, dated 23 February 1971, speculating on how to increase listenership even further, to "make the widest possible appeal." Evans had often written to the Choir director with the suggestion that they perform this or that piece he had recently heard. (If Condie replied, the documents seem not to have survived in Evans's files.) This was Evans's longest letter, burrowing into the very nature of Condie's choices. At the Tabernacle organ recitals, he wrote, the organists always included at least one "old melody" or "heart song." Shouldn't we include some on the broadcasts? He listed what he deemed to be apt possibilities: "The End of a Perfect Day," "Backward, Turn Backward, O Time in Your Flight," "Prayer Perfect, Not Understood," "The Old Refrain," "My Friend," "the better known Stephen Foster songs—and so many, many more." The Choir had covered the classics and contemporary works, Evans said, and had certainly done their share of hymns (although they could do more). Now, they needed to add this new "element in our repertoire," given how well such music had been received at the organ recitals. Evans then added—"if you'll pardon my provincialism"—that when he heard such songs "well and sincerely sung," he himself responded with "a bit of moistening of the eyes and a lump in the throat."[75]

By then, though, General Conference had become a cavalcade of fine choral music. On one typical Saturday in 1971, the Tabernacle Choir sang six hymns (two with the congregation) and six other full-scale pieces by the likes of Mozart, Fauré, and Randall Thompson. The Sunday morning session had three hymns (one with congregation) and five other pieces by Handel, Purcell, Mendelssohn, and others, while the afternoon session had one hymn (with the congregation) and three other pieces, including Gounod and another Mendelssohn. There was simply nowhere else on television where one could hear and see a choir perform so much of this sort of repertoire, especially without commercials—except, of course, the sermons given by LDS leaders between musical numbers.

At the same time, the Choir's recordings veered further into mass-market popular music. When Lowell Durham heard the rumor that Columbia was planning an album with the Tabernacle Choir backing Andy Williams, he wrote to new Church President Joseph Fielding Smith via Smith's wife, Jessie. Pleading for her to intercede with her husband to restore the Choir's high-toned reputation, he transcribed much of their joint appearance on KUED a decade earlier, where her husband had denounced the Choir appearing on Broadway.[76] Whether Jessie took the matter to her husband is not known. But the Choir's first and only album under Smith's presidency was, as it turned out, *Climb Every Mountain*, a collection of Broadway favorites.

The biggest setback to any unification of the Choir's ideals came that fall. On 1 November 1971, after a brief illness, Richard Evans died. Stewart tried to console the Choir by telling them that Evans had been "appointed unto death." He had a much greater work to perform on the other side. The Choir must go on without him. "There is no such thing as retrogression in the Church, only progression." But for the next four months, no one replaced him on *Music and the Spoken Word*. Instead, Allen Jensen read "spoken word" segments written by their departed leader. On 27 February 1972, the First Presidency announced the new spokesman for the broadcasts: Spencer Kinard, a KSL executive who immediately began writing and delivering his own Evans-esque messages tucked between the show's musical numbers.[77]

Smith's brief caretaker presidency ended after two and a half years. When the relatively vigorous Harold Lee took over as President in July 1972, he began the most massive reinvention of musical organization the Church had known. It included the dismantling of the post-Evans old guard of the Tabernacle.

SOFT SELL

WHEN HAROLD LEE ASCENDED to the Mormon Presidency, he ramped up the Church's musical forces, calling dozens of new personnel, most of them academics, to a new Church Music Department that replaced the old Church Music Committee. This department, which functioned under a new Music Committee of General Authorities, had its own committees and subcommittees, all charged with investigating and retooling every aspect of music in the Church, from hymnbooks to youth dances. Although the department did not directly oversee the Tabernacle Choir, it could not help but put the Choir under its aesthetic microscope. In so doing, it came up with one major recommendation: the removal of Richard Condie.

On 14 December 1973, Michael Moody, the executive secretary of the department, wrote a letter to Leslie Stone, the General Authority appointed to advise the department. Moody wrote that the Choir's morale was low, partly because of "less than desirable musical considerations." *Music and the Spoken Word* was now filled with love songs, popular songs, Broadway numbers, spirituals, and even "religious songs not in keeping with the spirit of the restored gospel." These things showed the "decline" of a great institution, not just of the Church but of the world. It was time to "take steps to restore the quality, dignity, and good spirit which has characterized our great Choir."[1]

Five days later, Harold Goodman, chair of the department, also wrote to Stone about the Choir. He reported that on a recent trip to New York, he heard "alarming concern" about the Choir from internationally renowned musicians. They, too, complained about the broadcasts veering further and further into vernacular music. Goodman hoped the Choir could return to spirituality that would appeal to "lay listeners" throughout the world, without relying so much on "popular expressions of music."[2]

With these letters in hand, on 21 December 1973 Stone drafted a letter, countersigned by Apostles Mark Petersen and Boyd Packer, addressed to the First Presidency. It referred to meetings that the signatories had had with the Presidency about the Choir, meetings in which Stone and others had questioned the Choir's choice of musical material for General Conference and especially for the radio and television broadcasts, the main media purveyor of the Church's image to the world. The broadcasts, they said, now abounded in "music about nature, love songs, ballads, serenades, etc., that could not be classified as devotional music." They specifically quoted lines from four numbers they had heard on the broadcast, whose lyrics they found particularly troublesome for their intimations of intimacy, or, in one case, blatant Catholicism:

- "Sleep thou not when affection seeks thine ear . . . When passion cries, oh my darling, open thine eyes."
- "The ancient passion wakes . . . Was that your kiss that touched me like a flame?"
- "O Shenandoah, I love your daughter, I'll take her 'cross the rollin' water . . . For seven years I courted Sally. For seven more he longed to hold her."
- "Virgin let me be protected . . . on the dreadful judgment day."

They then cited the letters from Moody and Goodman (which they attached) to show that their worries were broadly shared. The Choir was "hopefully an inspired organization" that the Church would lose if it became—echoing Clark's earlier warnings—more of a "chorus" than a "choir." The growing image of the Choir as an "entertainment" group, however "polished and competent," particularly vexed them. Then, backtracking a little, they admitted there was nothing "greatly out of order." But the "trend," they said, could be "detrimental to the influence of the Choir."[3]

Lee probably never read this last letter, if indeed it was ever sent: he died five days after it was drafted. His successor, Spencer Kimball was now the fourth man to hold the office of Church President in that many years. He was committed to the media mission of the Church. He tried hard to widen his followers' vision of proselyting to span the whole world and entwine with new technologies.[4] Radio and television would reach into realms impenetrable to door-knocking elders. And for Kimball that upped the ante on the Tabernacle Choir as missionaries. As far as the Church then could see, the Choir had seized the airwaves on its behalf. Indeed, the Choir had become a technology of its own, a well-run machine of image proclamation and reclamation. No huge rebuilds could be expected, only minor maintenance and tinkering. And that posed a problem for its conductors, who, like all conductors, often hope to remake their choirs in their own image.

In the year before Lee died, Condie and Lee's friendship had cooled. Condie had been insisting that he as conductor, not Church overseers—especially Ike Stewart—should have the final say in what, when, and how much the Choir sang. Condie's battles with Stewart had come to a head during the Choir's fall 1973 tour of Europe, in which Stewart had booked the Choir to sing in venues for as many as nine hours a day. Floods of complaints from Choir members made their way to Condie, who withstood Stewart as much as he could. "I'm sure he passed the word [about my resistance] on to President Kimball," Condie later said.[5]

Given Condie's conflicts with the Choir President, the complaints of the Music Department, and Condie's advanced age—at seventy-five, he was already the oldest Tabernacle Choir conductor ever—Kimball had to do something. After weeks of polling colleagues on suitable replacements, Kimball decided to release Condie and replace him with Jay Welch, who was the conductor of the Mormon Youth Symphony and Chorus, a secondary choir that McKay had approved in the last year of his life. On 12 June 1974, Kimball summoned Condie to his office. According to Condie, the First Presidency genially greeted him when he arrived, even though, he said, he knew that "this is it." Then, after an opening prayer, Kimball simply looked him in the eye and said perfunctorily, "Brother Condie, you are released from the Choir." Having seen the handwriting on the wall for a few months, Condie opted not to ask any questions, stood up, walked out, and muttered to himself, "That's a hell of a way to treat a man. I've given thirty-seven years of my life and worked just as hard as they work." He never recovered from what he considered this final insult.

Welch gladly stepped into the vacancy, receiving First Presidency approval to direct both the Tabernacle Choir and the Mormon Youth Symphony and Chorus, which he saw as the natural feeder group for the Tabernacle Choir, much as Stephens had used his youth choirs as training grounds for "his" Tabernacle Choir. Welch also set about revamping Choir logistics. He added Tuesday night rehearsals to the longstanding Thursday and Sunday times (though shortening the latter to forty-five minutes). He expanded the full-time Choir staff. He stopped requiring broadcast people to attend the Thursday night sessions. He reorganized and expanded the Choir staff (dress committee, stage management, executive secretary, etc.). He devised plans to use assistant and guest conductors more often—even asking the First Presidency to let Condie and Cornwall return to direct the Choir during General Conference in April 1975. He was successful in getting the First Presidency to approve a time limit to Choir membership, and was allowed to impose a twenty-five-year tenure term (raised from the ten-year limit he sought), with exemptions and extensions possible. He secured age limits, too: no members younger than thirty, none older than sixty-five.[6]

More important, and perhaps more risky for his position, he tried to deepen the broadcast repertoire, making it more serious, even academic, and featuring more tonally ambitious works by gentle modernists such as Howard Hanson. By the fall of 1974, the shift from Condie's more populist leanings on the broadcast was palpable. Welch's vision of Choir programming may have come partly from being aloof from the choral orthodoxy that typically bonded together conductors of choirs—common canon, procedures, and mutual regard—throughout the nation. New Tabernacle organist Robert Cundick summed it up well: "Jay was not a choral man, he was an orchestral man."[7]

But after only six months as conductor, Welch was forced to resign. Personality clashes and money problems had driven some intractable wedges. Choir President versus Choir conductor had been the sparring contestants in a now decades-long battle. And Welch had clashed with Stewart over authority from the outset. Russell Scott, Welch's personal assistant—an ad hoc position Welch had created without Stewart's permission—recalled that Welch "didn't have the best relations with some of the Choir officers" and did things that "didn't set well" with them. Welch did not understand that "they were still the boss," Scott said, which led to his being "released" because of "difficulties" he had with those up the ecclesiastical ladder. One of the difficulties was about money. In November 1974, the Church Auditing Department pored through the books Welch had been keeping for the Mormon Youth Symphony and Chorus. Whether through sloppiness or malfeasance on Welch's part, improprieties showed up that the auditors reported.[8]

On Thursday, 12 December 1974, Welch conducted the Choir at the annual First Presidency Christmas Program. The next day, President Kimball left for a trip to Mexico. Welch conducted the Choir broadcast on 15 December, the day before Kimball was due to return. At the end of the broadcast, Welch read a simple statement to the Choir: "Because of a convergence of personal problems which I cannot otherwise resolve, I have found it necessary to submit to the First Presidency my resignation as director of the Tabernacle Choir, effective immediately, and they have graciously accepted it. This has been done after considerable discussion of the circumstances involved." As he walked out, Stewart announced to the stunned Choir members that assistant conductor Jerold Ottley would be acting conductor till Welch was formally replaced. Most of the Choir understood what that meant: the odds were high that Ottley was about to succeed Welch.

Three days later the Choir performed its annual Christmas concert, which Welch had rehearsed but Ottley now conducted. At 10 A.M. the next day, Thursday, 19 December, Welch's wife came to the First Presidency alone to discuss with them what had just happened. President Kimball wrote of the meeting only that she "spoke highly" of her husband and that the Presidency "comforted her and assured her of our love and interest in her and in her lovely family and in Jay." Moments after she left at 10:30, they welcomed Ottley into their office to review his assignment.

The Monday after his announcement to the Choir, though, Welch had met with his mentor and boss at the University of Utah, Lowell Durham. In what Durham said at the time was a ninety-minute monologue, Welch unburdened himself. Durham then wrote to a friend that Welch's tale "is quite a lengthy one and could be misinterpreted if condensed." But Kimball's decision was final and irrevocable. Since the Church had made a nondisclosure agreement with Welch, he told Durham that if Durham wrote about any of what Welch had divulged, "remember you can't quote me." Welch would now return as a full-time faculty member at the university, although the Department of Music had already hired a replacement. He would also establish the Jay Welch Chorale, a smaller, non-university choir that soon sparked contention when Tabernacle Choir members began moonlighting in it.[9]

Twenty-one years later, Welch would publicly say only that "I got sick. It got to be too much to handle. So I asked for a release and they gave me one." At the time, though, those closest to him spoke of a far more "complicated" set of tensions with his overseers. Condie put it more bluntly, saying simply, "they had to put him out."[10]

Ottley's career as Tabernacle Choir director began with a simple premise: he never wanted to be the director of the Tabernacle Choir. He didn't believe in aspiring to callings in the Church—a common aspect of humility Mormons teach—and, having sung in the Choir for years, he too "didn't like the feel of the arena. It was too hectic, too big, too uncontrollable." He also disliked the uniformity of tone and style that Condie had promulgated. If that was the way the Choir was supposed to be, he thought, he wasn't interested.[11]

Like his two predecessors, Ottley was also on the faculty of the public University of Utah, instead of the now-estimable Church school, BYU. The two schools had a longstanding Church-state rivalry. And two of BYU's brightest musical luminaries had indeed migrated north to the state school—Leroy Robertson and choral conductor Newell Weight, who at one time McKay had nominated to conduct the Tabernacle Choir. But Condie and Welch's dual-salary arrangement with the University of Utah, machinated by Richard Evans, had primed the pump for conductors of the Choir. If the Church had pushed back against the state orchestra, the Utah Symphony, it welcomed the subventing of its own choral conductors with state educational money, at least for the present. The Church tried to maneuver another half-and-half split with the University of Utah. But the university, for the time being, would only let the Church get Ottley quarter-time, the other three quarters going to university departmental administration and teaching.[12]

When he suddenly took up the baton—even as an "acting" stand-in for Welch—some Choir members were "quite belligerent," Ottley said, angry about his swift ascension on the back of their beloved leader Welch. Welch had been, in Ottley's estimation, "the most charismatic conductor the Choir ever had."[13] Many members hoped Welch would be back soon and that Ottley was a mere caretaker. But the general Mormon acceptance of succession, the orderly, unquestioned transfer of authority, was so ingrained, that most Choir members accepted the replacement as pliantly as they would a new bishop.

Still, Ottley recalled that "a cloud hung over my head all the time." His conductorship felt adversarial, as though he were a new stepparent. After weeks of doing a creditable, but not overambitious, almost surrogate conductorship, there were "not too many defections." The Choir soon succumbed to both his charms and technique. After almost five months in titular limbo, the "acting" was removed from his title, prompted by the University of Utah's need to clarify its salary schedule for the coming year, which was now disrupted by Welch's return to full-time faculty status. The university initially kept Ottley on as half-time and the Church as three-quarter time, although Ottley felt he essentially had two full-time jobs. After a year of this arrangement, the university made him an adjunct and the Church hired him full-time.[14]

The First Presidency also called Don Ripplinger, a BYU choral educator, as an assistant conductor.

To make the new order complete, Church leaders released Ike Stewart as Choir President, announcing it at General Conference as the result of a letter from Stewart's doctor. Stewart had left his own trail of ill will, yet had presided over what most people would call the Choir's "golden" era. In his place, Kimball installed Oakley Evans, a former executive for J. C. Penney who had been in training with the ailing Stewart for months. Ottley was grateful for the change, feeling that, although he personally had gotten along with Stewart, he felt that Stewart had "molded some of the musical destiny of the Choir perhaps beyond what a president should do." For his part, Stewart reflected with pride that, because of his frugality, "when I left, the Choir had a large sum of finances in the treasury."[15] Among Evans's first assignments was to develop with Ottley a more systematic way of ascertaining the personal rectitude, sobriety, and morality of Choir members.[16]

The Choir had now become, a year and a half after he had taken charge of the First Presidency, the Tabernacle Choir according to Spencer Kimball. President Evans explained the working philosophy he and Kimball shared: "We had to evaluate where we could do the most good for the Church, because the Choir's main purpose was to be a tool to help spread the Gospel and build good will." Musical excellence, when achieved, was only a tool of that tool.[17]

Despite his earlier resistance to the job, Ottley now took it up with zeal. But the uncertain half-year trial period before his official appointment had robbed him of what would have been the customary honeymoon period with the Choir. He later said he felt "choked" by the circumstances, aggravated by the First Presidency's asking him to "soft pedal" innovation with the Choir. As if to assert his purview as conductor, he began allowing the Choir to sing some pieces with their original Latin texts, whether Renaissance motets or Verdi's *Requiem*.[18] But larger conflicts over repertoire were looming.

Back in 1967, lower-level General Authority Boyd Packer had given an address titled "Worthy Music, Worthy Thoughts." In it, he offered an antidote for evil thoughts that might poison the mind: sing a hymn to yourself. The sacred words would crowd other thoughts off of the "stage" in which thoughts appear as "characters" in the play of one's life. After becoming an Apostle when McKay died, Packer reiterated this message at October 1973's General Conference, whose proceedings were published to the entire Church. Packer's message led to a kind of behavioral folklore, especially among Mormon youth (and more specifically among temptation-beset young male missionaries), in which one needed to store hymns in the mind, making them part of one's everyday spiritual canon. This new principle, in which hymns had an almost talismanic power, gradually corresponded with increased—and eventually exclusive—use of hymns in the Tabernacle Choir's General Conference repertoire. A hymn could be arranged, but the tune had to be recognizable, familiar, and the words intact.

As though extending and broadening that sermon, Packer delivered a major new message on Church music during Ottley's trial period with the Choir. In February 1975, Packer spoke at BYU under the rubric "The Arts and the Spirit of the Lord." Spending most of his text on the requisites of "appropriate" music, some of his remarks seemed clearly to take aim at what the Choir and its last three conductors had largely pursued in General Conferences and broadcasts during the previous few decades. "Very frequently," he said, "when our musicians, particularly the more highly trained among them, are left to do what they want to do, they perform in such a way as to call attention to themselves and their ability. They do this rather than give prayerful attention to what will inspire. . . . To use the hymns of the Restoration for such a presentation, they feel, will not demonstrate their full capacities." Musicians may ask, Packer said, if he wanted the same hymns over and over, with nothing new introduced in Church meetings. "No, that is not what I would want, but it is close." He condemned any Mormon choir conductor who wanted "to win the acclaim of the world. He does not play to the Lord but to other musicians." In what seemed loud echoes of the arguments made against musical literacy in the Church's formative years, the speech created an unease in Mormon music making that lingered at all levels for decades. Although Packer did not mention the Tabernacle Choir by name, he spoke of music in "conferences" and knew well that, for the last century, this Choir had been the model for all other choirs in the Church.[19]

Ottley, though, occupied himself less with repertoire than with efficiency. Whereas the previous new conductors routinely reauditioned the Choir, Ottley slid past the potential rancor of such confrontations by changing the structure and terms of Choir membership. Some singers were over eighty, had been members of the Choir for more than fifty years, and sang—when they came at all—with a wide, unblending vibrato. Ottley proposed to the First Presidency a continuation of the age and length-of-service agreements Welch had gotten. The presidency, surprisingly, countered with even more conservative numbers: an age limit of fifty-five and a duration of fifteen years. After discussion, the two sides split the difference: Choir members had to quit after twenty years or when they turned sixty, whichever came first. Ottley and Evans also codified rehearsal attendance requirements (80 percent), assigned seating (with new members starting in the back), and exacting criteria for leaves of absence. In January 1978 the policies were delivered to Choir members in a three-sheet handout, the prototype of what would become, over the next twenty years, a full-fledged handbook.

Ottley's greatest structural innovation may have been the recruitment of his wife, JoAnn, as "Vocal Coach" for the Choir. Although family ties in the Choir had always been common, with as many as a half-dozen family members simultaneously serving in the Choir, no conductor's spouse had taken part like this before. But Jerold and JoAnn, both expert singers, had duetted for years, even in Tabernacle events. So now, while Jerold programmed, conducted, and made policy, JoAnn set up a virtual school in which she could train and coach singers, troubleshoot vocal defects, and even exhort them with memos, as in this one: "It seems too many get in vocal trouble by over-singing. It is easy to feel that in order to contribute fully, one should be 'heard' and in doing so, damages his voice and interrupts the blend. Actually we should not hear ourselves so much as feel ourselves in this big group."[20]

For his part, Jerold Ottley was determined to break free of the Choir's "one big locomotive kind of sound" and let it mold its sound to variant styles.[21] He wanted to tailor the group's sound to the particular styles of the pieces they sang—not wanting Bach and Brahms, for example, to sound alike, as they had under Condie.[22] He also wanted to extend the repertoire further into the present. Bernstein's *Chichester Psalms*, for example, became a favorite. And in the fall of 1977, Ottley even had the Choir sing its first truly avant-garde piece on the broadcast (Egil Hovlund's *Saul*). As part of Ottley's retooling, he played with different seating arrangements, finding that four eight-voice groups (two on each part) in each wing of the choir loft sounded best to him—though it did hamper the mastery of polyphonic music, admittedly not one of the Choir's staples. With all the structural, logistical, and timbral torquing that Ottley undertook, his transformation of the Choir's sound took about ten years.[23]

As the United States approached its bicentennial, though, seismic cultural changes shook the Tabernacle Choir. Nixon, at both of whose inaugurations the Choir had sung, had resigned in shame, and the nation was about to elect a president, Jimmy Carter, who would be more at home with the "country church" group the Tabernacle Choir had once been. And the Church itself had a new President who was reshaping the highest levels of Mormon administration, expanding the Church's international front, increasing its missionary force, bolstering financial and other support for Native Americans—the putative descendants of Book of Mormon peoples—and moving toward opening the priesthood to African Americans, whom some Church leaders still considered members of the race of Cain.

The recorded voice of Mormons was also being rocked. Columbia Records was curtailing its classical line and curbing repertoire into its profit margins, now almost entirely in popular music. John McClure, once the point man for the Choir at Columbia, had even argued that the sophistication of modern rock made it a valid aesthetic rival to the classical tradition. Every three years, the Choir had to renegotiate its contract with the label, and pressure was high to become more and more of a richly toned version of Columbia's Mitch Miller Singers, regularly delivering collections of sing-along favorites. Condie had been faulted by the Church Music Committee for veering too far into popular music. But record buyers counted on the Choir for just that. As a brand name, the Mormon Tabernacle Choir had long since dropped out of classical respectability, although they were still, along with Bernstein and the New York Philharmonic, effectively bankrolling the Columbia Masterworks line. "Ormandy and Bernstein's lighter works," Clive Davis later wrote, "were paying for nearly everything."[24] But the Tabernacle Choir's rival Robert Shaw had essentially dismissed them as a serious group. And the best-known musical representative of the Church was no longer its Choir, but the Osmonds, two of whom, Donny and Marie, began airing their hit television show on the American Broadcasting Company (ABC) network during the bicentennial year. The Tabernacle Choir appeared as guests on the *Osmond Christmas Show* in December 1976.[25]

In 1975, record labels had been scrambling to come up with products for the potential boom market of the upcoming U.S. bicentennial the following year. "American" was the new hallmark for proposals. That year, Columbia Masterworks director Tom Frost notified Ottley that the Choir was behind in its two-LPs-a-year contractual commitment to the label. Since the Tabernacle Choir had already done its share of Americana for the label, this seemed a good time to launch a new set for the upcoming national anniversary.

Determined to reclaim at least limited acreage on the musical high ground, Ottley negotiated with Frost to split the Choir's recordings henceforth between what the label needed for sales and the Choir needed for dignity. Two albums a year, yes, but one of them would be what Ottley wanted, the other what the label wanted. For this round they would do the bicentennial LP—what became the

LP called *Yankee Doodle Dandies*—but also an album of previously unrecorded American works, many of which the Choir had already performed under Condie but never taped.

Whether fortuitous or strategic, Ottley's plan was inspired. Goddard Lieberson, who had produced the *Mormon Pioneers* set ten years earlier, had also begun the Modern American Music series at the label in the 1950s, a series that was later extended into the Music of Our Time series championed in the late 1960s through early 1970s by John McClure. McClure, in turn, not only had produced some of the Tabernacle Choir's recordings in the 1960s, but was now Frost's boss, sitting in the position Goddard Lieberson formerly held. Columbia's 20th Century choral stable, led by the Gregg Smith Singers, favored high modernist works by Stravinsky and, lately, Ives, who was about to become the maverick darling of the bicentennial. An album of unrecorded new, slightly more accessible, American choral music at once fit the bicentennial market and filled a niche in the label's contemporary classical brand, however marginalized it was becoming.

The Choir's new LP, *A Jubilant Song*, appeared just after Christmas 1975. It mildly gratified critics and fans, who heard a new Choir: leaner, younger, crisper in diction, and slightly more progressive in material. The *American Record Guide* noted that none of the works on the album was "difficult," "trying," "obscure," or "forbidding," but the fresh programming overcame the Choir's somewhat "bland" manner of performance.[26] *High Fidelity* also noted the "very conservative" modernism of the collection but complimented the new sound of the Choir under Ottley, particularly the diction and the recording's engineering. "If this sort of material interests you, I'd urge you to buy your copy promptly. It is exactly the sort of thing that has a very short life span, and it would be foolhardy to predict that it will be available a year from now."[27]

Perhaps a more potent side effect of the Bicentennial was the official rapprochement of the Tabernacle Choir and the Utah Symphony. A bicentennial event in Utah initially led them to combine forces. But they then joined forces on a Columbia recording of war songs, with the Utah Symphony again being billed as the Columbia Symphony. In 1978, the two groups fulfilled Leroy Robertson's first intentions when they performed and recorded for Columbia Robertson's Book of Mormon oratorio, at which CBS Records (Columbia's new moniker) initially balked, then relented. The recording sold moderately well but served as a huge threshold in the exporting of "serious" Mormon music into the larger listening world.[28]

As of October 1980, the Church stopped sustaining any of the Choir personnel in General Conference. They gave no reason, just dropping the personnel from its list of people to be sustained by the vote of Mormons at General Conference. Apparently the Choir was now a curious semiprofessional appendage to the Church, no longer an "official" emissary, let alone auxiliary, but a reliable soft-sell media outlet.

That same year, the Church (through BYU) produced a half-hour television feature that enshrined the Choir in a new way. *Mr. Krueger's Christmas* featured the semilegendary Jimmy Stewart in the title role as an elderly janitor whose Christmas fantasies included conducting the Tabernacle Choir in the song "Sleigh Ride," which they sang on the *White Christmas* Choir album, which Krueger, in the show, had just put on his turntable. The Choir could be heard in that and other underscoring of the program, which is still broadcast on television around the world each Christmas. In equal parts a video Christmas card, a long ad for the 1977 *White Christmas* album, and a slightly unnerving melodrama about an old man's infatuation with a little blonde girl (played by the director's daughter), *Mr. Krueger's Christmas* sought to reaffirm and expand the Choir's reigning role in America's media Christmas, a role it had earned largely through the eight popular Christmas albums it had released over a twenty-year span.

A month after *Krueger's* first airing, the inauguration of Ronald Reagan gave the Choir its now pat nickname, America's Choir, boosting its quasi-populist image. They sang during the opening ceremony of the inaugural at the Lincoln Memorial—organized primarily by Osmond Entertainment—then rode a seventy-foot float in the inaugural parade, stopping (per Nancy Reagan's request) at the presidential review box to sing "The Battle Hymn of the Republic."[29] After the inauguration, the number of broadcast outlets for the Choir instantly jumped by 25 percent.[30] In February 1981, the Choir released an album of Walt Disney tunes. In March they sang backup for John Denver at a concert at the University of Utah. This was the Choir of the new, capitalist-populist America, neither a leader nor a champion of elitist art. The vernacular for which Condie had been fired arguably became, if not the Choir's native tongue, then its conversational one. The Church (and CBS) needed the widest audience, and that meant one disinclined to the elitism of "masterworks." What Alfred Frankenstein had discerned in 1941—the Choir falling "victim to the fetish of giving the public what it wants, to the detriment of more significant values"—had reached its apotheosis.

If the Choir's repertoire had turned motley and its schedule become a whirlwind, its summer tour of Europe in June 1982 showed that the organizing of such an excursion had become de rigueur. The planning and execution broke down into three categories that the Choir President—in this case, Evans—had to manage. First was financial: the group had to raise money to bankroll the tour so singers wouldn't have to pay their own way, and it had to work with Choir members' employers to grant them time off for the tour. Second was logistical: booking concert halls; contracting with concert agencies; chartering planes; booking a cruise ship, trains, buses, and hotel rooms for 550+ people (Choir and guests). The third was promotional: arranging for radio and television broadcasts of the concerts as well as planning receptions and luncheons for the Choir (and all its staff), with invitations to special guests in each city.[31]

This latest tour made more friends for the Church abroad, impressed some critics, and was immediately followed by a CBS gala honoring the Choir's fifty years on that network. But the tour had also allowed the Choir a refuge from the U.S. spotlight. Like Reagan and others in the conservative counterrevolution, the Church sternly opposed the Equal Rights Amendment, first approved by Congress in 1972 and now, via a legislative extension, in its final month of possible ratification. In addition to speaking and publishing against the amendment, Church leaders had organized Church members into rallies, door-to-door campaigns, and media events in key hold-out states such as Illinois. And for two years, protesters had intermittently picketed Temple Square and other Mormon sites, opposing the Church's stance on this issue. Like many observers, these protesters had the sense that the Tabernacle Choir was, in fact, that of Reagan's America, minstrels of a right-wing political hierarchy into which the new U.S. president had, in effect, anointed them.

When the October 1982 General Conference arrived, the ERA had failed, much to the Church's jubilation. Nevertheless, General Conference seats failed to fill, partly because high fuel costs hampered travel to the site, partly because local chapels now had satellite dishes to pick up broadcasts of the meetings, and perhaps because of the lingering unpleasantness of the recent anti-Mormon confrontations on Temple Square. The Choir soldiered on, increasingly confining its General Conference music to simple hymns, some arranged, some straight out of the congregational book.

For the next year and a half, the Choir continued its by-now pro forma round of duties and achievements: recordings, broadcasts, concerts, funerals, conferences, and the occasional commemoration or award. But the seeming alliance between the Church and the federal government—its sworn enemy a century earlier—had a symbolic moment when, in November 1983, Lieutenant Colonel Craig Jessop, a former member of the Choir under both Welch and Ottley, brought his military group the Singing Sergeants to the Tabernacle to sing for the Choir. It was a tender epilogue to the Reagan inaugural as well as the forecast of the Choir's future: Jessop would eventually succeed Ottley as the Choir's conductor. Six weeks after Jessop brought the Singing Sergeants to the Tabernacle, Ted Koppel interviewed Ottley on ABC's late-night show *Nightline*. But because the network station owners in Utah thought Koppel's show too heady, they didn't have it on their schedule. So no one in the state saw Ottley talking up the Church's musical missionaries on national television two days before Christmas.

By the mid-1980s, in lore and cliché at least, the Tabernacle Choir had become the main hub of U.S. choral culture (something Ottley had begun to realize when he attended his first national American Choral Directors Association meeting as the Choir's conductor in 1977).[32] Ottley had moved the Choir's sound from, as he put it, "opulent" (under Condie) to more "flexible" and "mobile."[33] When one referred to an ideal or standard or even Brand X Choir, the odds were that the Tabernacle Choir would be a default model. It was the happy stereotype of choirs. It had that reputation even though it did not resemble other choirs: it was the bull—or sacred cow—in the choral china shop. If you loved choir music, you had to hear them. If you conducted choral music, you wanted to conduct them. If you wanted to book a choir, they topped your list. If you wanted to film a choir, no other was as photogenic.

Along the way, because he conducted the Tabernacle Choir on CBS television each week, Ottley became the most recognized Mormon in the world, far more so than the Church President or Apostles. Still, his conductorship qualified the ways in which he was recognized. He was, for example, on vacation in Los Angeles with JoAnn and went into a little store to see if it had any good china. As they were digging around in the inventory, a Japanese American man tapped him on the shoulder and asked, "Are you Mr. Ottley?" He said, "Yes, I am." The man said, "I thought I recognized the back of your head."[34]

In their busyness, the Choir exemplified the Utah state symbol, the busy honeybee. In the single month of May 1984, for example, they entertained Danny Kaye, who conducted them in rehearsal; did a mini-concert for the Rotarian Western Region Convention; were filmed by a Japanese documentary crew; were recorded for a Florida Disney theater soundtrack; gave a concert for the Boy Scout National Council Meeting; and entertained the ambassador from New Zealand—all in addition to their regular rehearsing and broadcasting of multiple numbers each week.

But velocity always needs direction. So, in an era of internal social research and surveys about Church habits, the Tabernacle Choir undertook its own audience survey to learn what, if any, new directions the broadcasts should take. Mormon social psychologist Stan Weed—an employee of the Church's research division who would soon become a national leader in abstinence-centered sex education—designed a survey to be given to live audiences at six Sunday broadcasts in the Tabernacle during the summer of 1986.[35] The survey concerned three things: what type of person attends a broadcast, how do they react to it, and what outcomes result from the experience?

The survey had two sections, containing a total of twenty-two to twenty-five questions, depending on which of at least three versions of the survey one took. The questions surveyed such things as the audiences' religious background, their opinions about the broadcast generally (and certain facets of it in particular), why they decided to come on this day, and so forth. On a scale of one to five (1 = not at all true, 3 = somewhat true, 5 = very true), the survey participants would assess statements such as these:

THE CHOIR IN TODAY'S BROADCAST
—touched my heart.
—was enjoyable.
—was religiously uplifting.
—was boring.
—was too old fashioned.
—was what I expected.
—made me feel more positive toward the Mormons.
—would have been more enjoyable if the Choir sang without the organ accompanying it.
—was the kind of music I typically enjoy listening to.

In all, four thousand people took the survey. Only 3 percent of them were Utahns, with the rest from around the United States. Ninety-four percent were white, with an average age of fifty-three, and three-fourths were college-educated—this last characteristic was well above the national norm. Two thirds were Protestants (especially Lutheran and Methodist). How many said they were likely to change religions soon? A disappointing 4 percent.

The audiences came for a variety of reasons, mostly musical, they said (78 percent), cultural (71 percent), and architectural, (i.e., interest in the historic building, 57 percent). The top five musical preferences?—66 percent classical,

60 percent gospel, 59 percent big band, 42 percent country and western, and 21 percent rock and roll. Four out of five of them, however, had very positive reactions to what they heard in the broadcast, with the organ solos slightly less "uplifting" than the Choir. They gave Spencer Kinard high marks for his messages, with only 6 percent saying he was "boring."

As Weed and Oakley Evans's successor, Wendell Smoot, told the Choir on 29 January 1987, the survey showed that attending the Tabernacle broadcast made people slightly more likely to recommend attendance to friends, much more likely to go to a concert if the Tabernacle Choir came to their city, and not one iota more likely to convert to Mormonism. Weed explained that "in thirty minutes it's difficult to change one's religious philosophies." He recommended not changing the broadcast, except maybe to highlight more traditional, familiar hymns and religious music, as indeed Richard Evans had done in his day. "Our 'soft-sell' is impressing lots of people," Smoot said. But the audiences were "very select and not like the average convert, whose age is 18–36." The survey, that is, had confirmed what almost everyone's instinct told them: this was a show for older white Protestant audiences, who lacked much incentive to jump the religious fence.

The Choir, though, was at heart a musical unit, even more than a proselyting force. They performed in real time but turned out a constant string of albums in a variety of formats. Sacred music, whether great or merely serviceable, still dominated their repertoire. In 1987, amid a long, general slide in classical record sales, corporate shakeups, and realignments—including CBS's sale to Sony—and some "knock-down, drag-outs" between Ottley and CBS Records producers, the label and the Choir broke ties.[36] The Choir and the label were still receiving, as they had under Condie, letters describing how Choir recordings had helped console people in wartime and illness, after natural disasters, or amid emotional skirmishes, from death to divorce. Ottley's achievements in recording, though, still came in the shadow of Condie's. In 1985, for example, eleven years after Condie's departure, First Presidency counselor Gordon Hinckley publicly presented Condie (who would die that December) with two new Gold Records the RIAA had awarded to the Choir under his direction (both of them for Christmas albums). The accolades from Columbia accrued to the whole Choir, of course, whose past life was indivisible from its current incarnation. But the Choir now had to roam among other labels for the next decade, recording in fits and spurts with London/Decca, Argo, Telarc, and the Church's own media company, Bonneville International.

In 1988, though, a select group drawn mostly from the Choir's ranks made a recording that would be played more often and heard by more listeners than virtually any of their previous recordings. In 1955, the Church had begun using film for depicting portions of their sacred temple narrative, which included, as Apostle James Talmage put it, depictions of "the most prominent events of the creative period, the condition of our first parents . . . their disobedience and consequent expulsion from [Eden], their condition in the lone and dreary world," and so forth.[37] The film was remade in 1966, 1969, and 1974. Then, for its next remake in 1988, the First Presidency and quorum of Twelve Apostles tentatively approved adding a musical soundtrack. The film's director, Peter Johnson, hired composer Kurt Bestor to write what became a Hollywood-style score with echoes of everything from Ravel to the title theme for *Star Trek*. Throughout the score, Bestor included wordless choral singing à la "Neptune" in Holst's *The Planets*. To record this singing, he hired twenty-four singers drawn mostly from the Tabernacle Choir, then "stacked" the vocals electronically to get a fuller sound. "I wanted a British Choir sound," Bestor writes, "devoid of all the vibrato that is usually found in some American Choirs (and the Tabernacle Choir in those days)." The film soon began showing in LDS temples and since then has played hundreds of times a day, six days a week, for twenty-five years to millions of temple goers. In the process, after decades of reaching out to the world at large, the Tabernacle Choir finally, via a film soundtrack, penetrated the *ritual* core of its own faith.

The United States had great centrifugal force for its official choir. Kimball had wanted the Church's limbs to thrust further and further outward from the Church's homeland. From 1979 to 1993, the Choir, accompanied by the General Authorities, spouses, tech personnel, and others, toured parts of Asia, South America, the South Pacific, all sectors of Europe, and even Israel, where the Choir avoided the mistake another choir had committed in 1992 when it performed *Messiah* to an incensed audience. (The Tabernacle Choir performed Berlioz's *Requiem*, at the request of the Jerusalem Symphony, which accompanied them.) They even sang one concert before a Palestinian audience, prompting one of the hearers to say, "You have done more for the cause of peace in our country in the short time that you have been here than our negotiators have done in fifty years of talking."[38] Funding for all these tours came from royalties, concert earnings, and donors, most of whom could channel their funds through the Presiding Bishop's office or subsidiaries such as the LDS Foundation, which alone raised a half million dollars for the Australia/New Zealand tour in 1988.[39] As for logistics, every international tour, Smoot explained, was like transporting a small town across oceans and landscapes.[40]

Each tour had its particular charms and ambience, of course, but some tours seemed more overtly strategic than others. On 3 June 1990, for example, Hinckley announced a two-week, thirteen-concert tour of (mostly Eastern) Europe to a year later. This tour would be something of an aesthetic gauntlet thrown down: these would be some of the toughest audiences the Choir had ever faced, he said, because they sat in the deepest regions of Western musical sophistication. "You will never sing, I think, before more critical audiences," he said, "particularly [in] the eastern nations." The purpose? It was an "unprecedented opportunity, not only to bring credit to the Church, but also to our nation and the nations of the west."[41]

It was part hype, part challenge. In the following weeks, Ottley and Smoot echoed Hinckley's musical call to arms. Smoot was understandably general. This tour was designed, in effect, to show how much Mormon culture exceeded the parochialism people may have assumed about it. Ottley had "raised the Choir to the level where we can sing the music which will bring credit to the Church." Ottley, in turn, told the Choir that, although he had often heard them referred to as the Lord's Choir—a term Ike Stewart had often used in selling the Choir's uniqueness—"I can't say we have reached that goal." Ottley quoted eloquent reviews of the Choir from its 1911 East Coast tour and openly wished "that could be said again" (though he neglected to wonder to what extent the eloquence of music criticism itself had declined). Ottley then declared open season on vocal flaws in the Choir, promising a series of memos to the group addressing good vocal health, "correct modulated vibrato," a thorough knowledge of "linguatone" memorization, and so forth. "Complete involvement must be given. You can't pick and choose."[42]

But from the Church's point of view, this tour was to prime the pump for missionaries in Eastern Europe, a glittering new field of potential converts since Communism had collapsed there in the late 1980s. The First Presidency and Twelve Apostles had deliberated on this tour for two years and now expected massive goodwill through choral music. One major distraction along the way: in October 1990 the Choir's post–Richard Evans spokesman, fifty-year-old Kinard, was placed on "medical leave" for "stress-management problems" after his too-affectionate relationship with a single, twenty-four-year-old KSL anchorwoman came to light. "I expect to be back," he said. But within three weeks, he had resigned from both the broadcast and KSL. "I could no longer represent LDS

Church standards," he later explained. The Church auditioned new spokesmen for the *Spoken Word*, finally settling on another former KSL newsman, Lloyd Newell.[43]

Despite a successful tour—which had enormous saturation in European media, almost entirely glowing reviews, and a string of tearful, wildly applauding audiences—the Choir returned home to face a more mundane reaction from the nation that often treated it as more of a populist novelty than a profound arts group. One newspaper article in 1991 began with this cheery paragraph: "You don't need to be a Leonard Bernstein, a Jimmy Stewart or the nation's premier choral leader, Robert Shaw, to guest-conduct the world renowned Mormon Tabernacle Choir. Even Snoopy, Walt Disney's Donald Duck, and a 2½-year-old boy have led the 325-voice singing constellation." In 1994, a *Deseret News* headline read, "Shamu Makes 'Moonlight' Splash with Choir," referring to Sea World's mascot who was in town as part of the Great Salt Lake Boy Scout-O-Rama.[44]

Nevertheless, despite moments of novelty (or oddity), Choir minutes of the 1990s depict an avalanche of assorted events, visits, salutations from dignitaries, and announcements, not just of impending Choir duties and opportunities, but births, deaths, illnesses, retirements, all the things that one would announce in a Church meeting or even a family gathering. It was as though all Choir members, who had full lives outside of the relatively small percentage of time in the Choir each week, spent that Choir time in another world, another life that did not so much parallel their non-Choir life as match it, not in time but in mass and concentration, compression, intensity. To attempt to summarize it becomes confounding indeed.

Some moments stand out, as we have seen, though differently to different observers. But sometimes it is the less obvious that pull together strands from the Choir's history. Consider, for example, just one happenstance in 1995: Oliver Stone's *Nixon*, a cinematic survey of the now disgraced president, included in its soundtrack the Choir (under Ottley) singing the "Battle Hymn" and "Shenandoah." Both songs, of course, evoked the rustic America of Nixon's Ohio youth and even the Choir's presence at his inauguration. But the "Battle Hymn" arrangement was not the Choir's celebrated version by the American Peter Wilhousky but a newer one by the British composer John Rutter. And "Shenandoah" was one of the songs that twenty-two years earlier the Church Music Committee had singled out as breaching the Choir's *sacred* mission and eroding their trust in Condie. The movie was not only tough in its treatment of Nixon but was rated R by the Motion Picture Association of America. Movies with that rating were to be avoided by Mormons, according to Church President Ezra Taft Benson (Kimball's immediate successor), who had served in Eisenhower's cabinet when Nixon was vice president. And, as a touch of irony, the recording was owned by London Records and licensed by Polygram, so that British corporations presided over the recorded image of America's Choir.

Meanwhile, in the same year that Stone's *Nixon* was released, the Choir got the most scholarly attention it had yet received, though not the kind it would have courted. Beyond the promotional materials it published itself, the generally laudatory articles in Church and trade magazines, and the mixed bag of concert and record reviews, little academic attention had focused on the Choir. Cornwall's 1957 book (*Century of Singing*) had a pretense of it but remained mostly a memoir with a miscellany of facts from previous eras dropped in for context. Two coffee table books honoring the Choir's golden anniversary on radio appeared in 1979, one from BYU's in-house press, and the other from Harper & Row, authored by a young Sol Hurok booking agent, Jeff Calman. My own 1989 book, *Mormonism and Music: A History*, surveyed the Choir in the larger context suggested by its title. And in 1992, a learned book on the Choir's first and perhaps greatest hero, Evan Stephens, was self-published by its author, Ray Bergman, after winning the Utah Arts Council Writing Competition award for biography. But it was Michael Quinn's 1995 scholarly outing of Stephens as a case of winked-at "same-sex attraction" among pioneer Mormons that dragged the Choir into one of the most contentious realms of Mormon (and evangelical) rhetoric at the close of the twentieth century.[45]

Many people presumed that Stephens was gay because of his lifelong bachelorhood, seeming indifference to female companionship, and avid courting of young male roommates and protégés. Quinn, however, inferred coded messages to real and would-be partners in Stephens's writings. Despite, or perhaps because of, Quinn's eminence as an award-winning academic, defenders of Stephens fought back. Ray Bergman, Rhett James, and George Mitton (descendant of one of Stephens's alleged male partners) all faulted Quinn for sloppy handling of evidence and a blatant agenda (Quinn himself had come out a few years earlier). James and Mitton published an eighty-page online rebuttal to Quinn, insisting that—in an age-old defense of perceived homosexuality—Stephens behaved as he did because of an earlier lost (female) love.[46] And in Stephens's day, homosexuality—or as Victorians called it, "the sin that dare not speak its name"—may well have been in a "don't ask, don't tell" mode, even among Mormons, particularly if one followed the Mormon Creed, which was "let every man mind his own business." Intimate relations were so confusing in the days of polygamy that people often maintained an "I don't want to know" stance. But in Stephens's case, the fact that his leaders possibly *did* know that he would never be drawn into polygamy was a big plus for putting him at the head of the Choir in the very year that Woodruff had issued the Manifesto.

The Choir, of course, transcended such squabbles, both for their irrelevance to and distraction from the tasks at hand. Consider the year 1996. The Choir began with a full plate of broadcast, concert, and recording pieces to rehearse—hymn arrangements; works by Handel, Brahms, Copland, and Stephen Foster; even an Israeli folk song—all these in their first rehearsal of the year. They appeared on CBS' *This Morning* show. They sang for funerals, hosted guests at the Tabernacle, including visiting conductors and choirs who performed with them on *Music and the Spoken Word*. They sang in General Conferences, which Ottley told them in April was "the most important work we do." They launched another survey of rehearsal and broadcast audiences. They recorded their first full album of black spirituals, all arranged by Moses Hogan, who guest conducted. They sang for the Utah Arts Festival, for the rededication of the This Is the Place monument, and for assorted other commemorations and conferences. They did a small tour to San Francisco for the sesquicentennial of the arrival of the ship *Brooklyn*, which had sailed a group of New York Mormons around Cape Horn and enabled them to settle in the California Bay Area in 1846. And, among their most curious tasks that year, they had to confront the challenge of the diet drug combination Fen-phen. Women in the Choir were losing weight rapidly, and then usually regaining it. This was playing havoc with the harried Choir seamstresses, who, after taking in a Choir dress, couldn't let it back out if weight returned.[47]

At the end of 1996, as usual, they sang for the First Presidency Christmas Devotional, where Hinckley noted how "very expensive" the Choir had become and yet, in 1998 would be going on another European tour. Although he didn't announce it, this would be the now-traditional swan song European tour for the Choir's conductor.

The tour would span twenty-one days in June through July, with stops in London, Brussels, Geneva, Turin, Rome, Marseille, Barcelona, Madrid, and Lisbon—but no stops in Eastern Europe. The President of the Europe West Area of the Church, Dieter Uchtdorf, boldly said that "the Church's growth here in the next century will be built on the results of these concerts." Newspapers, radio, and television lapped up news of this small remigration from the Crossroads of the West, with one of the papers in Rome saying after a concert that "A company of angels appeared in the Auditorium in Via della Conciliazione." Non-Mormons took interest in the Church while, perhaps more importantly, the Choir's artistic success—a quality of performance that Ottley thought had not been exceeded on his watch—emboldened the relatively small brood of Mormon Europeans to acknowledge their presence in historically Catholic and High Protestant regions. This seemed to fulfill a Book of Mormon phrase Hinckley had taken up as a motto for the Church: "come forth out of obscurity."[48]

The approach to the year 2000 had a certain mystique for Mormons, as for many premillennialist evangelicals in the United States. To those who followed Bishop Ussher's famous chronology, which put the creation of the world at 4004 BC, any time after 1996 could signal the end of time itself. That was because the Book of Revelation suggested that the earth would enter the divine millennium after six thousand years. The official Mormon edition of the Bible indeed had Bishop Ussher's chronology in its timeline, with 4004 BC next to "The Fall of Man." And section 77 of the Church's Doctrine and Covenants claimed that the earth would last only seven thousand years: six thousand and then the return of Christ. So, just as the imminence of 1890 had provoked Mormon fears that the end was here, now the end of the 1900s—especially the looming "Y2K" (Year 2000) computer problem that threatened a worldwide shutdown—alarmed many Mormons. As 2000 drew near, the First Presidency, it seemed, had to make changes that said, as Jesus himself once had done, "the end is not yet." That meant undertaking new things, the physical symbol of which was a new Conference Center, which would take the place of the Tabernacle for all major Church events. At the same time, the musical symbol of continuance would be the next revamping of the Tabernacle music team.

In February 1999, Craig Jessop—now the assistant conductor—led the Choir and Utah Symphony in a performance of Brahms's *Requiem*, then recorded it for Telarc. For the recording, everyone in the Choir was told to bring two blankets apiece to cover the entire center section of the Tabernacle. (While the members and leaders could be changed out, of course, the Tabernacle's acoustic quirks remained.) The following month, Smoot told the Choir that big changes would come after General Conference in April. Until then, "Do not bother Jerry or Craig with questions."[49]

April Conference arrived, and by now the Choir repertoire consisted entirely of hymns and hymn arrangements. Packer's emphasis on hymns—or at least the bureaucratic construal of that emphasis—had taken root so strongly throughout the Church that bishops, stake presidents, and other leaders were mandating that nothing but hymns be sung in any meetings. The Tabernacle Choir provided no counter example in General Conference. Although the Choir was the model for local Church choirs, Hinckley, as close to an aesthete as the Church had at the helm, took note of this disturbing trend. He grew so concerned at the massive constriction in musical breadth in Church meetings that in 2002 he wrote a letter to leaders at all levels to try to correct it. Hymns were "standard" for congregational singing. But prelude, postlude, and Choir music should be open to "other appropriate" music (a phrase used twice in the brief letter).[50] Determining propriety never goes smoothly, of course. But the "hymns-only" approach had become too tight. Yet the leading choir of the Church, apparently by constraint, had done nothing in the Church's main conferences to illuminate the realms of non-hymn propriety.

In one sense, Ottley summarized the criteria by which conductors had come to be prized. As Ottley prepared to retire after twenty-five years of service—the first conductor of the Choir since C. J. Thomas to leave the post without rancor (or, in Lund's case, death)—Lowell Durham's son Tom, a member of the Choir, published a sixteen-point summary of Ottley's legacy in the Choir's biennial magazine, *Keeping Tab*. Many of the achievements noted there could be credited to Ottley's predecessors, as well: getting new seats installed, changing the seating arrangement, refining attendance policies, training members' musicianship, continuing their touring and recording, maintaining ties with the professional choral world, and promoting new Mormon-composed music. But a few tangible accomplishments indeed were new: he utterly revamped the Choir's music library system, irrevocably settled the retirement age, had the Choir stand during broadcasts, and shared the baton with guests far more than ever before.

On Sunday, 9 May 1999, Smoot introduced the three new conductors to the Choir, a trio designed like ecclesiastical presidencies or bishoprics: Craig Jessop, conductor, with Mack Wilberg (choral conductor from BYU) and Barlow Bradford (director of the Utah Chamber Artists) as associate conductors. At the announcement, Ottley revealed to the Choir one of Wilberg's chief tasks: "We put Mack into his office, shut the door, turned off the outside world and put him to work arranging music for you." His first new hymn arrangement, sung on the 13 June broadcast, was a reverent, almost monastic version of the originally jaunty gospel song "Did You Think to Pray?" President Hinckley found it so moving that he was said to have wept when he heard it. Jessop was not shy thereafter in calling Wilberg a "musical genius."[51]

That July, a fire in the Tabernacle broke out when a spotlight on the organ ignited a drape next to it. A month later, a block north of the Tabernacle, a tornado—unheard of in Salt Lake City—struck the Conference Center construction site, toppling cranes and injuring four workers. But the new building would be ready for occupancy at the first General Conference of the year 2000. And by the time it opened, the First Presidency had taken another huge step in enlarging the Choir's image.

CHAPTER 8

THE ENDLESS POSTLUDE

SINCE 1982, Ottley had asked the First Presidency for the Choir to have its own orchestra. After they had lost Ormandy and the Philadelphia Orchestra as partners in 1967, the Choir had returned to organ accompaniment or pick-up groups—mostly drawn from the Utah Symphony—for its recordings. And it had never had an orchestra for its broadcasts. The Choir obviously longed for its golden years, with a renowned orchestra acting as its accompanist. But the Church had relied on Columbia to fund that accompanist, with the Choir's cut of the record profits having not to fund anything but the conductor, the technicians, and a secretary or two. Now, the Choir had the solid audience and reputation, but no orchestra.

Hinckley seems to have favored Ottley's proposal from the beginning but had no authority to make it happen while Kimball, Benson, and Hunter had been Presidents of the Church. With Hinckley now at the Church's helm, he disbanded the Mormon Youth Symphony and Chorus in 1998, the twenty-fifth year of the conductorship of Robert Bowden, who had replaced Welch in 1974. Behind the scenes, Hinckley told Barlow Bradford, the associate conductor of the Choir, that "it is time for orchestra music to come forward in the Church and take its rightful place."[1] Named the Orchestra at Temple Square, the new in-house ensemble essentially represented the return of Beesley's Tabernacle Orchestra of the 1880s.

But unlike its century-old forerunner, this orchestra's pretenses now mirrored the Choir's huge accomplishments. "The vision of the First Presidency," Hinckley's counselor James Faust explained, "is that over time this orchestra could achieve excellence and prestige in national and even world-wide musical circles." The motivation seemed both aesthetic—to lift instrumental music's stature in the Church—and propagandistic—to draw even more cultivated non-Mormons into the church's orbit, listeners who liked classical music but not solely in its choral incarnation.

So the invitations went out. Smoot and his cohorts believed that BYU would help stock the 110-piece orchestra with its student players. BYU president Merrill Bateman even floated the idea of granting students university credit for playing in the new orchestra—an idea the BYU School of Music rejected. After more discussion, it became clear that students at the Church's largest university would not be the default roster. It would have to be a community orchestra populated by eager players who would audition for their new Church calling. In that sense, at least, it would mimic the Tabernacle Choir. At the group's first official rehearsal, 16 October 1999, Faust divulged what seemed the new group's proximate cause: the Church was making a film about Jesus in the Old and New Worlds to show in its Salt Lake visitors center. The filming was done, the soundtrack had been written, and they needed a top-notch orchestra to record it.

Initially, President Hinckley had asked Wendell Smoot if they should pay the players of this new in-house group. Smoot said no. The orchestra must volunteer their time and efforts in just the same way as the Choir. But he didn't foresee the big problem that lurked behind the scenes: the Choir and orchestra's first two commercial recordings together were contracted with Telarc, a major label that, as it turned out, was a signatory agent for the American Federation of Musicians. Attempting to dodge the union scale requirements for any orchestra recording on Telarc, the Church had its attorneys draft a letter to the label explaining why, since this was volunteer orchestra—indeed, one whose members considered themselves called by God—all references to "employees" or "employed" musicians in the union contract were invalid. The attorneys even floated a First Amendment argument: "members of the Choir and the Orchestra value their participation as an experience of worship. We hope that both Telarc and the AFM will understand and respect their beliefs."[2] That meant: no pay for the musicians.

Puzzled by this tactic, Telarc wrote to the New York AFM headquarters to see if they concurred with the Church. The New York office forwarded the matter to Local 104, the Salt Lake area branch of the AFM. This prompted a meeting at the Church Office Building with Bradford, Smoot, and a Church attorney on one side, and three union representatives on the other. Soon after the meeting, Local 104's attorney Joseph Hatch fired off a reply to the New York AFM, insisting on the difference between "religious exercise" and "commercial enterprise." The Tabernacle Choir singing at General Conference was a religious exercise. Recording "Battle Hymn" for Columbia was a commercial enterprise. Local 104 completely rejected the idea that the Orchestra at Temple Square recording for Telarc was a religious matter. The players must be paid union scale wages plus benefits and pension. If, after being paid, players wanted to donate the money back to the Church, the union had no objection.[3]

At their inaugural rehearsal, the Church announced to the orchestra that they would be paid for at least the first of two contracted albums with Telarc, a Christmas CD—leaving Choir members who heard the announcement to wonder why the singers were not being paid, whereas their "volunteer" accompanists were. Given the feeling of inequity between singers and players and also among orchestra members themselves—some of whom were "off the books" and weren't getting paid for the recordings, while most of their colleagues were—the Telarc-AFM-Choir-orchestra conglomeration became intolerable.

Within a year, it also became clear that a world-class orchestra was implausible with a group of freelance volunteers. A decent studio-grade orchestra, though, was plausible. And that's what the Church really needed. The idealism of the orchestra's prospectus soon faded as pragmatism took over. The Orchestra at Temple Square would perform one or two concerts a year by itself, but mostly accompany the Choir in Church broadcasts, recordings, movie soundtracks, and some public events—though not at General Conferences, presumably since there was no room for them in the new Conference Center with a full contingent of General Authorities at the front of the hall.

After the two Telarc CDs that featured the orchestra, *A Mormon Tabernacle Choir Christmas* (2000) and *The Sound of Glory* (2001), the Church quit the label and started its own, a subsidiary of the Bonneville Corporation, which allowed the Choir and orchestra to make their own recordings with volunteer players in a right-to-work state. The name of the Choir, so mutable throughout its history, was enshrined as its own audio dispensary: the Mormon Tabernacle Choir was now a recording label.

Recording revenues shot up, of course. New Choir President Mac Christensen (who had succeeded Smoot in 2000) summed it up coyly: "Instead of 10 cents for every CD, we do a lot better."[4] But just two weeks after the new label was announced, Barlow Bradford quit as associate conductor. "Many moments on broadcasts were inspiring," he said in his public letter of resignation, and he fondly recalled a performance of Robert Cundick's *Redeemer* and conducting the orchestra with the Choir at the dedication of the rebuilt Nauvoo Temple. But he didn't mention the recordings he had overseen. His stated reasons for resigning had a boilerplate tone: "at this time in my life there are a number of things I want to pursue I may not have the chance to do later."[5] But he had witnessed that the orchestra's original status had been downgraded to that of one more accompanist for the Choir. Even the organists had their own solos on *Music and the Spoken Word*. But the orchestra now played on broadcasts only when the Choir sang. The lateral, quasi-equal pretense on which the orchestra had been formed had mutated into a vertical relationship, with the Choir and Jessop decidedly on top.

Jessop seemed shaken by the resignation. He felt he had shared the podium generously with both Wilberg and Bradford. And his military and Church training had both taught him a sense of loyalty that Bradford had breached. From then on, Jessop and Wilberg took over the orchestra—neither of them well-suited for the task—in broadcasts and recordings. Soon, former BYU faculty member Igor Gruppman was hired to lead the players through their meager but proficiently played concert schedule. Still, some players, sensing what Bradford had sensed, also quit.[6]

Although the Choir cherished and touted its status as America's Choir, the term needed burnishing. When it came to presidential inaugurals, they had staked a claim, but, since LBJ, only a claim on the Nixon-Reagan-Bush lineage. Democratic presidents had overlooked or avoided them for the inaugurals. They looked more and more like *Republican* America's Choir, ambassadors for a hardcore conservatism increasingly polarized from liberal and progressive U.S. values. They seized every opportunity to counter that image. Some opportunities came through rhythm-and-blues singer Gladys Knight's 1997 conversion to the Church. Suddenly the Church had gone further than ever against the tide of its old-time "colored problem." The opening of the priesthood to black members in 1978 was one thing. But now the Mormon gospel had penetrated into the iconic heart of American gospel music. Knight sang for Hinckley and a full house at the Conference Center for his ninetieth birthday in June 2000, noting over the pulpit that, no matter how much she loved Mormon music, she missed her old shouting and clapping church music. She then sang with the Choir on their Christmas program that December. Still, feeling that Mormonism deserved a taste of the gospel choirs she grew up with, in 2002 Knight formed a new inter-racial Mormon gospel choir, Saints United Voices. Their debut album *One Voice* won the 2005 Grammy Award for *Best Gospel Choir or Chorus Album*, for which, of course, the Mormon Tabernacle Choir would never be a contender.[7]

But if the Church's best prospects for massive growth seemed to lie mostly outside the bounds of North America, the Choir needed to improve its international credentials. Tours helped and, from the Choir's *Cielito Lindo* album under Condie, to an international anthems project they carried out under Ottley, the Choir had made recorded efforts to slough off its U.S.-myopic image. The February 2002 Winter Olympics in Salt Lake City offered a vast global stage for doing so in their own backyard.

Church members, including General Authorities, differed on how to react to the 1995 announcement that the Winter Olympics would be coming to town. The mixed feelings resembled those that surrounded the coming of the railroad to Utah almost a century and a half earlier: would this be progress or pollution? Would this allow the Church to shine in its best light to a faltering world, or would the world flood in and drag the Church down with it? A master of public relations, Hinckley guided the Church into the same soft-sell approach the Tabernacle Choir had used for years, "downplaying, in fact, their urge to convert," as Jan Shipps put it. The Church's "great opportunity" with the Olympics would be to show its generosity and yet restraint. The motto for the 2002 Winter Olympics was "Light the Fire Within." Mormon humorist Robert Kirby said the Church's strategic response was "contain the fire within."[8]

Before the onset of two weeks of nonstop television images from the heart of Mormondom, the Church had donated land near Temple Square for the medals plaza, hung a huge Olympic banner on the Church Office Building, mustered 5,400 volunteer hosts for tourists to the state, and offered the Choir not only for the opening ceremonies but for daily concerts and mini-concerts for curious tourists. Throughout their Olympic appearances, the Choir leaned strongly toward the middle-of-the-road European-U.S. soundtrack one would have expected in any other circumstances, with odd pop moments such as singing backup for Sting. Hank Stuever at the *Washington Post* wrote that these Winter Olympics became "a coming-out party for Mormons that gave people a vernacular about Mormonism they didn't have before." Candy Thomson of the *Baltimore Sun* called the Games "a great warm-up act for everything that's followed" for Mormons in media—the "everything" ranging from polygamy-themed shows like *Big Love* and *Sister Wives*, to successful competitors on *American Idol* and *So*

You Think You Can Dance, to the Mormon-authored *Twilight* book and movie series, to the *Book of Mormon* Broadway musical, and many more entrées of Mormons into mainstream popular culture.

But it was an "in-house" event that best underlined the Church's pursuit of international public relations: the Choir's performance at the Church's normally quite formal General Conference in April 2004, in which they sang backup for Brazilian pop star Liriel, who soloed in both English and Portuguese in an arrangement of the hymn "I Know that My Redeemer Lives." Part assimilation and part neocolonialism, the elevation of a foreign female pop singer above the Choir in the Church's most hallowed public gathering broke cultural barriers for the Choir, as well. But it was a one-off event, since then unanswered in subsequent Church General Conferences.[9]

That same year, PBS hung the "America's Choir" marquee on the group once again in an hour-long documentary on the Choir (funded mostly by Mormon donors) under that name. An oblique sequel to the earlier PBS Mormon documentary *Trail of Hope*, this was a history and unbridled celebration of the Choir featuring testimonials by collaborators on Christmas programs PBS had shown (e.g., Angela Lansbury), the Salt Lake Winter Olympics (Sting), and the corporate media king who had anointed the Choir decades earlier: Charles Osgood, host of *Sunday Morning* (the featurette show that preceded *Music and the Spoken Word* each week), and CBS news demigod Walter Cronkite, who narrated the whole PBS program. As had become customary, a video version, titled *America's Choir: The Story of the Mormon Tabernacle Choir*, was marketed along with a tie-in CD as well as a coffee table book by the scriptwriter, Heidi Swinton. The book was lean and glossy, its cover drenched in red, white, and blue tones.[10]

Under Jessop, the Choir kept up and intensified the almost-breakneck circuit that he had inherited from Ottley. As a kind of focused consolidation of its past into the present, a few months after the 2002 Winter Olympics the Choir had sung at the dedication of the rebuilt, restored, and revamped Nauvoo Temple—the site where Stephen Goddard had led the Church's main choir before transplanting it to the Salt Lake Valley. At the same time, to keep reaching out into the world, Jessop's Choir broadcasts featured an increasing number of guests—solo artists, small ensembles, and choirs—who often brought with them repertoire well outside the Choir's norms. At times, *Music and the Spoken Word* seemed like a clearinghouse for all things musical in the United States, a kind of high-class "open mike" forum for anyone from opera divas to family folk bands.

Jessop, an outspoken champion of black musical heritage in the States, devoted at least one show each February to Black History Month, emphasizing old-time spirituals, though nothing that echoed more current black styles or did more than faintly mimic the American gospel church choir tradition. But on 24 February 2008, Newell's *Spoken Word* segment celebrated Rosa Parks and the Choir and organist performed spirituals. New black Choir member Alex Boyé did true gospel-style melismatic solos on "When the Saints Go Marching In," while a rousing Dixieland band accompanied the singers. A BYU blog captured some of the college audience's reactions to this 2008 performance: "I really like the 'new' Music & Spoken Word"; "They're freshening it up for the MTV generation"; and, more equivocally, it "did not sound like MoTab."[11]

Meanwhile, the sixteen compact discs the Choir issued under Jessop's direction heavily favored easily marketable hymns and Christmas offerings. These generally climbed high on the *Billboard* classical charts, which, given the shrunken classical market, would happen if only a slice of Mormons bought the recordings. (A choral CD that sold 30,000 would be considered a huge success.)[12] Tucked among the less challenging offerings, one also found notable discs of Brahms's German *Requiem* (in English) and a Randall Thompson collection. One disc in 2008, though, stood out: a new Latin *Requiem* composed by Wilberg himself.[13] As many other composers had done, Wilberg trimmed some liturgical movements and inserted tropes, setting the texts in a style that palpably echoed Ralph Vaughan-Williams, a favorite composer of both Jessop and Wilberg. Its compendium of rich chordal voicing suited the Choir well. Still, many Mormon listeners wondered why one of their quasi-official composers had prepared a Catholic mass instead of, say, another Book of Mormon oratorio.

But by the time the Wilberg CD hit the shelves, Jessop had resigned.

Given the awkward history of Choir conductors' exits for a century and a half, Jessop's resignation seemed unremarkable, even though he had served less time as conductor than anyone except Welch since the Salt Lake Tabernacle was built. But, given its suddenness, seeming lack of provocation, and tight-lipped aftermath, his departure stoked more rumors than had any others. What emerged amid the rumors was a contest of implausibilities. On one extreme was the claim that Jessop refused to "out" gay members of the Choir and orchestra to his overseers and so was fired. This was a time of great Mormon angst about gay matters, particularly as the Church at the time of Jessop's resignation was about to bankroll and muster volunteers for California's anti–gay marriage amendment, Proposition 8. And the Choir had its own odd connection: Bradford was becoming less reticent about his own sexuality and would soon marry a man.

On the opposite extreme was Jessop's claim that he simply had accomplished far ahead of schedule everything in his personal twenty-year plan for the Choir. If he stayed on, he said, the Choir would stagnate. But the statement's premise was that he in fact had a twenty-year plan.

Whatever skeins of truth any of these claims contained, three facts are clear. First, Jessop was weary. Some Choir members noticed it weeks ahead of his resignation. The whirlwind schedule, the added weight of conducting the orchestra—not part of his original assignment—added to the bureaucratic nitty-gritty that all Tabernacle Choir conductors had to endure, took a toll. Jerold Ottley had warned Jessop not to stay in the position as long as he, Ottley, had; and JoAnn Ottley had told Jessop that the conductorship was like trying to take a drink from a fire hydrant—a phrase Jessop repeated to a friend who asked the conductor how he was doing just eight days before he quit.

Second, the departure came on the heels of Thomas Monson's ascendancy to the Presidency of the Church. Monson took the reins and within a month Jessop was out. On this proximity of dates, Jessop says simply that he and Monson both decided "the time was right" for Jessop to leave.

The third evident fact of Jessop's resignation is that it was unplanned. Some sudden incident or epiphany prompted an ungainly exit. At their Thursday rehearsal four days after the "Rosa Parks" episode of *Music and the Spoken Word*, Jessop called an extra Saturday rehearsal for organist Cundick's popular oratorio *The Redeemer*, their next recording project. When Saturday came, Jessop, without explanation, didn't show up. Sunday's broadcast came and, again, Jessop failed to appear. At the following Tuesday's rehearsal, Jessop stood to read his letter of resignation, then walked out quickly. Mac Christensen steadfastly refused to explain to inquirers the cause of the abrupt severance. And that refusal cast a shadow even on Jessop's own untenable explanations. With a soldier's mindset, Jessop seems to have fallen on his sword for some larger cause.[14]

Less than a month after resigning, Jessop interviewed to become the head of the Utah State University Department of Music in Logan. He got the position and went on to build up a busy schedule of guest conducting around the country and beyond. Meanwhile, as suddenly as Ottley had been thrust into an acting conductorship after Welch, Wilberg now had to assume Jessop's podium. At first in an "acting" position—the usual fallback—and then a continuing appointment, Wilberg knew the full range of choral music perhaps better than any previous conductor. His training and experience were impeccable. He was businesslike and efficient, yet, as one Choir member described him—in decidedly Cornwallesque terms—"pleasant, funny, and precise."[15] But the lamentation and rumormongering over Jessop's leave-taking blunted the onset of Wilberg's new career.

For the first time since Evan Stephens, the conductor of the Tabernacle Choir was a prolific composer. But Wilberg's situation differed fundamentally from Stephens's. Stephens thrived in an era when Church leaders wanted *new* hymns, anthems, cantatas, and other sacred pieces, anything that would exemplify Mormon self-reliance and, indeed, flow from the unique reservoir of the spirituality that the Church claimed for itself as the "only true church." Stephens was the court composer for the Kingdom of God. Wilberg came into his own in an era in which familiarity and allegiance to the past governed the making of art that was "useful" to the Church. New *arrangements* of canonized hymns suited the Church, but not the abundance of new *compositions* that Stephens had delivered to grateful ears. Wilberg had a choir at the ready for any new pieces he might write, of course, especially given his conservative compositional voice. He could program those new pieces in the occasional broadcast or concert or recording. But he seldom did so and never did so for General Conference, for which he rolled out a series (still ongoing) of well-crafted, though formulaic, arrangements of numbers from the LDS hymnbook.

As for singing style, the Choir now seemed almost to be retrograding through its previous conductors. Jessop had pursued a richer, darker sound, one that his conducting itself seemed to portray. While he seconded Bradford's suggestion that the women needed to put on a lot of pounds—sonically, not literally, he assured them—he conducted as though a latter-day Sisyphus, pushing the large mass of the Choir from one note to the next. At the same time, with the orchestra in place, the musical mass doubled. The resultant sound harked back to Condie's "classic" dark Choir sound, the one that Columbia had captured so faithfully.

Now, in his wake, Wilberg adopted a lighter, more workmanlike conducting style that harked back to Cornwall. Whereas Jessop had displayed often garish emotion in his facial expressions, Wilberg tended to a severe, unemotive mien, his gestures suggesting a technician at the controls of a huge machine. Unlike Jessop, he told the women of the Choir not to gain sonic pounds but, in fact, to brighten their tone, indeed to try and sound "younger"—possibly to sail their timbre through the wave of orchestral sound in front of them, but also to subliminally appeal to a more youthful audience. Indeed, reaching younger and broader audiences has been the explicit (and necessary) quest of the most recent

Choir President, Ron Jarrett. One detects it especially in the Choir's collaborations from 2010 through 2014; these have ranged from backing Bryn Terfel on a *Deutsche Grammophon* recording—their first departure from their own label in years—to singing backing tracks for a remix of "If It's Magic" for a Stevie Wonder symphonic remix album. The Choir now has—and, Jarrett would say, needs to have—both a Facebook page and a YouTube channel. One could even envision a collaboration with the Brooklyn Tabernacle Choir.[16]

By now, though, amid attempts to remix itself through pop collaborations and repertoire and to renew itself through the term limits of its members, the "retirements" of its conductors, and the evolution of sound media, all the routines of the Mormon Tabernacle Choir's existence have long since been set down, formalized, distilled, and codified. Once one understands the Choir's routines, forged through a century of inspired trial and error, the specific incidents of its ongoing lifespan make less of a difference. With that in mind, one might well look out at the Choir's ongoing career as the simple persistence of three distinct ideas: a brand, a system, and a spectacle.

Indeed, the Mormon Tabernacle Choir brand name has astonishing cachet. In 2007, for example, the Tabernacle Choir sold out Denver's Pepsi Stadium—fifteen thousand seats—three days before the Rolling Stones, another major brand name, sold just thirteen thousand seats in the same venue.[17] Like most venerable brand names, this one conveys all one needs to guarantee dependability, though not innovation or inventiveness. The term *iconic*, so promiscuously used in popular media, must be applied to this Choir. Like the name CBS itself, the Mormon Tabernacle Choir's name proudly carries the plump baggage of its pioneering history. That baggage sometimes can feel like dead weight. Yet the authority of its heft, even in the Choir's sappiest pseudo-pop moments, cannot be flouted.

In the twenty-first century, one might well speak of the brand as having a "Christmas Division." Jessop had once said flatly, "We should own Christmas."[18] The Choir's Christmas albums from the 1950s onward had sold prodigiously. Starting in 2001, high-production-value DVDs of each multimedia celebrity-hosted Christmas concert began to fill the marketplace. Extending the symbiotic résumé-building relationship between celebrities and the Choir that had grown since the 1960s, these new concerts and DVDs featured hosts ranging from actors (e.g., Jane Seymour, Peter Graves, Claire Bloom, Michael York) to legitimate crossover singers such as Frederica von Stade and Renée Fleming to overt pop artists such as Natalie Cole and David Archuleta (the last was the young Mormon who had been a runner-up on television's *American Idol*). Indeed, the fusion of "America's Choir" and *American Idol* suggested a blurring of categories not just in the Church but in the culture at large, in which "classical"—at least in *Billboard* chart terms—meant anything that had the trappings of symphonic instrumentation or "trained" vocal technique and (usually) few or no drum tracks.

But despite its cultural ecumenism, the Choir tends its brand carefully. Several choirs and even orchestras throughout the United States have used the word "Mormon" in their names, the best-known—until recently—being the Southern California Mormon Choir.[19] But in 2007, saying that a new unofficial venture was "inspired and needed," Brandon and Brett Stewart formed the Mormon Choral Organizations of America (MCO), a coalition that soon included choirs and even orchestras of various age groups in several states (Arizona, California, Texas, and Utah). Their 2011 recording of Brett Stewart's original Book of Mormon–based oratorio, *Messiah in America*, shot to the top of the *Billboard* classical charts in its first week of release. That, their sold-out concerts in multiple states, rapid growth, and word-of-mouth popular appeal—including a hyperbolic endorsement by popular right-wing commentator Glenn Beck, who said they were "better than the Mormon Tabernacle Choir"—made the Church take notice.[20]

In 2010, the Church had issued a new General Handbook with this policy, doubtless provoked primarily by the burgeoning MCO coalition: "Standing community choirs directed by and consisting primarily of Church members [but] not sponsored by the Church. . . . should not use references to the Church such as 'LDS,' 'Latter-day Saint,' or 'Mormon' in their names." Although MCO was initially able to begin drafting an agreement with the Church allowing them to use "Mormon" in the trademark license of their name, the MCO's massive market success and geographic expansion led Church officials to tell the Stewarts that they were likely to cause "confusion" if they continued to use "Mormon" in a name connected with choirs: in other words, Mormon Choral Organizations were not a subsidiary of the "Mormon" religio-corporate brand.

After several MCO member organizations appeared together at the prestigious American Choral Directors Association in 2013, the Stewart brothers changed the group's name to *Millennial* Choral Organizations, a less felicitous and, indeed, more confounding name that obscures the Mormon roots of the concept and the membership of its leaders. It was indeed, more ecumenical, which both expanded and diluted its famous-Mormon-choir-derived connotations. The logo, though, remained the initials *MCO*, a pragmatic repurposing of the original initials and, in turn, an inferential wink at the policing of the term *Mormon*.

The Mormon Tabernacle Choir is now the firmament that presides over three other entities: the Orchestra at Temple Square, the Temple Square Chorale, and the Bells at Temple Square—a Protestant-style handbell choir that functions as a sort of portable carillon, with individual players sounding their bells in sequence, machinelike and lockstep as a well-trained militia. The fifty-six-page 2010 policy handbook for all four groups is fastidious.

The handbook begins with an outline of worthiness to be a member of these groups, all of which are "goodwill ambassadors for The Church of Jesus Christ." Brief mission statements follow, and then a list of choir-related positions, everything from the conductors, organists, announcer, and president, to paid administrative staff (including secretaries and a paralegal), to a populous team of volunteers—hosts, historian, stage manager, librarians, wardrobe committees, medical advisors, newsletter editor, website committee, and more. The book then details how members should handle their personal deportment and social interactions in the choir. These include rules for inviting guests to rehearsals, taking pictures, and parking; the need to avoid speaking to "the media" without permission and disclosing Choir matters on blogs; the need to avoid scented products (due to "serious allergies suffered by many" members of the groups); dress and grooming standards; proper care (and returning) of scores; and so on. Decades of experience had sprouted policies for every circumstance one would encounter in rehearsals, broadcasts, and tours.

To say that a group of *artists* "got it down to a science" seems like a contradiction. But the phrase fits, almost poignantly, the Tabernacle Choir, which is now and probably always will be locked in a network of tasks and duties, hyper-committed to maintaining its spotless reputation, and therefore almost desperate for efficiency. Today's Choir does not so much exemplify music as it carries out one of God's own mission statements: as Brigham Young put it, "that we may know how to systematize everything that we are engaged in."[21]

The Choir always needed to look their best for concerts and behave their best in public when offstage. The members were missionaries and had to look the part (this is not just metaphorical: letters of admission to the Choir and release from it have referred to membership as a "mission call").[22] But when the Choir sang on the radio and for recordings, it had no visual obligation to its mass-media fans. Television changed that. They now had to be fussier about clothing color, how well dresses fit, how their individual faces would look in tight close-up, how focused their eyes were on their conductor, and, of course, how imposing the Choir as a whole loomed onscreen. Yet, in a sense, television resuscitated something the Choir had long relied on: spectacle.

Part of the great transition that Evan Stephens had effected was to make of the Choir something worthy of P. T. Barnum: a grandiose, slightly unmanageable, and therefore overpowering sight. Stephens had created massive spectacles of children's choirs before he became conductor of the Tabernacle Choir. Once he had the Choir under his baton, he continued the tradition of spectacle by touring with—as advertised—the largest choir one might ever see on a stage. Cornwall, too, could not resist the lure of the spectacular in his colossal, staged versions of *Elijah*. Oratorio alone did not suffice: it had to be joined with a visual sight worthy of the mountain country the Choir inhabited. Cornwall leading the Choir in song at the foot of the Red Rocks cliffs in 1956 was pure spectacle. Condie extended the tradition—with the grateful complicity of CBS—by moving the Choir from the Tabernacle to Mount Rushmore for its first satellite telecast. And, of course, the very idea of a satellite telecast itself was a global spectacle, one that purported to encompass the whole world with the help of the cosmos itself.

In the twenty-first century, the Choir's network show now features flashier, more agitated music as a prefix to its opening song, "Gently Raise the Sacred Strain." Video clips of nature scenes now accompany the singing, appeasing the eyes of viewers who might find it boring to focus solely on disciplined singers plying their collective art. And the Conference Center itself, which the Choir increasingly uses—despite unremarkable acoustics—is laid out for visual thrall, with mammoth ranks of organ pipes, brightly backlit.

One could go on listing assorted examples of the Choir's quest for spectacle. But perhaps the 2012 Christmas concert-broadcast-video recording will suffice: A small forest of light-bejeweled Christmas trees, bowers, red, white, and blue banners, and even huge sculpted snowflakes adorned the Conference Center. Red- and green-costumed teens holding large gold- and red-wrapped packages pranced and twirled through the aisles and across the stage, where they deposited their packages and danced, sometimes with dry-ice fog teasing the eye. Underscored by the orchestra, newsman Tom Brokaw stood at the front of the stage and told the elaborate story of the Mormon "Candy Bomber," Gail Halvorsen, who dropped small, candy-laden parachutes to German children during the Berlin Airlift. Bathed in blue light, a tableau of downcast children behind barbed wire stood alongside the stage. Soon an indoor blizzard of small parachutes drifted onto the Conference Center crowd.

Christmas, of course, brings us back to the founding spectacle of Christianity, the one not only found in the Book of Luke, but cited in many carols:

> And there were in the same country shepherds abiding in the field, keeping watch over their flock by night. And, lo, the angel of the Lord came upon them, and the glory of the Lord shone round about them: and they were sore afraid. And the angel said unto them, Fear not: for, behold, I bring you good tidings of great joy, which shall be to all people. For unto you is born this day in the city of David a Saviour, which is Christ the Lord. And this shall be a sign unto you; Ye shall find the babe wrapped in swaddling clothes, lying in a manger. And suddenly there was with the angel a multitude of the heavenly host praising God, and saying, Glory to God in the highest, and on earth peace, good will toward men. And it came to pass, as the angels were gone away from them into heaven, the shepherds said one to another, Let us now go even unto Bethlehem, and see this thing which is come to pass, which the Lord hath made known unto us.

One carol distills the essence of the angels' loud, panoramic appearance into a single word: *hark.*

In 1848, just as the Mormons were accomplishing their grand exodus to Utah, Søren Kierkegaard wrote in another context: "In all eternity it is impossible for me to compel a person to accept an opinion, a conviction, a belief. But one thing I can do: I can compel him to take notice."[23] That is precisely what the spectacle of angels singing on that one night in Palestine was meant to do. Just so, seizing people's attention remains the better part of Mormon missionary work for its allegedly most powerful proselyting group, a Choir that has long traded on a comparison to angels. This Choir offers no direct message, no sermon in song to the world. Indeed, the demands of public-service broadcasts in law and in the network rules disallows any overt Mormonness in their half hour of music and the spoken word. But in an age of imponderable rivalry for attention, this Choir reaches to grasp any tool it can find to compel you to take notice. As if great music were not enough—which, sadly for the twenty-first century, it no longer is.

NOTES

INTRODUCTION

1. On the inaugural introduction, see Joseph Berger, "A Church Choir's Show at the Inauguration Brings a Burst of Brooklyn Pride," *New York Times*, 22 January 2013. For the "civil religion" quote, see David W. Stowe, *How Sweet the Sound: Music in the Spiritual Lives of Americans* (Cambridge, Mass.: Harvard University Press, 2004), 89.

2. Heber G. Wolsey, "The History of Radio Station KSL from 1922 to Television," PhD dissertation, Michigan State University, 1967, 136–37.

3. Choir President Ron Jarrett, quoted in Shane Warby to Michael Hicks, email 13 December 2012.

4. Vivian Gornick, *The Situation and the Story: The Art of Personal Narrative* (New York: Farrar, Strauss and Giroux, 2011), 16.

5. I found the epigraph on a single page in the papers of Tracy Cannon, who had been a Tabernacle organist, assistant conductor, director of the LDS School of Music, and chairman of the Church Music Committee.

CHAPTER 1. BOOKS AND ANGELS

1. The citations for these scriptures are in Mosiah 2:28 and Mormon 7:7 (on "choirs") and 1 Nephi 1:8 and Alma 36:22 (on "concourses").

2. The most comprehensive biography of Joseph Smith is Richard Bushman, *Rough Stone Rolling: A Cultural Biography of Mormonism's Founder* (New York: Knopf, 2005).

3. Swedenborg described celestial choirs and spiritual choirs, the two distinguishable by their tone colors. There were choirs of little children, detectable because they were not mature enough to act as one. There were strictly "gentile" choirs, noted for their coarser sound. There were also choirs associated with voluntary breathing, others with involuntary; the former became active in waking hours, the latter in dreams. The timbre of angel choirs sometimes seemed indistinguishable from violins and, apparently most often, was merely a feeling, conveyed without sound, of a large group all thinking the same thing at once. Some choirs, he said, acted only by "representations," others by representations and voices, still others by voices alone, and so on—a diverse inventory indeed. I have assembled these ideas from the citations in the massive, four-volume work of John Faulkner Potts, *The Swedenborg Concordance: A Complete Work of Reference to the Theological Writings of Emmanuel Swedenborg Based on the Original Latin Writings of the Author* (London: Swedenborg Society, 1888), 614–15.

4. For this quotation and a fuller discussion of the relationship between Smith and Swedenborg, see J. B. Haws, "Joseph Smith, Emanuel Swedenborg, and Section 76: Importance of the Bible in Latter-day Revelation," in *The Doctrine and Covenants, Revelations in Context: The 37th Annual Brigham Young University Sidney B. Sperry Symposium*, ed. Andrew H. Hedges, J. Spencer Fluhman, and Alonzo L. Gaskill (Provo and Salt Lake City: Religious Studies Center, Brigham Young University, and Deseret Book, 2008), 142–67.

5. From Aubrey de Vere's lyrical drama *The Waldenses: or, The Fate of Rora*, in which angels sing these words to the character of Agnes; quoted and discussed in *Dublin University Magazine* 21 (February 1843): 203.

6. The comments on the Presbyterian choir appear in the *Wayne Sentinel*, 25 February 1824. On the Methodist choir see G. A. Tuttle, "A Historical Sketch of Palmyra Methodist Episcopal Church" (1911), microfilm of typescript in L. Tom Perry Special Collections, Harold B. Lee Library, Brigham Young University (hereafter cited as SC-HBLL).

7. Arthur Mees, *Choirs and Choral Music* (London: John Murray, 1901), 186.

8. For a concise sampling of the patristic arguments concerning music, see Oliver Strunk, ed., *Source Readings in Music History* (New York: Norton, 1965), 59–75.

9. See George Fox, "Some Queries" (broadside), in *Gospel Truth Demonstrated in a Collection of Doctrinal Books*, 3 vols. (Philadelphia: M. T. C. Gould, 1831), also the Quaker documents quoted in Frederick John Gilman, *The Evolution of the English Hymn* (London: George Allen and Unwin, 1927), 176–96.

10. See http://www.cblibrary.org/biography/cartwright/pc10.htm (accessed 8 October 2013).

11. Mees, *Choirs and Choral Music*, 186.

12. *Charles G. Finney: An Autobiography* (Westwood, N.J.: Revell, 1908), 102.

13. From the Presbyterian "Directory for Worship," quoted in David Steele, *Continuous Singing in the Ordinary Worship of God . . .* (ca. 1870), available online at http://www.covenanter.org/Steele/continuoussinging.htm.

14. From the autobiography of James Jackson McIlyar (1816–1907), cited in Wallace Guy Smeltzer, *Methodism on the Headwaters of the Ohio: The History of the Pittsburgh Conference of the Methodist Church* (Nashville, Tenn.: Parthenon, 1951), 213.

15. See the anonymous *Brother Mason the Circuit Rider; or, Ten Years A Methodist Preacher* (Cincinnati: H. M. Rulison, 1856), 157–58, 230; the quote is on 278.

16. The quotations are from the article by "M.R." titled "Ancient and Modern Mode of Singing the Psalms," *Associate Presbyterian* 4 (September 1862): 462–66.

17. William Smith, "Notes Written on 'Chambers' Life of Joseph Smith" (ca. 1875), in Dan Vogel, comp. and ed., *Early Mormon Documents*, vol. 1 (Salt Lake City: Signature Books, 1996), 487.

18. The statements by Campbell are quoted in Dale A. Jorgenson, *Theological and Aesthetic Roots in the Stone-Campbell Movement* (Kirksville, Mo.: Thomas Jefferson University Press, 1989), 198, 206–7.

19. Mees, *Choirs and Choral Music*, 189–90.

20. Dean C. Jessee, comp. and ed., *The Personal Writings of Joseph Smith* (Salt Lake City: Deseret Book, 1984), 124. Versions of this account published by the Church politely change "altercation" to "discussion." Jessee's is faithful to the original manuscript, though.

21. "Our Father Adam," *Latter-day Saints' Millennial Star* (hereafter cited as *Millennial Star*) 15 (1853): 780.

22. Benjamin Brown, *Testimonies for the Truth* (Liverpool: S. W. Richards, 1853), 11.

23. Quoted in Pearl of Great Price (one of the Mormon "standard works" of scripture), Joseph Smith-History, 1:28.

24. On 29 March 1837, one brother was actually brought before the elders for "Disturbing the Singing School several times." Kirtland Elders Quorum Record, http://www.boap.org/LDS/Early-Saints/Kirt-Elders.html (accessed 8 October 2013).

25. "Choir of the Stake of Zion in the City of Nauvoo," *Times and Seasons* 3 (1 January 1842): 653.

26. The full citations are Lowell Mason, *Manual of the Boston Academy of Music for Instruction in the Elements of Vocal Music on the System of Pestalozzi* (Boston: J. H. Wilkins and R. B. Carter, 1839) and William S. Porter, *The Musical Cyclopedia: or the Principles of Music Considered as a Science and an Art . . .* (Boston: James Loring, 1834).

27. For the quotations and information in this and the preceding paragraphs, see Porter, *Musical Cyclopedia*, 73–76.

28. "Music," *Times and Seasons*, 15 January 1842.

29. See the paternity settlement concerning Hills and Clift in the Newell K. Whitney Papers, SC-HBLL.

30. The Young and Woodruff quotations are from, respectively, Young to Mary Ann Angell Young, letter 12 November 1840, Philip T. Blair Family Papers, Special Collections, J. Willard Marriott Library, University of Utah; *Times and Seasons* 2 (1 March 1841): 331.

31. Henry Caswall, *The City of the Mormons; Or, Three Days in Nauvoo, in 1842* (London: J. G. F. and J. Rivington, 1842), 9.

32. "The Funeral of Ephraim Marks," *Wasp*, 16 April 1842.

33. See Bessie Louise Pierce, *A History of Chicago*, vol. 1, *The Beginning of a City 1673–1848* (New York: Knopf, 1937), 305.

34. Helen Mar Whitney, "Scenes in Nauvoo," *Woman's Exponent* 10 (15 September 1881): 58, and 11 (15 November 1882): 90.

35. "Nauvoo Music and Concert Hall," *Nauvoo Neighbor*, 30 October 1844.

36. "On the Laws of Nature," *Nauvoo Neighbor*, 23 April 1845.

37. All the quotations in this paragraph are from Joseph F. Smith to Susa Young Gates, letter 2 December 1915, Emma Lucy Gates Bowen Papers, SC-HBLL.

38. William Phillips letter, 17 May 1851, in Ronald D. Dennis, trans. and ed., *Zion's Trumpet: 1851 Welsh Periodical* (Salt Lake City: Brigham Young University Religious Studies Center and Deseret Book, 2012), 153.

39. Quoted in Ronald Dennis, "John Parry and the Mormon Tabernacle Choir," http://welshmormon.byu.edu/Resource_Info.aspx?id=4077 (accessed 15 August 2013). See also Ronald D. Dennis, *The Call of Zion: The Story of the First Welsh Mormon Emigration* (Provo: Religious Studies Center, Brigham Young University, 1987), available at http://rsc.byu.edu/es/archived/call-zion-story-first-welsh-mormon-emigration/9-council-bluffs-salt-lake-city%E2%80%941849 (accessed 8 October 2013).

40. One finds references to the group by that name in *Deseret News*, 3 and 16 August 1850, 60 and 66. The Gunnison quotation is from J. W. Gunnison, *The Mormons, or, Latter-day Saints, in the Valley of the Great Salt Lake* (Philadelphia: J. B. Lippincott, 1856), 37.

CHAPTER 2. BUILDINGS AND PROFESSORS

1. See "Minutes of the General Conference," *Latter-day Saints' Millennial Star* (hereafter cited as *Millennial Star*), 31 July 1852.

2. Jules Remy and Julius Brenchley, *A Journey to Great-Salt-Lake City*, 2 vols. (London: W. Jeffs, 1861), 2:56.

3. The quotations and information in this paragraph are from "Deseret Philharmonic Society," *Deseret News* (hereafter cited as *DN*), 1 March 1855.

4. For more on these setbacks, see Michael Hicks, *Mormonism and Music: A History* (Urbana: University of Illinois Press, 1989), 46–47.

5. For a good overview of Calder's efforts, see William J. McNiff, *Heaven on Earth: A Planned Mormon Society* (Oxford, Ohio: Mississippi Valley Press, 1940), 175–77. On the association's concertizing, see Levi Edgar Young, *The Great Mormon Tabernacle with Its World-famed Organ and Choir* (Salt Lake City: Bureau of Information, 1930), 11–12. For more on these enterprises (and information pertaining to the following paragraph), see "New School House," *DN*, 12 December 1860; "The Concert in the Theatre," *DN*, 30 September 1863; and "The Concert This Evening," *DN*, 16 December 1863.

6. See, for example, Orson F. Whitney, "Charles John Thomas," in *History of Utah*, 4 vols. (Salt Lake City: George Q. Cannon & Sons, 1892–1904), 4:349–50; William Earl Purdy, "The Life and Works of Charles John Thomas: His Contribution to the Music History of Utah," master's thesis, Brigham Young University, 1949, 12–14.

7. Edward W. Tullidge, *History of Salt Lake City and Its Founders* (Salt Lake City: Edward W. Tullidge, 1886), 771–72.

8. John Tullidge in *Utah Magazine* 3 (2 October 1869): 347–48.

9. Mrs. M. G. Clawson, quoted in Sterling S. Beesley, *Kind Words the Beginnings of Mormon Melody: A Historical Biography and Anthology of the Life and Works of Ebenezer Beesley, Utah Pioneer Musician* (n.p.: Sterling S. Beesley, 1980), 248–49.

10. This handwritten remedy is pasted into the Charles John Thomas Scrapbook, L. Tom Perry Special Collections, Harold B. Lee Library, Brigham Young University (hereafter cited as SC-HBLL).

11. From an address given before the Deseret Dramatic Association, 1 March 1861, in the Deseret Dramatic Association Papers, Church History Library, the Church of Jesus Christ of Latter-day Saints (hereafter cited as CHL).

12. See Fred C. Collier, ed., *The Office Journal of President Brigham Young: 1858–1863 Book D* (n.p.: Collier's Publishing, 2006), 388–89 (1 August 1863).

13. John Tullidge, "The Concert of the Deseret Musical Association," *DN*, 2 March 1864.

14. E.R. Snow, "That Concert," *DN*, 2 March 1864.

15. Scott C. Esplin, ed., *The Tabernacle: "An Old and Wonderful Friend,"* (Provo: Religious Studies Center, 2007), 170.

16. On the Boston comparison, see George Albert Smith to N. S. Elderkin, letter 11 November 1869, and to Mary O. Pope, letter 9 May 1870. On the cost of the instrument, see George Albert Smith to Hannah P. Butler, letter 28 January 1869. All in the Historian's Office Letterpress Copybook, CHL.

17. See George D. Pyper, *The Romance of an Old Playhouse* (Salt Lake City: Deseret, 1937), 155–57; Susa Young Gates, *Life Story of Brigham Young* (New York: Macmillan, 1930), 247; and Howard Hoggan Putnam, "George Edward Percy Careless: His Contributions to the Musical Culture of Utah and the Significance of His Life and Works," master's thesis, Brigham Young University, 1957, 95. For helpful surveys of Careless's career, see "George Careless" in Whitney, *History of Utah*, 4:351–52; George D. Pyper, "In Intimate Touch with George Careless," *Juvenile Instructor* 59 (1924): 113–18, 173–77, 233–36, 287–88; and Bruce David Maxwell, "George Careless, Pioneer Musician," *Utah Historical Quarterly* 53 (spring 1985): 131–43. The statements about being "chief director of music throughout the church," and "immediately [beginning] development of the Tabernacle choir" are in "Pioneer Choir Leader Tells Story of the Early Day Music Activities," *DN*, 28 February 1925; these statements are important because of the confusion about when Careless took on the Choir and under what circumstances.

18. For the pertinent mentions of Sands and Careless, see the respective front pages of *Millennial Star*, 23 November 1867 and 3 November 1869.

19. From a newspaper article (apparently *DN*), 13 October 1869, in Charles John Thomas Scrapbook, SC-HBLL.

20. Charles Raymond Varley, comp., "Thomas Cott Griggs 1845–1903: A Biography" (typescript), CHL, 6–7.

21. Pyper, "In Intimate Touch with George Careless," 233.

22. *Journal of Discourses*, 26 vols. (London: Latter-day Saints' Book Depot, 1855–86), 13:345.

23. "The Singing during Conference," *Millennial Star*, 31 May 1870.

24. The letter appeared in *DN*, 23 October 1872.

25. This information comes from an article about the Choir by Paul V. C. Whitney, in J. Spencer Cornwall Scrapbook, J. Spencer Cornwall Papers, SC-HBLL.

26. See the letter to the editor from George Goddard, 10 August 1875, published in the *DN* (date unknown), in the Charles John Thomas Scrapbook. Other notices on Sunday school choir concerts appear throughout the same source. For more on Sunday school music in this era, see George Goddard, "Thanks and Facts," *Juvenile Instructor* 9 (1 August 1874): 182; "Sunday School Matters," *Juvenile Instructor* 9 (28 August 1874): 206; and *Jubilee History of Latter-day Saints Sunday Schools*, 1849–99 (Salt Lake City: Deseret Sunday School Union, 1900), 27–28.

27. On this kind of pay for musicians, see Thomas McIntyre Journal, 2 June 1867, 12 March 1873, 15 and 26 November 1874, and many other dates through August 1875, CHL. For an overview of Careless's insistence on pay for his players, see Pyper, *Romance of an Old Playhouse*, 158.

28. The amount is based on Ebenezer Beesley's request to be paid what Careless had been and being granted that amount. Beesley, *Kind Words*, 364–65.

29. On the Brigham Young anecdote, see Gates, *Life Story of Brigham Young*, 247–48.

30. Tullidge, *History of Salt Lake City and Its Founders*, 775, 777. (The surrounding pages in this source also give some of the information in the previous paragraph.)

31. *Utah Musical Times* 2 (1 August 1877): 74.

32. On his resignation and the vote to elect Griggs, see the Thomas McIntyre Journal, 16 and 19 August 1880.

33. For a biographical overview of Griggs, including his relationship with the Tabernacle Choir, see Edwin F. Parry, "Some of Our Composers: Thomas C. Griggs," *Juvenile Instructor* 36, no. 23 (1 December 1901): 723–26. On Griggs's perspective on being elected Choir conductor in absentia, see Varley, "Thomas Cott Griggs 1845–1903," 11.

34. The entire run of the minutes during Beesley's tenure appears in Beesley, *Kind Words*, 673–717. All the information in this paragraph is found in these minutes.

35. Thomas McIntyre Journal, 22 August 1880.

36. See Varley, "Thomas Cott Griggs 1845–1903," 12.

37. The information and quotations in this sentence and the previous paragraph come from Beesley, *Kind Words*, 364–66.

38. The lighting issues are covered in the George Goddard Diaries, 8 and 14 June, 21 July, and 10 August 1882, CHL.

39. The subject of Mormon polygamy and its prosecution has been treated often in the scholarly world. For perhaps the best and most engaging overview, see B. Carmon Hardy, *Solemn Covenant: The Mormon Polygamous Passage* (Urbana: University of Illinois Press, 1992).

40. See, for example, "Biography of Thomas Broadbent," (29 October 1889, Mormon Diaries collection, SC-HBLL, 15; and Kate B. Carter, comp., *Our Pioneer Heritage*, 20 vols. (Salt Lake City: Daughters of Utah Pioneers, 1975), 10:309–10.

41. On this journalistic back and forth, see the minutes in Beesley, *Kind Words*, 696, 698.

42. These quotations are from Ernest Ingersoll, "Salt Lake City," *Harper's New Monthly Magazine* 69 (August 1884): 395–97.

43. Beesley's letter is reproduced in his *Kind Words*, 379–80.

44. See Beesley, *Kind Words*, 369–70.

45. The exchange of letters and other information on this project are found in ibid., 433–34.

46. This and the quotations that follow in this paragraph are from Tabernacle Choir Minutes, CHL, February 1885, transcribed in Beesley, *Kind Words*, 703–4. On the prevalence of incarcerations of "prominent citizens," see John Caine and Hiram Clawson to A. Chizzola, letter 15 October 1885, Deseret Dramatic Association Letterbooks, CHL.

CHAPTER 3. "MY TABERNACLE 'MORMON' CHOIR"

1. For a good overview of the evidence on this statement, see http://www.shields -research.org/General/LDS_Leaders/1stPres/Joseph_Smith/56_Year.htm (accessed 22 July 2013).

2. The quotations are from Abraham H. Cannon Journal, 7 October 1889 and 5 October 1890, Church History Library, the Church of Jesus Christ of Latter-day Saints (hereafter cited as CHL). This journal has been published in two edited forms: Edward Leo Lyman, ed., *Candid Insights of a Mormon Apostle: The Diaries of Abraham H. Cannon, 1889–1895* (Salt Lake City: Signature Books, 2010); Dennis B. Horne, *An Apostle's Record: The Journals of Abraham H. Cannon* (Clearfield, Utah: Gnolaum Books, 2004). The prophecies and expectations about 1891 are discussed in Malin L. Jacobs, "The Alleged Fifty-Six-Year Second Coming Prophecy of Joseph Smith: An Analysis," http:// www.shields-research.org/General/LDS_Leaders/1stPres/Joseph_Smith/56_Year.htm (accessed 11 October 2013).

3. Abraham H. Cannon Journal, 24 and 31 October 1890.

4. Evan Stephens has been written about more than any other Tabernacle Choir conductor. Sources range from his own autobiographical articles to scholarly treatments. The book that remains definitive is Ray L. Bergman, *The Children Sang: The Life and Music of Evan Stephens with the Mormon Tabernacle Choir* (Salt Lake City: Northwest Publishing, 1992). Among the most useful shorter works are B. F. Cummings Jr., "Shining Lights: Professor Evan Stephens," *Contributor* 16 (September 1895): 651–63; Orson F. Whitney, "Evan Stephens," *History of Utah* (Salt Lake City: George Q. Cannon & Sons, 1892–1904), 4:365–67; Evan Stephens, "The Great Musician" (memoir), in Kate B. Carter, comp., *Our Pioneer Heritage*, 20 vols. (Salt Lake City: Daughters of Utah Pioneers, 1975), 10:85–91; and Steve Dube, "The Music Mormon: Evan Stephens of Pencader," http://welshmormon.byu.edu/Resource_Info.aspx?id=2152 (accessed 26 August 2013). The Chadwick story is in *Richard P. Condie Interviewed by Jerold D. Ottley* (n.p.: Richard P. Condie, n.d.) (interviews conducted in 1978 and 1982), 14.

5. *Alexander Schreiner Reminisces* (Salt Lake City: Publishers Press, 1984), 104.

6. "Echoes of Music in Utah," *Salt Lake Tribune*, 6 January 1895.

7. See Ray L. Bergman, comp., "Evan Stephens's Compositions: A Compilation of 515 Known Titles of Evan Stephens's Musical Compositions" (typescript), CHL.

8. This letter, the source for this paragraph and the two that follow, appears in "The Tabernacle Choir," *Deseret Weekly* 45 (22 October 1892): 561–62. For a complete, though brief, history of the organ, see Barbara Owen, *The Mormon Tabernacle Organ: An American Classic* (Salt Lake City: Temple Square, 1990).

9. Reid L. Neilson, *Exhibiting Mormonism: The Latter-day Saints and the 1893 Chicago World's Fair* (Oxford: Oxford University Press, 2011).

10. The history of this contention and its relation to this eisteddfod is detailed in William D. Jones, *Wales in America: Scranton and the Welsh, 1860–1920* (Cardiff: University of Wales Press, 1993), 135–41.

11. The information in this and the next paragraph is covered in great detail in Neilson, *Exhibiting Mormonism*, 114–21. See also Phillips G. Davies, ed. and trans., "William D. Davies Visits the Welsh in Utah in 1891," *Utah Historical Quarterly* 49, no. 4 (fall 1981): 374–87.

12. Thomas Griggs Journal, 9 July 1893, CHL.

13. Ibid., 27 August 1893.

14. Ronald W. Walker, *Qualities That Count: Heber J. Grant as Businessman, Missionary, and Apostle* (Provo: Brigham Young University Press, 2004), 131.

15. See Edna Coray Dyer, "Music in Church Service" (typescript), Edna Coray Dyer Papers, L. Tom Perry Special Collections, Harold B. Lee Library, Brigham Young University (hereafter cited as SC-HBLL).

16. See Craig S. Campbell, *Images of the New Jerusalem: Latter Day Saint Faction Inter-*

pretations of Independence, Missouri (Knoxville: University of Tennessee Press, 2004), 150.

17. Evan Stephens quoted in "The Tabernacle Choir," *Deseret Weekly* 49 (1 September 1894): 340.

18. Quoted in Dyer, "Music in Church Service."

19. Quoted from the scrapbook of the event, excerpted in Linda Louise Pohly, "Welsh Choral Music in America in the Nineteenth Century," PhD dissertation, Ohio State University, 1989, 72. (For an overview of the event, see 68–71 of this source.)

20. "Editorial Department," *Pennsylvania School Journal* 42 (December 1893): 259.

21. Lyman, *Candid Insights of a Mormon Apostle*, 415; Scott Kenney, ed., *Wilford Woodruff's Journal 1833–1898*, 9 vols. (Salt Lake City: Signature Books, 1984), 9: 261. See also A. Karl Larson and Katharine Miles Larson, ed., *Diary of Charles Lowell Walker*, 2 vols. (Logan: Utah State University Press, 1980), 2:765.

22. The information and quotations in this and the following paragraph are from "The Famous Singing Contest," *Deseret Weekly* 47 (30 September 1893): 467–68.

23. "The Welsh Eisteddfod," *Music* (Chicago) 6 (September 1893): 545.

24. "Tabernacle Choir" (1894).

25. On Stephens's talk of resigning, see Thomas Griggs Journal, 25 October 1894 and 3 January 1895. On the salary increase, see Lyman, *Candid Insights*, 591–92.

26. Joseph F. Smith quoted in Charles Raymond Varley, comp., "Thomas Cott Griggs 1845–1903: A Biography" (typescript), 19, CHL.

27. Smith's letter appears in James R. Clark, ed., *Messages of the First Presidency*, 6 vols. (Salt Lake City: Bookcraft, 1965–75), 3:267–68.

28. The judge's review of the Salt Lake Chorus is found in *Salt Lake Tribune*, 5 October 1895.

29. Thomas Griggs Journal, 7 and 10 October 1895.

30. The reviews are excerpted in E. H. Pierce, comp., *Mormon Tabernacle Choir: Being a Collection of Newspaper Criticisms and Cullings from Metropolitan Magazines and Musical Journals* (Salt Lake City: n.p., 1910), 25–27.

31. Thomas Griggs Journal, 2 September 1896; "Denver's Musical Festival," *San Francisco Call*, 2 September 1896; "This Week in Church History," *Church News*, 24 August 1996; "Musical Progress in Utah," *Millennial Star* 58 (1896): 617–18. Edward H. Anderson, "Utah, We Love Thee," *Improvement Era* 20 (July 1917): 767.

32. See Bergman, "Evan Stephens's Compositions."

33. Evan Stephens, letter of recommendation for Franklin Madsen, 1 April 1916, in Franklin and Florence Jepperson Madsen Papers, SC-HBLL.

34. These events are listed in the Eli H. Pierce Diary, July 1897, CHL. His charge for absenteeism is noted in Thomas Griggs Journal, 12 January 1896.

35. These quotations appear in Choir brochures of the time.

36. Agnes G. Murphy, *Melba: A Biography* (New York: Doubleday, 1909), 222. The earlier accounts of Stephens and Melba are taken from Mary Jack, interviewed by Mabel Jones Gabbott and Lucille Reading, typescript, 5–6, CHL.

37. The "choir member" mentioned is Edna Coray Dyer; see Edna Coray Dyer Journal, 17 April 1898, SC-HBLL. The Griggs quotes are from Thomas Griggs Journal, 15 and 21 April 1898.

38. The information and quotations in this and the following three paragraphs are in the front-page stories about the event in the *Salt Lake Tribune*, 8–10 October 1898. The conference remarks in question appear in the *Deseret Weekly* 18 (15 October 1898): 545. For more on this General Conference episode with John W. Taylor, see Dennis B. Horne (with materials prepared by Orson F. Whitney, 1890), *Latter Leaves in the Life of Lorenzo Snow* (Springville, Utah: Cedar Fort, 2012), 278–81, 519 n41.

39. The "czarlike autocracy" and "Stephens' Tabernacle Choir" statements are both in Thomas Griggs Journal, 9 January 1902.

40. About Stephens's threats (or "offers") to resign, see Edna Coray Dyer Journal, 1 August 1904.

41. See "The Old and New Tabernacle Organ" and "The Tabernacle Organ," both in *Deseret News* (hereafter cited as *DN*), 20 April 1901. The *Tribune* notices on this topic appear in the 19 and 21 April 1901 issues. See also Edna Coray Dyer Journal, 21 April 1901.

42. The aftermath of the organ debate is outlined in Thomas Griggs Journal, 26 August and 6 November 1902.

43. For the information in this paragraph, see E. Pierce, *Mormon Tabernacle Choir*, 25–28.

44. On plans for the St. Louis trip, see Stan Larson, ed., *A Ministry of Meetings: The Apostolic Diaries of Rudger Clawson* (Salt Lake City: Signature Books, 1993), 713.

45. On the Reed Smoot hearings, see Michael Harold Paulos, ed., *The Mormon Church on Trial: Transcripts of the Reed Smoot Hearings* (Salt Lake City: Signature Books, 2008).

46. In Clark, *Messages of the First Presidency*, 4:104–5.

47. Edna Coray Dyer Journal, 28 April 1904. The quotation in the next paragraph is from the same source, 17 October 1904.

48. See Kenneth L. Cannon II, "'And Now It Is the Mormons': The Magazine Crusade against the Mormon Church, 1910–1911," *Dialogue: A Journal of Mormon Thought* 46, no. 1 (spring 2013): 1–63.

49. Quoted in E. Pierce, *Mormon Tabernacle Choir*, 29.

50. "The Phonograph," *DN*, 21 September 1878; on the 1900 recording attempt, see Griggs Journal, 29 March 1900.

51. The standard account of this episode—on which I heavily rely—is Richard E. Turley Jr., "'Epoch in Musical History': The Mormon Tabernacle Choir's First Recordings," *Utah Historical Quarterly* 79, no. 2 (Spring 2011): 100–121. Turley is the scholar to whom

I refer in the following paragraph. For a complete listing of the recordings (including the Tabernacle Choir as "the Handelian Choir"), see Tim Brooks, *The Columbia Master Book Discography*, vol. 1, *U.S. Matrix Series 1 through 4999, 1901–1910* (Westport, Conn.: Greenwood Press, 1999), 401–2.

52. E. Pierce, *Mormon Tabernacle Choir*, 45–48.

53. Ibid., 45.

54. Presiding Bishop Charles Nibley's comment is recorded in the Anthon Lund Journal, 17 April 1911, CHL. The contract letter to E. Pierce and all other information and quotations in this and the following three paragraphs come from the pertinent tour papers (box 15) in the George D. Pyper Papers, Special Collections, J. Willard Marriott Library, University of Utah. For the tour in a larger Church context, see James B. Allen and Glen M. Leonard, *The Story of the Latter-day Saints* (Salt Lake City: Deseret Book, 1976), 474–75.

55. Glenn Dillard Dunn, "In the World of Music: Mormon Chorus Sings Praises of Irrigation," *Chicago Daily Tribune*, 27 October 1911.

56. A copy of the July 1915 program is in the Emma Lucy Gates Bowen Papers, SC-HBLL.

57. Pyper's characterization in his article "Evan Stephens," *Improvement Era* 36 (July 1933): 573.

CHAPTER 4. THE POWER OF THE AIR

1. "Choir Will Reorganize Big Tabernacle Choir," *Salt Lake Telegram*, 19 October 1915, excerpted in Ray L. Bergman, *The Children Sang: The Life and Music of Evan Stephens with the Mormon Tabernacle Choir* (Salt Lake City: Northwest Publishing, 1992). All of the information and quotations in this and the following three paragraphs comes from this source, 10–14, and Evan Stephens's letter to the *Salt Lake Telegram*, 22 October 1915, reprinted at 271–74.

2. See Joseph F. Smith to Anthon H. Lund, letter 15 August 1916, First Presidency Letterbooks, excerpted and transcribed in Scott Kenney Collection, Special Collections, J. Willard Marriott Library, University of Utah.

3. This characterization of Lund comes from William King Driggs, "L.D.S. Church Academies Music Departments-1904 to 1924" (manuscript), L. Tom Perry Special Collections, Harold B. Lee Library, Brigham Young University (hereafter cited as SC-HBLL); Mary Jack, interviewed by Mabel Jones Gabbott and Lucille Reading, typescript, Church History Library, the Church of Jesus Christ of Latter-day Saints (hereafter cited as CHL); letters relating to the divorce and his physical condition in the Cornelia Sorenson Lund Papers, SC-HBLL; "Anthony C. Lund," *Salt Lake Telegram*, 13 June 1935; and the editorial on Lund's passing in *Deseret News* (hereafter cited as *DN*), 12 June 1935.

4. W. Driggs, "L.D.S. Church Academies Music Departments," 2.

5. "New Leader for Tabernacle Choir," *Salt Lake Tribune*, 17 August 1916.

6. John P. Hatch, ed., *Danish Apostle: The Diaries of Anthon H. Lund, 1890–1921* (Salt Lake City: Signature Books, 2006), 615.

7. Joseph F. Smith to Evan Stephens, letter 19 July 1916, Scott Kenney Collection.

8. "Pete" [Cecil Gates] to Lucy Gates, letter 27 October 1916, Emma Lucy Gates Bowen Papers, SC-HBLL.

9. John Hatch, *Danish Apostle*, 626.

10. Benjamin Mark Roberts, "Anthony C. Lund, Musician, with Special Reference to His Teaching and Choral Directing," master's thesis, Brigham Young University (1952), 32.

11. John Hatch, *Danish Apostle*, 622.

12. His letter was published in "Tabernacle Choir Director Resigns," *Salt Lake Tribune*, 28 July 1916.

13. Roberts, "Anthony C. Lund," 34–35.

14. John Hatch, *Danish Apostle*, 635.

15. See Evan Stephens to Samuel Bailey Mitton, letters 28 July 1916 to 2 May 1927, published in Bergman, *The Children Sang*, 227–46.

16. All of these quotations come from Lund's undated, unpublished talk titled "What Shall We Do for Our Singers?" (holograph in Cornelia Sorenson Lund Papers).

17. Cornelia Sorenson Lund Papers.

18. See "Evan Stephens Lauded as Genius at Funeral," *DN*, 1 November 1930.

19. On the critical reception, see Michael Hicks, *Mormonism and Music: A History* (Urbana: University of Illinois Press, 1989), 174. The quotation from Grant about the work's quality comes from Heber J. Grant to Emma Lucy Gates, letter 31 March 1916, Emma Lucy Gates Bowen Papers.

20. This quotation and those in the next paragraph are from Albert Bowen to Emma Lucy Gates, 14 April 1922, Emma Lucy Gates Bowen Papers.

21. A detailed listing of all their recordings during these years may be found at victor.library.ucsb.edu (accessed 17 August 2013).

22. Madeline Davis quoted in J. Spencer Cornwall, *A Century of Singing: The Salt Lake Mormon Tabernacle Choir* (Salt Lake City: Deseret Book Co., 1958), 201.

23. J. S. Cornwall, *Century of Singing*, 84–85.

24. Charles N. Boyd, "Choir Development since 1876, and the Preeminent Choirmasters," in Karl W. Gehrkens, ed., *Volume of Proceedings of the Music Teacher's National Association: Twenty-Third Series* (Hartford, Conn.: MTNA, 1929), 70–71.

25. A copy of the brochure may be found in Scrapbooks, Cornelia Sorenson Lund Papers.

26. Rudolf Arnheim, *Radio* (London: Faber and Faber, 1936), 258–59.

27. Paul Valéry, "The Conquest of Ubiquity," in *Aesthetics*, trans. Ralph Manheim (New York: Pantheon Books, 1964), 225.

28. Earl J. Glade, "Preaching the Gospel through Radio," *Improvement Era* 28 (January 1925): 245.

29. For these quotations and more on the advent of KZN, see Heber G. Wolsey, "The History of Radio Station KSL from 1922 to Television," PhD dissertation, Michigan State University, 1967, 10–11.

30. Earl Glade, interviewed by Alma Heaton, 15 November 1984, SC-HBLL.

31. The most comprehensive source on these events is Wolsey, "History of Radio Station KSL," 133–55. See also the few details in " . . . a Legend in Radio," *Wasatch Front Focus* (April 2009): 5. For the larger context of religious broadcasting in the early days of radio, see Tona J. Hangen, *Redeeming the Dial: Radio, Religion, and Popular Culture in America* (Chapel Hill: University of North Carolina Press, 2002), 21–36.

32. "Tabernacle Choir Rehearses Tonight for Big Broadcast," *DN*, 10 July 1929.

33. For more on the first broadcast and its reception, see J. S. Cornwall, *Century of Singing*, 227–28.

34. Earl J. Glade, "To the Ends of the Western Hemisphere," *Improvement Era* 34, no. 4 (February 1931): 223. The quotation in the next paragraph is from this same page.

35. Roberts, "Anthony C. Lund," 64.

36. W. C. Holt letter cited in ibid., 38–39.

37. This and all subsequent quotations from broadcasts, as well as information on the titles, come from the bound scripts in Richard L. Evans, Files, CHL.

38. Savage is quoted in Varley, "Thomas Cott Griggs," 23.

39. Wayne B. Hales, "Acoustical Properties of the Salt Lake Tabernacle," *Journal of the Acoustical Society of America* 6 (January 1930): 291–92.

40. See Tracy Cannon to Ed Kimball, letter 13 May 1930, Edward P. Kimball Collection, SC-HBLL.

41. David Smith quoted in Jack Sears, "Anthony C. Lund and Tracy Y. Cannon Sponsor New Movie Star," *News Advocate* (Price, Utah), 13 February 2013, 6–7.

42. In this account I rely chiefly on Kenneth Fielding McAllister and Maridon McAllister Morrison, *The Life of Our Parents: G. Stanley and Donnette McAllister* (n.p.: Kenneth McAllister, 2012), 35. On the birth of the *Church of the Air* series, see "Religion: Church of the Air," *Time*, 24 August 1931.

43. Roberts, "Anthony C. Lund," 65.

44. The article, 15 December 1932, Adeline Ensign Scrapbook, CHL.

45. *The Seventies Manual 1934–1935: The Basic Principles of Spiritual Progress* (Salt Lake City: Deseret News, 1934), 54.

46. Roberts, "Anthony C. Lund," 66. For an overview of the fair and its layout, see David L. Lewis, *The Public Image of Henry Ford: An American Folk Hero and His Company* (Detroit, Mich.: Wayne State University Press, 1987), 302–3; Robert W. Rydell, *World of Fairs: The Century of Progress Expositions* (Chicago: University of Chicago Press, 1994).

47. A copy of the Church's fair brochure is in the Lund Scrapbooks.

48. For more on the Choir's itinerary, see the articles about the tour in *DN*, 11, 12, 14, 15, 17, and 19 September 1934.

49. *The Diaries of J. Reuben Clark, 1931–1961, Abridged* (Salt Lake City: n.p., 2010), 11 (18 February 1934).

50. This is taken from a timeline of the Church Music Committee in the Tracy Y. Cannon Papers, CHL.

51. *The Diaries of Heber J. Grant, 1880–1945, Abridged* (Salt Lake City: n.p., 2010), 407 (4 and 10 April 1935).

52. J. Spencer Cornwall Oral History, interviews by Carol Cornwall Madsen, 1980, typescript, CHL, 1–2.

53. Sylvester Q. Cannon to J. Spencer Cornwall, letter 10 June 1935, J. Spencer Cornwall Papers, SC-HBLL.

54. J. Spencer Cornwall Oral History, 3.

CHAPTER 5. FROM WITHIN THE SHADOW

1. On the cutting of members and new audition requirements, see J. Spencer Cornwall, *A Century of Singing: The Salt Lake Mormon Tabernacle Choir* (Salt Lake City: Deseret Book Co., 1958), 9, 11–15; Gail Martin, "In the Major Key," *Deseret News* (hereafter cited as *DN*, 11 April 1936. The quotation ("A person can't sing well . . ."), as well as other information in this and the following paragraph is taken from E. R. Zaloudez, "'And He Shall Gently Lead Them,'" *Bee* (date unknown), in J. Spencer Cornwall Scrapbook, J. Spencer Cornwall Papers, L. Tom Perry Special Collections, Harold B. Lee Library, Brigham Young University (hereafter cited as SC-HBLL).

2. The Ottley quotations are from Jerold Ottley, interviewed by Gordon Irving (January-September 1983), typescript, Church History Library, the Church of Jesus Christ of Latter-day Saints (hereafter cited as CHL), 225. The Schreiner quotation is from *Alexander Schreiner Reminisces* (Salt Lake City: Publishers Press, 1984), 104. The "cute" quotation is from Mary Jack, interviewed by Mabel Jones Gabbott and Lucille Reading, typescript, 10, CHL. The joke and other details of Cornwall's rehearsal techniques appear in Evan M. Wylie, "'Gently Raise the Sacred Strain': The Story of the Great Mormon Tabernacle Choir," *Collier's*, 7 January 1950, 60–62.

3. Cornwall recounted this meeting variously over the years. This account relies on J. S. Cornwall, *Century of Singing*, 48.

4. For a lengthy account of this episode, see J. S. Cornwall, *Century of Singing*, 202–5.

5. Edward P. Kimball, "A Reprehensible Practice," *Improvement Era* 35 (June 1932): 490.

6. As quoted in an AP "special report," included in Larry Kurtz to Richard L. Evans, letter 7 December 1967, Richard L. Evans, Papers, CHL.

7. The time sheets and scripts for these years of broadcasts are in Richard L. Evans, Files (a collection distinct from "Papers"), CHL.

8. The salary information is in *Richard P. Condie Interviewed by Jerold D. Ottley* (n.p.: Richard P. Condie, n.d.) (interviews conducted in 1978 and 1982), 5.

9. *Richard P. Condie Interviewed by Jerold D. Ottley*, 23.

10. For an article and picture about Hewlett's Supreme Coffee, see "Hewlett's Install Latest Vacuum Sealing Plant," *Utah Payroll Builder* 8, no. 9 (May 1921): 37.

11. Quoted in Ronald W. Walker, *Qualities That Count: Heber J. Grant as Businessman, Missionary, and Apostle* (Provo: Brigham Young University Press, 2004), 279.

12. Joseph Smith et al., *History of the Church of Jesus Christ of Latterday Saints*, edited by B. H. Roberts, 7 vols., 2nd ed. rev. (Salt Lake City: Deseret Book, 1948 printing) 6:254.

13. J. S. Cornwall treats this performance at length in his *Century of Singing*, 165–69.

14. Gail Martin, "Fanfare: Presentation of 'Elijah' at Tabernacle Recalls Genius of Mendelssohn, the Composer," *DN*, 1 October 1938.

15. A. F. Maisch to Richard L. Evans, letter 9 September 1939, Richard L. Evans Files.

16. *The Diaries of J. Reuben Clark, 1931–1961, Abridged* (Salt Lake City: n.p., 2010), 18 (14 December 1938).

17. Schreiner became one of the most popular (and best-paid) of the organists at the Tabernacle and, more to the point, on the broadcast. Like other Tabernacle organists, he is overshadowed by the Choir in this treatise. For an in-depth treatment of his career, see Daniel Frederick Berghout, *Alexander Schreiner: Mormon Tabernacle Organist* (Provo: Joseph Fielding Smith Institute for Latter-day Saint History and BYU Studies, 2001). See also Schreiner's scattered but delightful quasi-memoir, *Alexander Schreiner Reminisces*.

18. *The Diaries of Heber J. Grant, 1880–1945, Abridged* (Salt Lake City: n.p., 2010), 385.

19. For an anthology of the more positive fan mail received by the Choir under Cornwall, see J. S. Cornwall, *Century of Singing*, 277–313.

20. All the information and quotations in this paragraph are from the *Diaries of J. Reuben Clark*, 26–28 (22–23 June 1939). See also the entry for 3 February 1939 (22).

21. Tabernacle Choir Minutes (hereafter cited as TCM), 26 April 1942, CHL.

22. James R. Clark, ed., *Messages of the First Presidency*, 6 vols. (Salt Lake City, Bookcraft, 1965–1975), 6:88. The letter itself is in the Tracy Y. Cannon Papers, CHL. The First Presidency reaffirmed this letter in 1951 (TCM, 18 October 1951).

23. M. O. Ashton (for Presiding Bishopric) to Harvey Fletcher, letter 12 August 1939, Harvey Fletcher Papers, SC-HBLL; Harvey Fletcher to M. O. Ashton, letter 18 August 1939, Harvey Fletcher Papers. See also *Diaries of J. Reuben Clark*, 32–33 (22 August 1939).

24. The papers related to this affair are in the J. Spencer Cornwall Papers, including his 1940 diary, from which "accomplished" quotation is taken (21 January 1940).

25. "Super-Volume Concert Records Scare Audience," *New York Herald Tribune*, 10 April 1940; "Sound Waves 'Rock' Carnegie Hall as 'Enhanced Music' Is Played," *New York Times*, 10 April 1940.

26. Greg Milner, *Perfecting Sound Forever: An Aural History of Recorded Music* (New York: Faber and Faber, 2009), 51.

27. The report and other correspondence related to this request are in the Fletcher Papers.

28. This episode is recorded in *Diaries of J. Reuben Clark*, 49–51 (7, 15, 19, 27–28 March and 1 April 1941).

29. Quoted in the *Tabernacle Organ* (official publication of the Choir), 27 July 1941.

30. A copy is in the J. Spencer Cornwall Papers.

31. Isabel Morse Jones, "15,000 Hear Concert by Tabernacle Choir," *Los Angeles Times*, 21 August 1941. Alfred Frankenstein, "Mormon Choir Upholds Tradition in S.F. Concert" [August 1941] in J. Spencer Cornwall Scrapbook.

32. Heber J. Grant to J. Spencer Cornwall, letter 18 February 1942, J. Spencer Cornwall Papers.

33. On the "drafting" into the Choir, see TCM, 9 April 1942.

34. The "desperate" quotation is in TCM, 3 September 1942. The statement about striking the piano is in TCM, 22 October 1942.

35. William O. Shaddix to Columbia Broadcasting Co., letter 26 January 1941, in Richard L. Evans Files.

36. Cornwall's quote about being "on guard" is in TCM, 5 July 1942. On the hats issue, see TCM, 25 June 1942 and 30 March 1944. The hair combing incident is mentioned in TCM, 16 April 1950.

37. *Diaries of Heber J. Grant*, 465 (13 August 1942).

38. See John E. Dewey to J. Reuben Clark, letter 11 July 1944, J. Spencer Cornwall Papers.

39. Dimitri Tiomkin to J. Spencer Cornwall, letters 27 June and 21 July 1944, J. Spencer Cornwall Papers.

40. *Diaries of J. Reuben Clark*, 85 (29 November 1944).

41. TCM, 10 August 1944.

42. First Presidency to J. Spencer Cornwall, letter 22 December 1947, J. Spencer Cornwall Papers. On the *Creation* performance, see Conrad B. Harrison, "Tabernacle Choir Thrills Audience with Its Rendition of 'The Creation,'" *DN*, 2 July 1947. On Elijah, see Conrad B. Harrison, "Tabernacle Choir Outstanding in Impressive 'Elijah' Performance," *DN*, 9 August 1947.

43. TCM, 21 April 1946.

44. On this whole episode (including the quotation), see First Presidency to Adam Bennion, letter 9 September 1946, and J. Reuben Clark to Adam Bennion, letter 4 November 1946, in J. Reuben Clark, Papers, SC-HBLL. The "catspaw" quotation is from *Diaries of J. Reuben Clark*, 96 (5 August 1946).

45. For the fullest account of the symphony's encounters and disputes with the Choir, see Maurice Abravanel interviewed by Jay M. Hammond (typescript), 24 September 1981, Utah State Historical Society Archives, 3, 8–16, 19–25, 42–43.

46. TCM, 17 October 1948.

47. Tracy Y. Cannon to First Presidency, letter 17 October 1935, Tracy Y. Cannon Papers.

48. The *Saturday Review* review is quoted in J. S. Cornwall, *Century of Singing*, 215; see also *High Fidelity* 6, no. 2 (February 1956), 96. The Presbyterian record playing is mentioned in TCM, 20 January 1955.

49. TCM, 17 August 1952.

50. TCM, 28 February 1957.

51. TCM, 22 February 1951.

52. TCM, 27 March 1955. The "bunk" quotation is from TCM, 5 February 1953.

53. TCM, 29 October 1950.

54. The "beer programs" issue is discussed at length in *Diaries of J. Reuben Clark*, 179–84 (16–17, 22, 24 October 1951).

55. Mary Jack interview, 20.

56. Warren John "Jack" Thomas, *Salt Lake Mormon Tabernacle Choir Goes to Europe—1955* (Salt Lake City: Deseret News Press, 1957), xv. This book is the most detailed single source on the tour.

57. See Thomas, *Salt Lake Mormon Tabernacle Choir Goes to Europe*, 50–51.

58. The Hanson and other celebrity quotations are from "Nation's Top Music Groups Congratulate LDS Choir," newspaper clipping from (15?) July 1954 in the J. Spencer Cornwall Scrapbook; the *Life* quotation is from "The Chord of a Choir," *Life*, 26 July 1954, 20. The "angels" quotation is from Lamont E. Tueller to J. Spencer Cornwall, 16 October 1954, J. Spencer Cornwall Papers.

59. Allen S. Cornwall to Mark E. Petersen, 13 April 1955, in Salt Lake Tabernacle Tour Files, CHL.

60. The best overview of the whole *Book of Mormon* oratorio saga from its outset, see Marian Robertson Wilson, *Leroy Robertson: Music Giant from the Rockies* (Salt Lake City: Blue Ribbon Publications, 1996), 201–7, 271–72.

61. I base the generalizations in these two lists on the various relevant newspaper articles in Salt Lake Tabernacle Tour Files; Warren Thomas, *Salt Lake Mormon Tabernacle Choir Goes to Europe*; J. Spencer Cornwall Scrapbook. See especially the *London Times* review, 29 August 1955.

62. The quotations are from J. S. Cornwall, *Century of Singing*, 153 and 114, respectively.

63. For Cornwall's full account of this tour, see J. S. Cornwall, *Century of Singing*, 101–57.

64. See Fern Denise Gregory, "J. Spencer Cornwall: The Salt Lake Mormon Tabernacle Choir Years, 1935–1957," DMA dissertation, University of Missouri-Kansas City, 1984, 44.

65. *Richard P. Condie Interviewed by Jerold D. Ottley*, 25.

66. On this controversy, see TCM, 17 and 21 April 1955.

67. TCM, 8 September 1957.

CHAPTER 6. A CULTURAL NECESSITY

1. *Richard P. Condie Interviewed by Jerold D. Ottley* (n.p.: Richard P. Condie, n.d.) (interviews conducted in 1978 and 1982), 34.

2. On the Weight (misspelled "Waite") appointment and the subsequent discussion, see David O. McKay Diary, 20 August 1957, David O. McKay Papers, Special Collections, J. Willard Marriott Library, University of Utah.

3. This Cornwall conversation and the Condie conversation that follows (quoted as transcribed by his secretary, Clare Middlemiss) are from a telephone conversation between David O. McKay and Stephen L. Richards, 13 September 1957, David O. McKay Papers.

4. David O. McKay Diary, 15 September 1957.

5. Transcripts of McKay's telephone conversations with Stephen Richards, 18 September 1957, David O. McKay Papers; David O. McKay Diary, 26 September 1957.

6. These figures come from Harper Carraine to Jay W. Wright, letter 15 December 1960, Richard L. Evans, Files, Church History Library, the Church of Jesus Christ of Latter-day Saints (hereafter cited as CHL).

7. Tabernacle Choir Minutes (hereafter cited as TCM), 14 January 1958, CHL.

8. On the difference in style, Mary Jack, interviewed by Mabel Jones Gabbott and Lucille Reading, typescript, CHL, 10.

9. TCM, 29 September 1957.

10. TCM, 19 December 1957.

11. The information and quotations in this paragraph are from TCM, 8 April 1958.

12. Ottley discusses this in Jerold Ottley, interviewed by Gordon Irving (January–September 1983), typescript, CHL, 73–74, from which the ensuing discussion of Condie's rehearsal methods is found.

13. An interesting account of Condie from an outsider watching a broadcast in the Tabernacle may be found in Wallace Turner, *The Mormon Establishment* (Boston: Houghton Mifflin, 1966), 29–32.

14. TCM, 14 May 1959.

15. For the quotes and analogies, see Vicki Alder, *Under My Baton: Richard P. Condie with the Mormon Tabernacle Choir* (Salt Lake City: Promontory, 2008), 37–39.

16. TCM, 10 February 1958.

17. The standard works on the split in repertoire, as dictated primarily by Columbia Records, are Mark David Porcaro, "Secularization of the Repertoire of the Mormon Tabernacle Choir, 1949–1992," PhD dissertation, University of North Carolina, 2006; and Mark David Porcaro, "'We Have Something Really Going between Us Now': Columbia Records' Influence on the Repertoire of the Mormon Tabernacle Choir, 1949–1992," http://www.ncco-usa.org/tcs/issues/vol1/no1/porcaro/TCS_Porcaro_MTC.pdf (accessed 30 October 2013).

18. Review of *The Lord Is My Shepherd*, *High Fidelity* 8, no. 12 (December 1958): 70.

19. Porcaro deals at length with Columbia's desire to emulate and rival both Shaw and Wagner's choirs in his "We Have Something Really Going between Us Now," 48–58.

20. See TCM, 25 May and 30 September 1958.

21. Ray Ericson, review of *The Beloved Choruses*, *High Fidelity* 9, no. 6 (June 1959): 77.

22. As quoted in Marian Robertson Wilson, *Leroy Robertson: Music Giant from the Rockies* (Salt Lake City: Blue Ribbon Publications, 1996), 237.

23. The budget is outlined in TCM, 13 July 1958. Isaac Stewart referred to these "two wealthy members" as funding Choir tours generally in his interview with Ronald W. Walker, 5 October 1981, typescript, CHL, 2.

24. For the details of the making of this recording, I have relied heavily on the first-hand account in Alexander F. Schreiner, interview by Nancy Furner Hurtado (1973–75), 40–43, typescript, CHL.

25. *High Fidelity* 10, no. 1 (January 1960): 64.

26. The "interesting" quotation is from TCM, 16 November 1958. The invitation and the Choir members' lack of televisions are discussed in "Famed Choir Invited for Telecast," *Deseret News* (hereafter cited as *DN*), 26 November 1958, and TCM, 21 December 1958.

27. Lester Hewlett to George Romney, letter 17 February 1958, Tabernacle Choir Tour Files, CHL.

28. Tallies and samples from these letters are found in Richard L. Evans, Papers (a collection distinct from "Files"), CHL.

29. See the file on this broadcast, April 1960, in Richard L. Evans Papers.

30. Richard L. Evans to Lester F. Hewlett, letter 29 February 1960, Richard L. Evans Files.

31. Paul H. Evans to Lester F. Hewlett, letter 5 April 1960, Richard L. Evans Files.

32. David O. McKay Diary, 18 May 1962.

33. Ibid., 26 and 27 September 1962.

34. Schuyler G. Chapin and John T. McClure to Lester F. Hewlett, letter 22 April 1960, reprinted in Porcaro, "Secularization of the Repertoire of the Mormon Tabernacle Choir," 294–96.

35. Ted Cannon to Lester F. Hewlett, letter 29 May 1962, Richard L. Evans Files.

36. These and other transcribed excerpts are in Lowell Durham to Jessie Evans Smith, letter 30 March 1970, Lowell M. Durham Papers, L. Tom Perry Special Collections, Harold B. Lee Library, Brigham Young University.

37. Ted L. Cannon, "Re: Satellite T.V. Broadcast," memo 8 May 1962, Richard L. Evans Files.

38. The story of this Rushmore switch appears in Kirk Johnson, "Mormons on a Mission," *New York Times*, 20 August 2010.

39. The information and quotations in this paragraph come from the voluminous correspondence on this listenership campaign (1961–63) in Evans Papers.

40. Richard Evans quoted in an AP Special Report included in Larry Kurtz to Richard Evans, letter 7 December 1967, Richard L. Evans Files.

41. On the network's removal of the five minutes, see Richard L. Evans to Arch Madsen, letter 1 December 1961, Richard L. Evans Files. On this matter in 1962, as well as the others discussed in this paragraph, see David O. McKay Diary, 29 December 1962.

42. All of the information in this and the next two paragraphs comes from the very detailed accounts in David O. McKay Diary, 6 June and 3 September 1963.

43. For quasi-official overview of the recording sessions, see "Two Historic Occasions Feature Choir with JFK and Bernstein," *Keeping Tab*, 6 October 1963. A useful recollection of the sessions appears in a comment made by Julie Bevan on 6 August 2005 in the thread at http://www.amazon.com/The-Christmas-John-Francis-Wade/dp/B0000029Z6 (accessed 28 June 2014).

44. The proposal was first made to the Choir in Carlos Moseley to Lester F. Hewlett, letter 3 April 1962, Richard L. Evans Files.

45. For vivid descriptions of this episode, see Mary Jack interview, 19; Ottley interviewed by Irving, 78.

46. On the overlap of the Oswald shooting and the Choir broadcast, see Richard L. Evans to Fred Friendly, letter 30 November 1964; on the reimbursement proposal, see Richard L. Evans to Isaac M. Stewart and Ted Cannon, letter 3 January 1964; both are in Richard L. Evans Files.

47. The quotations are from Richard L. Evans to Isaac M. Stewart, Richard P. Condie, et al., letter 17 December 1962, Richard L. Evans Files.

48. As quoted in Hank Reineke, *Ramblin' Jack Elliott: The Never-Ending Highway* (Lanham, Md.: Scarecrow Press, 2010), 168. For the *Saturday Review* quotation and other excerpts from that review, I relied on Harold Lundstrom, "Critic Lauds Mormon Disc," *DN*, 19 February 1966.

49. David O. McKay Diary, 10 February 1965.

50. See ibid., 9 April 1965, and the 1 April 1965 personnel request forms in Richard L. Evans Papers.

51. See Isaac M. Stewart and Theodore L. Cannon to David O. McKay, letter 18 November 1965, Richard L. Evans Files.

52. David O. McKay Diary, 26–28 July and 20 August 1965.

53. Richard L. Evans to Isaac M. Stewart and Ted Cannon, letter 24 August 1965; Isaac M. Stewart and Theodore L. Cannon to First Presidency, letter 30 August 1965; both in Richard L. Evans Papers. For an overview of the Church's acquisition and exploitation of television stations during this era, see Gregory Prince and William Robert Wright, *David O. McKay and the Rise of Modern Mormonism* (Salt Lake City: University of Utah Press, 2005), 124–38.

54. Isaac M. Stewart and Theodore L. Cannon to First Presidency, letter 30 August 1965, Richard L. Evans Files.

55. On this matter, see David O. McKay Diary, 9 June and 4 August 1964.

56. TCM, 1 October 1964. Non-Tabernacle Choir music for the conference was taken up by BYU Choirs and the Relief Society's women's chorus, the Singing Mothers.

57. Porcaro provides a comprehensive track-by-track list of the Choir's albums, 1949–92, in "We Have Something Really Going between Us Now," 70–115.

58. Ezra Taft Benson to Isaac M. Stewart, letter 19 November 1965, Richard L. Evans Files.

59. Review of *Ein Deutsches Requiem* by Johannes Brahms, *High Fidelity* 13, no. 12 (December 1963): 73.

60. Harold Lundstrom, "Maestro Lauds Tabernacle Choir," *DN*, 17 June 1967.

61. Isaac Stewart to Richard Condie, letter 30 November 1967, Richard L. Evans Files. See also "RCA Victor Woos Ormandy from Columbia," *New York Times*, 29 November 1967.

62. Isaac Stewart to Richard Condie, letter 30 November 1967, Richard L. Evans Papers.

63. See Lester Hewlett and Richard Condie to William R. Johnson, letter December 1960, in Porcaro, "Secularization of the Repertoire of the Mormon Tabernacle Choir," 299. Their basic argument was that the symphony was a group of professionals, the Choir amateurs with only proselytes for their reward. Collaborating could set a bad precedent and cause union troubles, as well.

64. Isaac Stewart to David O. McKay, letter 9 May 1967, Richard L. Evans Files.

65. See David O. McKay Diary, 27 March 1967; Mark E. Petersen in a memo attached to a letter from David O. McKay to himself (27 March 1967) and copied to Richard Evans. Richard L. Evans Files.

66. Boyd K. Packer to Harold B. Lee, letter quoted in Lucile C. Tate, *Boyd K. Packer: A Watchman on the Tower* (Salt Lake City: Bookcraft, 1995), 154.

67. David O. McKay Diary, 21 November 1967.

68. Stewart interview with Walker, 3.

69. From a letter by Richard Nixon to Isaac Stewart included in *Keeping Tab*, 6 October 1968.

70. See Charles J. Weber to Richard L. Evans, letter 12 December 1969, and Evans's letter of reply, 22 December 1969, both in Richard L. Evans Papers.

71. Lowell M. Durham, "The State of Church Music-1970" (dated 22 September 1969), Lowell M. Durham Papers.

72. Wynetta Martin tells the story of her admittance into and tenure with the Choir in *Black Mormon Tells Her Story* (Salt Lake City: Hawkes, 1972).

73. All of the information and quotations in this paragraph are from Isaac M. Stewart to Harold B. Lee, letter 21 July 1970, Richard L. Evans Papers.

74. See Richard L. Evans to First Presidency, letter 23 February 1971, Richard L. Evans Papers.

75. Richard L. Evans to Richard P. Condie, letter 20 January 1971, Richard L. Evans Papers.

76. Durham to Smith, 30 March 1970.

77. The quotations and information in this paragraph are from TCM, 7 November 1971 and 27 February 1972.

CHAPTER 7. SOFT SELL

1. Michael F. Moody to O. Leslie Stone, letter 14 December 1973, Music Department Office Files, Church History Library, the Church of Jesus Christ of Latter-day Saints (hereafter cited as CHL).

2. A. Harold Goodman to O. Leslie Stone, letter 19 December 1973, Music Department Office Files.

3. Church Music Committee (signed by Stone, Petersen, and Packer) to First Presidency, letter draft 21 December 1973, Music Department Office Files.

4. See Edward L. Kimball, ed., *The Teachings of Spencer W. Kimball* (Salt Lake City: Bookcraft, 1982), 587–88.

5. All the statements of fact and quotations in this and the next paragraph come from *Richard P. Condie Interviewed by Jerold D. Ottley* (n.p.: Richard P. Condie, n.d.) (interviews conducted in 1978 and 1982), 33–34; Lowell M. Durham, "Changing of the Guard at the Crossroads," unpublished paper in Lowell M. Durham Papers, L. Tom Perry Special Collections, Harold B. Lee Library, Brigham Young University, 6–8; and Vicki Alder, *Under My Baton: Richard P. Condie with the Mormon Tabernacle Choir* (Salt Lake City: Promontory, 2008), 91–92. On Condie's actual resignation in front of the Choir, see Orvilla Allred Stevens, *Looking Back to Learn, Looking Ahead with Faith* ([Provo?]: Orvilla Allred Stevens, 1989), 258.

6. On the Mormon Youth Chorus as a feeder group, see Jerold Ottley, interviewed by Gordon Irving (January-September 1983), typescript, CHL, 105. On the age limits, see 113.

7. Comment in the autobiographical document "History of Robert Milton Cundick," typescript, 24, CHL.

8. The only extensive history from which my account draws its facts appears in Ottley interviewed by Irving, 108–12. The quotations by Scott are from Russell Scott, interviewed by Don Ripplinger, typescript, 31–32, CHL. On Welch's resignation in front of the Choir and its emotional aftermath, see Orvilla A. Stevens, Oral History, interview by Charles Ursenbach (1975), 156–59, CHL.

9. Ottley discusses the Jay Welch Chorale in Ottley interviewed by Irving, 182–83. On the return to the University of Utah, see J. Boyer Jarvis to Pete D. Gardner, memo 16 December 1974, University of Utah Personnel Files, Special Collections, J. Willard Marriott Library, University of Utah.

10. *Richard P. Condie Interviewed by Jerold D. Ottley*, 33.

11. Ottley interviewed by Irving, 62.

12. On this arrangement, see ibid., 101.

13. Ottley interviewed by Irving, 117.

14. These employment details are found in ibid., 120–21.

15. Isaac Stewart Reminiscence (1980), typescript, 3–4, CHL. The quote from Ottley is from Ottley interviewed by Irving, 123.

16. Ottley interviewed by Irving, 122; for more on Evans's administration, see 131.

17. Oakley S. Evans, *Merchandising, Memories, and Me* (Provo: Family History Services, Brigham Young University, 1988), 166.

18. Ottley interviewed by Irving, 143.

19. The quotations come from Boyd K. Packer, "The Arts and the Spirit of the Lord," *BYU Studies* 16, no. 4 (summer 1976): 5–6.

20. JoAnn Ottley to "New Members," undated memo (ca. 1980), copy in author's possession.

21. Quoted in Mark David Porcaro, "Secularization of the Repertoire of the Mormon Tabernacle Choir, 1949–1992," PhD dissertation, University of North Carolina, 2006, 30.

22. Ottley interviewed by Irving, 74.

23. Ibid., 31–32.

24. Clive Davis (with James Willwerth), *Clive: Inside the Record Business* (New York: William Morrow, 1975), 232. (See also 240 on the problems with selling classical records, especially McClure's new avant-garde titles.)

25. On Columbia's shift during this period, see Ottley interviewed by Irving, 181.

26. Review of *A Jubilant Song, American Record Guide* 40, no. 1 (November 1976): 49.

27. Review of *A Jubilant Song, High Fidelity* 26, no. 11 (November 1976): 140.

28. Ottley interviewed by Irving, 136–37, 187.

29. "Church Representatives at Reagan Inauguration," *Ensign* 11, no. 3 (March 1981): 74.

30. "Reagan Thanks Choir for 'Gift of Love for America,'" *Church News*, 20 March 1981.

31. This is my taxonomy of the unsorted list given in O. Evans, *Merchandising, Memories, and Me*, 172–73.

32. Ottley interviewed by Irving, 172.

33. See ibid., 195.

34. Ibid., 134.

35. Copies of the 3 August 1986 surveys, titled "Mormon Tabernacle Choir Audience Survey," and their results (announced in a meeting at the Assembly Hall, Temple Square, 29 January 1987 and recorded by Thomas Durham) are in my possession.

36. The quotation is from Porcaro, "Secularization of the Repertoire of the Mormon Tabernacle Choir," 306.

37. James E. Talmage, *The House of the Lord* (Salt Lake City: Bookcraft, 1962), 99. For more on the evolution of the temple endowment, including its use of film, see David John Buerger, *The Mysteries of Godliness: A History of Mormon Temple Worship* (Salt Lake City: Signature Books, 2002).

38. On the *Messiah* faux pas, see "History of Robert Milton Cundick," 40; for the Palestinian quotation, see "Don Ripplinger History" (interview with Mike Ohman, 2 March 2009), 5, Franklin S. Harris Fine Arts Center Archive, School of Music, Brigham Young University.

39. See Melinda Sowerby, "LDS Foundation Helps Fund Education, Choir, Missionaries," *Salt Lake Tribune*, 18 December 1989.

40. See Jay M. Todd, "A Company of Angels," *Ensign* 28, no. 10 (October 1998): 30–37.

41. Tabernacle Choir Minutes (hereafter cited as TCM), 3 June 1990, CHL.

42. TCM, 7 June 1990 (for Smoot) and 26 June 1990 (for Ottley).

43. Vern Anderson, "Mormon Tabernacle Choir Announcer Off the Air," 27 October 1990, http://www.apnewsarchive.com/1990/Mormon-Tabernacle-Choir-Announcer -Off-the-Air/id-186d7c9ea6e84be568cde091ee046e3f (accessed 18 October 2013); Margaret Traub, "Voice of Mormon Tabernacle Choir Quits Over Relationship with Newswoman," 2 November 1990, in www.apnewsarchive.com/1990/ (accessed 6 August 2013); Scott D. Pierce, "Kinard Resigns as Vice President of News and Public Affairs for KSL," *Deseret News* (hereafter cited as *DN*), 1 November 1990; "Kinard Says He Suffered Depression after Resigning," *DN*, 13 December 1992.

44. See Quig Nielsen, "Tabernacle Group Has Sung under Direction of Celebrities from Snoopy to Jimmy Stewart," *DN*, 9 January 1991; "Shamu Makes 'Moonlight' Splash with Choir," *DN*, 6 May 1994. Reviews for the Choir on its 1991 tour were collated in a thick booklet for Choir members titled *The Salt Lake Mormon Tabernacle Choir: Historic Tour to Europe and USSR, June 8–29, 1991*, copy in CHL.

45. See Gerald A. Petersen, *The Mormon Tabernacle Choir: More than Music* (Provo: Brigham Young University Press, 1979); Charles Jeffrey Calman, *The Mormon Tabernacle Choir* (New York: Harper & Row, 1979); D. Michael Quinn, *Same-Sex Dynamics among Nineteenth-Century Americans: A Mormon Example* (Urbana: University of Illinois Press, 1996). This last volume was based on earlier papers Quinn had given at Mormon-related conferences. Ottley talks about the Calman book in some depth in Ottley interviewed by Irving, 193–94.

46. http://maxwellinstitute.byu.edu/publications/review/?vol=10&num=1&id=280 (accessed 17 August 2013). A fascinating footnote to this discussion came in the assertion that Stephens's sacred temple apron was passed along to a friend's quasi-adoptive son because of the latter's gay status. See http://people.ucsc.edu/~odonovan/evan.html (accessed 27 August 2013).

47. The list of achievements is collected from TCM, 1996. The General Conference quote is from 2 April 1996.

48. The quotations about the tour are found in Todd, "A Company of Angels." The Book of Mormon quotation is from 2 Nephi 1:23.

49. The information and quote in this paragraph are in TCM, 14–16 February and 18 March 1999.

50. First Presidency to General Authorities; Area Authority Seventies; Stake, Mission, and District Presidents; Bishops and Branch Presidents, 7 November 2002, copy in my possession. The letter had no discernible effect, and General Conference music remains similarly narrow.

51. The information and quotes in this paragraph are in TCM, 9 May and 15 June 1999.

CHAPTER 8. THE ENDLESS POSTLUDE

1. The quotations in this paragraph come from Tabernacle Choir Minutes (hereafter cited as TCM), 16 October 1999, Church History Library, the Church of Jesus Christ of Latter-day Saints (hereafter cited as CHL). Facts about the orchestra's formation, negotiations with BYU, and related matters come from the same source; personal interviews I conducted with Kory Katseanes and Mark Ammons in 2013; electronic correspondence with Alisha Ard and Justin Findlay; "The Orchestra at Temple Square," *Keeping Tab* 51, no. 2 (October 2000); Craig Jessop and Barlow Bradford, form letter of invitation to potential orchestra members, 27 May 1999; David Randall to BYU Performance Faculty (memo), 26 August 1999; and David Randall to BYU [Music] Faculty, 17 October 2002; copies of all nonrepository sources here are in my possession.

2. Jon E. Waddoups to Evelyn K. Mowbray, letter 12 July 1999, copy in my possession.

3. The information here comes from Erich Graf, telephone conversation with the author, 1 October 2013. Also, Evelyn K. Mowbray to Debbie Newmark, letter 3 August 1999, and Joseph E. Hatch to Debbie Newmark, letter 3 September 1999, copies in my possession.

4. Mac Christensen quoted in Lee Benson, "About Utah: Leading the Choir Suits This Mac Very Well," *Deseret News* (hereafter cited as *DN*), 13 January 2011.

5. Barlow Bradford to "Dear Choir," letter 31 March 2003, copy in my possession.

6. On Jessop's sharing of the podium, see Christopher Michael Redfearn, "The Choral Philosophies and Techniques of Craig Jessop," DA dissertation, University of Northern Colorado, 2012, 113. On Jessop's observed reaction to Bradford's resignation, I rely on interviews with personal friends of his, notes in my possession.

7. For the best overview of her conversion and later involvement with LDS Church music, see Mark Albright, "The Gladys Knight Conversion Story," *Meridian Magazine*, http://www.ldsmag.com/12092/article/1/page-1 (accessed 15 September 2013). See also "Celebrating President Hinckley," *Keeping Tab* 51, no. 2 (October 2000).

8. Jan Shipps's comment is in a column posted at http://www.beliefnet.com/Entertainment/Olympic-Games/The-Mormon-Olympics.aspx?p=3 (accessed 13 August 2013). Robert Kirby is quoted in Peggy Fletcher Stack, "Remembering the 'Mormon' Olympics that Weren't," *Salt Lake Tribune*, 24 February 2012.

9. For an analysis of this event, see Judd Case, "Sounds from the Center: Liriel's Performance and Ritual Pilgrimage," *Journal of Media and Religion* 8, no. 4 (2009): 209–25.

10. On Mormon donors and PBS sponsorship, see Redfearn, "Choral Philosophies and Techniques of Craig Jessop," 113.

11. www.cougarboard.com/board/message.html?id=3514973 (accessed 17 April 2013).

12. Redfearn, "Choral Philosophies and Techniques of Craig Jessop," 113.

13. Review of Mack Wilberg's *Requiem*, http://blog.ldsmusicnow.com/mack-wilberg-requiem-and-other-choral-works/ (accessed 1 October 2013).

14. For the initial announcement and useful comments, see "Craig Jessop Resigns from Mormon Tabernacle Choir," http://www.acappellanews.com/archive/001801.html (accessed 1 October 2013). Jessop's explanation of these events is in Redfearn, "Choral Philosophies and Techniques of Craig Jessop," 103–4. For the context and reception of the resignation, I thank Thomas Durham, who has shared with me details he collected when Jessop resigned. A simple search of the internet reveals various theories. On the "fire hydrant" phrase, see Darrell Babidge to the author, email 21 June 2013.

15. Cecelia Fielding, quoted in Charlene Winters, "Wilberg Transposed to Tabernacle Choir," *BYU Magazine* (summer 1999), http://magazine.byu.edu/?act=view&a=211 (accessed 17 August 2013).

16. Joseph Walker, "New Mormon Tabernacle Choir President Aspires to Young Adult Playlists," *DN*, 20 September 2012; R. Scott Lloyd, "LDS Church's Mormon Tabernacle Choir Launches YouTube Channel," *DN*, 30 October 2012.

17. www.mormonchurch.com/782/the-mormon-tabernacle-Choir (accessed 6 August 2013).

18. Redfearn, "Choral Philosophies and Techniques of Craig Jessop," 114.

19. For examples of how the name "Mormon" might be adapted and transformed in local contexts, see Kent Larsen, "Doctrines of Localization" (essay and comments) at http://timesandseasons.org/index.php/2008/09/doctrines-of-localization/ (accessed 2 October 2013).

20. For the Brandon Stewart quote ("inspired and needed") and the Glenn Beck quote, see http://www.glennbeck.com/2013/08/23/glenn-speaks-to-brandon-stewart-of-the-millennial-choir/ (accessed 8 October 2013). Most of the treatment that follows comes from Brett Stewart to the author, email 9 October 2013.

21. For this quotation and its context, see Michael Hicks, "Notes on Brigham Young's Aesthetics," *Dialogue: A Journal of Mormon Thought* 16, no. 4 (winter 1983), 127–28.

22. See, for example, Mac Christensen and Craig Jessop to Thomas Durham, letter 30 April 2002, copy in author's possession.

23. Søren Kierkegaard, *The Point of View for My Work as an Author: A Report to History*, trans. Walter Lowrie (New York: Harper & Row, 1962), 35.

INDEX

MICHAEL HICKS is a professor of music at Brigham Young University and the author of *Mormonism and Music: A History* and *Sixties Rock: Garage, Psychedelic, and Other Satisfactions.*

My Lord, What a Morning: An Autobiography   *Marian Anderson*
Marian Anderson: A Singer's Journey   *Allan Keiler*
Charles Ives Remembered: An Oral History   *Vivian Perlis*
Henry Cowell, Bohemian   *Michael Hicks*
Rap Music and Street Consciousness   *Cheryl L. Keyes*
Louis Prima   *Garry Boulard*
Marian McPartland's Jazz World: All in Good Time   *Marian McPartland*
Robert Johnson: Lost and Found   *Barry Lee Pearson and Bill McCulloch*
Bound for America: Three British Composers   *Nicholas Temperley*
Lost Sounds: Blacks and the Birth of the Recording Industry, 1890–1919   *Tim Brooks*
Burn, Baby! BURN! The Autobiography of Magnificent Montague   *Magnificent Montague*
    with Bob Baker
Way Up North in Dixie: A Black Family's Claim to the Confederate Anthem   *Howard L. Sacks*
    and Judith Rose Sacks
The Bluegrass Reader   *Edited by Thomas Goldsmith*
Colin McPhee: Composer in Two Worlds   *Carol J. Oja*
Robert Johnson, Mythmaking, and Contemporary American Culture   *Patricia R. Schroeder*
Composing a World: Lou Harrison, Musical Wayfarer   *Leta E. Miller and Fredric Lieberman*
Fritz Reiner, Maestro and Martinet   *Kenneth Morgan*
That Toddlin' Town: Chicago's White Dance Bands and Orchestras, 1900–1950
    Charles A. Sengstock Jr.
Dewey and Elvis: The Life and Times of a Rock 'n' Roll Deejay   *Louis Cantor*
Come Hither to Go Yonder: Playing Bluegrass with Bill Monroe   *Bob Black*
Chicago Blues: Portraits and Stories   *David Whiteis*
The Incredible Band of John Philip Sousa   *Paul E. Bierley*
"Maximum Clarity" and Other Writings on Music   *Ben Johnston, edited by Bob Gilmore*
Staging Tradition: John Lair and Sarah Gertrude Knott   *Michael Ann Williams*
Homegrown Music: Discovering Bluegrass   *Stephanie P. Ledgin*
Tales of a Theatrical Guru   *Danny Newman*
The Music of Bill Monroe   *Neil V. Rosenberg and Charles K. Wolfe*
Pressing On: The Roni Stoneman Story   *Roni Stoneman, as told to Ellen Wright*
Together Let Us Sweetly Live   *Jonathan C. David, with photographs by Richard Holloway*
Live Fast, Love Hard: The Faron Young Story   *Diane Diekman*
Air Castle of the South: WSM Radio and the Making of Music City   *Craig P. Havighurst*
Traveling Home: Sacred Harp Singing and American Pluralism   *Kiri Miller*
Where Did Our Love Go? The Rise and Fall of the Motown Sound   *Nelson George*
Lonesome Cowgirls and Honky-Tonk Angels: The Women of Barn Dance Radio
    Kristine M. McCusker
California Polyphony: Ethnic Voices, Musical Crossroads   *Mina Yang*
The Never-Ending Revival: Rounder Records and the Folk Alliance   *Michael F. Scully*
Sing It Pretty: A Memoir   *Bess Lomax Hawes*
Working Girl Blues: The Life and Music of Hazel Dickens   *Hazel Dickens and Bill C. Malone*
Charles Ives Reconsidered   *Gayle Sherwood Magee*
The Hayloft Gang: The Story of the National Barn Dance   *Edited by Chad Berry*
Country Music Humorists and Comedians   *Loyal Jones*